PREFACE

THE object of the pages that follow is, first, to show the importance of a study of creative thought and to develop an interest in it; next, to offer some suggestions as to the natural history of mind in its most inspired moments; finally, to institute a regime for the individual whereby he may secure the highest mental efficiency.

That the programme is ambitious I know only too well, but I desire to draw attention to the limits imposed upon my treatment of the subject. I have addressed myself to general readers of the more thoughtful type, not to psychological students, except in so far as all intelligent people are nowadays included in that category. This, whilst compelling an observance of the scientific method, has naturally demanded a practical study of the mind at work—*i.e.* psychology caught in the very act, not the formal science of the text-book. Such a method, however, cannot be safely pursued without the assistance of experts, and my pages bear ample witness to the fact that I have consulted their views. But it is a method that selects *practical values* as the criterion of worth in preference to systematic treatment on theoretical lines.

The civilised world appears to be preparing for a new era in which the strategy and tactics of war are to be applied to commerce. Will the race go to the swift and the battle to the strong? Possibly; but I should prefer to say that the race will be won by those whose minds possess the finer

creative forces, especially as executive ability has now
reached a high degree of efficiency. We may not care for
the idea of continued warfare, even on a peaceful basis, but,
despite the new cosmopolitanism which is bound to succeed
the pronounced nationalism of the past, the nations are not
yet likely to surrender their individuality as separate peoples ;
and in science, in literature, and in the fine arts generally,
there is certain to be a renaissance of national traditions and
ideals. In some respects this is a most desirable tendency,
because it prevents the uniformity which is the accompaniment of large combinations. Herein the smaller nations
will have an abundance of opportunity.

I have only touched the fringe of a great and ever fascinat-
ing subject, but the one thing I have aimed at in this book,
apart from its discussions, is *stimulus* ; and if I succeed
in arousing an interest that shall bear fruit in practical
endeavour I shall feel that my labours have received their
reward.

London, 1917.

CONTENTS

SECTION I

THE NATURAL HISTORY OF GENIUS

vii

CONTENTS

CONTENTS

SECTION III

BIOLOGICAL FACTORS

CONTENTS

SECTION IV

HINDRANCES TO ORIGINALITY

CONTENTS

CONTENTS

CHAPTER VII.—*continued*

Civil Service Mind—War Censorship Ineptitudes—
Army and Navy Officers—A Theological Colonel—The
Right Kind of Military Intellect—Why the Naval
Officer is Mentally " Free "—Professional Mind tends
to Dogmatism—Isaac Taylor on Lay Inventions

SECTION V

LOOKING AHEAD

CONTENTS

SECTION VI

PRAXIS

Originality cannot be "taught"—But even Poets
are "made"—Professor Giddings on the Fewness of
Great Men—"1" in every 450,000—The Waste of
Talent—Professor Butcher on σοφία—Two Factors:
Physical and Mental—Can Physical and Mental
Ability be trained together?—W. R. Greg says No
—Health Culture *v.* Muscle Culture—Does Mind Train-
ing injure Health?—Use and Disuse—J. S. Mill and
Ethology—Our Lack of a Human Science—The
Questionnaire—Thought and Bodily Position—De-
pression and Fatigue—The Need for Self-Knowledge
—Professor D. F. Harris on Nerves—The Virtue of
Sensibility—Jastrow on *Feeling*—Logic is a *Test* of
Thinking—Sensibility is not Mere Observation—Da
Vinci on *Wonder*—Also Aristotle and Goethe—Opposed
to Modern *Antagonism*—Türck on Disinterestedness—
Maeterlinck's View of *Admiration*—The Moralists and
Rapture—Pater and his Gospel of Sensitiveness—
Mental Labels—Sir Thomas Browne's *Sympathy*—The
Psychology of *Moods*—The Folly of Haste—Dangers

CONTENTS

ORIGINALITY

INTRODUCTION

I

THE reader of modern psychological literature is impressed by two facts: first, the skill, learning, and industry of the professional psychologist; next, the undue emphasis placed upon noetic processes. It is this second fact that is the more surprising to the private student; for to him mind is energy *par excellence*, therefore it is a mistake to give attention to its more static conditions rather than its fundamental dynamic qualities: it is unwise to spend money and labour on studying aspects of the knowing process when the mind's creative aspects are awaiting the first signs of serious attention on educative lines. In making such statements there is always a danger of being misunderstood, so we propose to offer evidence in support of our contention. Take, for example, the record of experimental psychology, from the first efforts of Fechner and Wundt up to the present moment. On what is most emphasis laid? Not on mental *energetics*, but on those processes which end in themselves, and have no direct or immediate importance in relation to practical life. It is just as if a motor engineer, lecturing to students, never dealt with a motor engine in action on the road, but confined his remarks to the intricacies of its mechanism, displayed whilst working in a fixed position. That we need to know the intricacies of the mental machine is obvious, and we are greatly indebted to laboratory psychologists for their skilful and often exhaustive work in this respect. But, after all, it is the mind in action—on the great highroads of experience—that matters most; psychology in the class-room should have a more living association with the psychology of the crowd, of the assembly, and of the individual in his struggles towards an ideal. To glance through the annual index of a modern psychological journal, published monthly or quarterly, is to be convinced that two-thirds of the discussions are on matters of more or less speculative interest, the other third being given over to Volition, to Emotion, or to new developments. We do not presume to say what the proportional relationships should be, but all that is represented by the word Feeling should certainly have a much larger place than it has in the arguments and discussions of scholars. The usual answer to this contention is that only academic subjects can be dealt with by academic people in academic associations. That, no doubt, is the fact at the moment, but is it not time to change it ? A society for the study of psychology ought not to be satisfied if it has simply compared opinions on debated issues old and new : it will need to do this, of course, but its work should transcend the passive mind and acquire the ability to offer practical guidance to all who want it, whatever their station in life. We never hear of a Professor of Psychology being sent for to assist a Cabinet Minister in estimating the effect of a new law on the public imagination, but we do hear of the professors of other sciences being consulted by the Government. Why this difference ? Presumably, because the Cabinet Minister is his own psychologist, or else because psychology as we know it in text-book form has been almost entirely confined to *exposition*, to the comparative neglect of *application*. Of late years American psychologists have made a strong effort to realise their teaching in practice, notably W. Dill Scott and the late Hugo Münsterberg. But there is still room for much development work, and we are still in the atmosphere of the *book* instead of being in the presence of the *man*.

II

Before the war everybody went to Germany to study book psychology, for in that country it was alleged that the internal mechanism of the mind had been investigated with more success than elsewhere; but although Germans claimed to know more about the mental engine than anybody else, they know vastly less about men and nations—hence their errors in the field of practical psychology were positively colossal. They misjudged everybody and everything, and will become in future years a sad illustration of the difference between studying a subject and knowing the reality. In one department alone was Germany unique, and that was in auto and hetero-suggestion. Therein she led the world.

To *know*, to *feel*, to *resolve*—these are the functions of mind which appear to occupy the attention of those men and women who act as leaders of the community. Rightly construed, such functions embrace the whole of our possible existence, but, unfortunately, they are seldom construed in the right way. Invention or creation is the highest mental activity of which we are capable, and yet in education, in religion, in science, in everything, it is an activity which does not receive its due. This is owing, in part, to the immense growth of knowledge, and to the intense interest in acquiring it; a tendency is set up to live mentally by amassing information; and the more individual tendencies of the mind are gradually eclipsed. It is a noteworthy achievement to master the literature of education; but it is more masterly to know less about it and to be a Montessori. It is indicative of great memory power to be able to recite the poems of John Milton; but it is better to be able to indite a new poem that shall equal one of his. It is distinctive to be an oracle of reference on all matters financial or economic; but it is a finer thing to offer an original contribution to the solution of the problems of currency. The feeling of superiority that is associated with the creative mind is not difficult to understand, and it is appreciated to the full by most people; nevertheless there appears to be no attempt worthy of the name to discover and develop the mental processes leading to originality, presumably because genius has always been regarded as a gift, needing neither training nor experience.

One of the objects of this book is to plead for a greater recognition of individuality by allowing more scope to the creative principle in the education of mental ability. As matters stand at present our schools and universities are like factories which turn out the manufactured article by the thousand—according to pattern. To change these factories into establishments where individual differences will be recognised and developed is a task of supreme difficulty, but that is no reason why it should not be attempted, or that it should be attempted in a revolutionary spirit, for in nothing is a finer sense of discrimination more necessary than in balancing the claims of the older system of education with those of the new.

III

"Something new" : that is the popular conception of originality, and, as a conception, it has more than a germ of truth in it; although, as a definition, it would not satisfy even the moderately critical person. The poet who writes a ballad that seizes the imagination; the physicist who invents a new method of using etheric waves; the engineer who substitutes the explosive pump for the suction pump; the statesman who contrives taxation on hitherto unthought-of lines—these men have the power of original thought and action, mainly because they have the power to bring something new into the world. Thus far the popular conception is right. But it is possible to be original without adding anything new to the world's intellectual treasures, or to the conveniences of civilisation. The mathematician who believes he has made a new discovery, only to find later that he has been anticipated, is none the less an original worker. Adams' share in the discovery of Neptune is not cancelled because Le Verrier was thinking, calculating, and perhaps observing on the same lines, at the same time. Originality is the expression of the individual self in relation to its environment; its significance does not lie in newness so much as in sincerity—as Carlyle long ago pointed out. It is obedience to the injunction "Be a Person." Every man who is *himself*, and not a careful copy of others, is an original person. His originality may not have any great value or

4

distinction, inasmuch as his essential self may have no inward illumination, deep knowledge, fine sensibility or vast experience, but these deficiencies do not decide the matter. Mrs Poyser has more originality, as a country dame, than many a Newnham graduate, even though the latter might make the former blush for her ignorance of Latin and Algebra.[1]

In these pages, however, we shall not deal with originality in character and conduct except incidentally; our chief concern will be the intellectually new and striking. And what is meant by *new*? The only new thing we ever know is a new personality; and even he—or she—has many similarities with other personalities. But that which separates an individual from the surrounding mediocrities is some well-nigh undefinable *difference*: a way of speaking, a mental outlook, a charm of manner, a gift of control. This suggests, and rightly so, that we must look for the meaning of the word *new* in the conception of difference, not in absolute creation. Take a simple illustration: Pitman's phonography. Was it new? Certainly, but Sir Isaac Pitman was not the first to invent a system of shorthand. Shorthand methods of varying values had been in use for centuries when the first *Teacher* was issued in Bath; but Pitman, advancing on the merits of his predecessors, engineered a difference in his favour. Shorthand had had a long history, but it reached an apex in the Pitman signs. They were *new*, not merely novel. A man who invents a new face for a clock produces a novelty, but the man who invented the clock itself was genuinely original.

IV

Take another illustration: that of the Humphrey Explosion Pump. Here there is no piston and no connecting

---

[1] "What rare and racy originality do we often find in the sayings of the poor and uneducated! Their conversation may be often richer in this golden ore than that of those who are called their betters; for, having heard less of other men's views, their shrewd, observant minds are driven to their own."—"Conventional and Original Minds," in *The Spectator*, 31st December 1892.

rod : a column of water does service for both. Were
Torricelli alive he would be among the first to say it was
a new thing altogether, at any rate so different from the
ordinary apparatus for lifting water that the word pump is
hardly applicable. In consequence Mr H. A. Humphrey's
originality is all the more distinctive ; its value is in proportion to the range of difference that separates his invention
from similar instruments previously used. And this is the
criterion we have to employ in judging all originalities in
relation to the quality of newness. The vital difference
between Judaism and Christianity lies in the fact that Truth
and Law are translated from a Code into a Living Person,
and Christianity thus becomes the most original of all
religions, having in its Founder, as Lecky puts it, "an
enduring principle of regeneration."

Prof. S. H. Butcher remarks that "Greek literature is the
one entirely original literature of Europe. With no models
before their eyes to provoke imitation or rivalry, the Greeks
created almost every form of literary art—the epic, the lyric,
the elegy, the drama, the dialogue, the idyll, the romantic
novel, history, and oratory ; and the permanence of the
types so created shows that they rest on no arbitrary rules
or on the mannerisms of a people, but answer to certain
artistic laws of the human mind."[1] Perhaps the Greeks
were not so badly off for models as we imagine them to have
been. We do not know enough about early Greece to be
able to say, with confidence, how far the great poets and
dramatists had the oral and literary efforts of others to guide
them. But even though it is impossible to suppose they
created, in the almost absolute sense, all the forms of literary
art just enumerated, they imparted to them a wealth of
achievement that no other nation has surpassed ; hence the
unfading glory which still surrounds their names and their
works.[2]

[1] *Harvard Lectures on Greek Subjects*, p. 129.
[2] Mahaffy in his *What the Greeks have done for Modern Civilisation*
(p. 42) says of the *Iliad* and *Odyssey* that they appeared like
Melchizedek without father, mother, or descent. This is going too
far. A truer view is found in K. O. Müller's *History of the Literature
of Ancient Greece*, vol. i., p. 35.

INTRODUCTION

V

Newness ? It is relative—but real. Its relativity is seen in the oft-repeated phrase of Emerson, that "every house is a quotation from a quarry as every man is a quotation from his ancestors." Give us time, say the critics, and we will take the gilt off every loudly proclaimed originality by tracing its origin to some previous idea that has escaped notice ; and even that previous idea will turn out to be a copy of something still more previous. When the investigations thus begun have been concluded (the critics remark finally) we shall fall into line ourselves by imitating those who have gone before us, exclaiming : " There is nothing new under the sun." But will any reasonable man venture to say that since this Hebrew sceptic coined his hopelessness into words there has been nothing new ? Have we made no sort of advance in Europe since the days of Solomon ? That we hold some of the same truths to-day much in the spirit in which he held them, and that human nature in its fundamentals has remained unchanged, may be conceded ; we may even concede that in his days there were intelligent anticipations of future developments, but to accept his dictum with the sense of conviction, as many people do, is palpably absurd. As in the world of Nature, so in the history of thought, there is an organic connection between past and present ; but this does not preclude departures from what seems to be the fixed course of things ; and these variations in Nature have their counterpart in the originalities of thought. The problem therefore is to decide what is relatively new and what is really new in every contribution of the human mind that we designate original. This demands a discussion of plagiarism in its wider sense, and of the function of imitation. If we had the time and the necessary knowledge of languages we could go through the whole world of literature and find that every thought has had expression *in some form or other*, often inadequate, even in circumstances where plagiarism was quite an impossibility.

Plagiarism is purely a question of degree. When Charles

ORIGINALITY

Reade in *The Wandering Heir* bodily appropriated twenty or
thirty lines of a little-known poem of Dean Swift, and was
later found out, he became angry and complained of " masked
batteries manned by anonymuncula, pseudo-nymuncula, and
skunkula "; but it was a case of direct plagiarism—*i.e.*
borrowing without acknowledgment.[1] But when we study
closely other charges of plagiarism we may be allowed to
express our doubts. Bacon wrote : " A little philosophy
inclineth men's minds to Atheism, but depth in philosophy
bringeth men's minds about to religion." Pope wrote :

> " A little learning is a dangerous thing ;
> Drink deep, or taste not the Pierian Spring."

Are we justified in saying, as some have said, that Pope
borrowed the idea from Bacon ? He *may* have done so, but
a plagiarism is a palpable theft, not a similarity. Besides,
as Pope expressed the idea in a phrase that has become
classic, is he to have no recognition of merit in that respect ?
Again, when Gibbon described history as " little more than
the register of the crimes, follies, and misfortunes of mankind," he is said to have been indebted to a phrase of Voltaire :
" En effet, l'histoire n'est que le tableau des crimes et des
malheurs." Which of the two was the more likely to understand history in its sordid aspects ? And was there not
enough originality in Gibbon to save him from so petty a
charge ? These ideas, which find an embodiment in the
language of every intellectual epoch—*i.e.* are in the
common currency of thought—were taken up by two writers
of eminence and phrased according to individual perception
and sense of fitness.

VI

One of the most curious instances of unconscious plagiarism, by means of which ideas in the memory come forth
naked and thus without the clothing of their original associations, is provided by Prof. Jung. He first quotes from

[1] " Literary Plagiarism." Article in *The Contemporary Review*,
June, 1887.

INTRODUCTION

Thus Spake Zarathustra. We quote from Common's translation, and side by side give the notes provided by Jung showing the origin of Nietzsche's ideas :

Now about the time that Zarathustra sojourned on the Happy Isles, it happened that a ship anchored at the isle on which standeth the smoking mountain, and the crew went ashore to shoot rabbits. About the noontide hour, however, when the Captain and his men were together again, they saw suddenly a man coming towards them through the air, and a voice said distinctly: "It is time. It is the highest time!" But when the figure was nearest to them (it flew past quickly, however, like a shadow in the direction of the volcano) then did they recognise with the greatest surprise that it was Zarathustra ; for they had all seen him before except the Captain himself, and then loved him as the people love: in such wise that love and awe were combined in equal degree. "Behold!" said the old helmsman, "there goeth Zarathustra to Hell."[1]

An extract of awe-inspiring import from the log of the ship *Sphinx* in the year 1686 in the Mediterranean.

Just. Kerner, *Blatter aus Prevorst*, vol. iv., p. 57. The four captains and a merchant, Mr Bell, went ashore on the island of Mount Stromboli to shoot rabbits. At 3 o'clock they called the crew together to go aboard, when to their inexpressible astonishment, they saw two men flying rapidly over them through the air. One was dressed in black, the other in grey. They approached them very closely, in the greatest haste ; to their greatest dismay they descended amid the burning flames into the crater of the terrible volcano, Mount Stromboli. They recognised the pair as acquaintances from London.

The analogies here are too familiar to be mere coincidences ; indeed we know they are not, for Nietzsche's sister told Prof. Jung that her brother had read Kerner's works at the age of fifteen or sixteen but had not renewed his acquaintance with them since. Then did Nietzsche recall the incident at the moment of writing the episode ? We cannot think that he did, for, as Jung points out, it could never have been his intention "to commit a plagiarism from a ship's log ; if this had been the case he would certainly have omitted the very prosaic 'to shoot rabbits' which was, moreover, quite

[1] *Thus Spake Zarathustra*, pp. 155-156.

ORIGINALITY

unessential to the situation." [1]   The only conclusion is that after a lapse of twenty-four years Nietzsche recollected the Stromboli *material* but not its origin, and reformed it to suit the purpose he had in hand.   There could hardly be a better illustration of the manner in which the mind unwittingly will utilise old experience in the construction of a new undertaking.   But the use of previous material may be conscious and intentional, as in the case of Shakespeare, of whom Professor Brander Matthews says, "he reached out again and again to possess himself of another man's work, but he was an imperial conqueror.   His imagination was set free to work most amply and most boldly when it was set in motion by the invention of an uninspired predecessor." [2] Here, as before, the newness, and consequently the originality, is due to the difference between the material as it previously existed and the metamorphosis to which it has been subjected.

VII

How far is imitation a constituent of all originality? Imitation is a treacherous word to handle, partly because the greatest genius is something of an imitator, and partly because the word is used in an offensive sense ; to call a man an imitator is intended to humiliate him.   But imitation is a matter of degree : it stretches from the servile copyist to the man who, as Aristotle said, imitates Nature in such a way as to fulfil her unfinished designs.   In social life, in economic matters, and in the intellectual sphere, also, imitation is a method of progress. [3]   All sociologists are agreed on this point, and it is obvious to every student of mankind.   The Red Indian, proud, aloof, and lacking the power of imitation, is dying off, and many tribes have dis-

[1] *Analytical Psychology*, p. 88.
[2] "Was Shakespeare a Plagiarist?" (*Munsey's Magazine*.)   De Goncourt believed that Balzac was greater than Shakespeare because he invented his own characters. *Journal*, p. 343.
[3] "The copying of socially fruitful variations in the ideas and ideals of the individuals is the real method of progress in human society."—Prof. Ellwood, *Sociology in its Psychological Aspects*, p. 304.

appeared already : the negro, on the other hand, has an eye to being like "the others," and he survives : imitation is saving him. From this method of progress we naturally conclude that the really important person is the man who sets up our standards and creates our values—those standards that guide our conduct and those ideals that give us our sense of worth. And we further conclude that the last thing such a man could be called would be *imitator*. No doubt ; but let us beware of the subtlety of words. When Nietzsche tried, without success, to recreate our moral conceptions he aspired to be a second Christ by becoming an anti-Christ : that is, he was an imitator of a previous teacher, but with a personal note that constituted a decided difference —he aimed at a complete eclipse of his predecessor. Every pronounced individuality must imitate other individualities ; the very permanence of the earth, of human conditions, of language, and evolution render this a necessity. But with the truly original mind there is a margin of *difference*, as we have already remarked, and it is this which causes the new standards to be set up and the new values to be created.

There is, however, an aspect of the subject wherein imitation is used as a means to a higher end. This need not occasion surprise when we recall the immense range of the imitative principle,[1] for a new imitation, if we may so speak, is an added interest to the sense which hears echoes everywhere. Onomatopœia—the harmony of word sounds and sense in poetry—is an example. Take Shakespeare's imitation of the bubbling in the witches' cauldron :

> "For a charm of powerful trouble,
> Like a hell-broth boil and bubble.
> Double, double toil and trouble,
> Fire, burn ; and, cauldron, bubble."[2]

That, however, is but an elementary illustration of the use of the imitative principle to secure new unities ; we see it to better advantage in music and the fine arts generally, where that which is familiar is reproduced in associations that

[1] A handy guide to this is Steel's *Imitation : the Mimetic Function in Human Nature and in Nature*. Liverpool, 1910.

[2] *Macbeth*, IV.

suggest an extension of it; or as Quatremère de Quincy phrases it: *to imitate in the fine arts is to produce the resemblance of a thing, but in some other thing which becomes the image of it.*[1] It may be questioned whether this can apply to more material spheres of life and effort; by its very nature it does not lead to the highest originality, and in some instances has already led to eccentricity, as seen in the work of Ivan Meshtrovic. Asked as to why some of his figures have arms, hands and feet missing, he replied: "Who would care to look on a Venus de Milo with arms? We love and admire her as she is, and out of that love and admiration arises a desire to imitate. You will remember, doubtless, the remark attributed to Michael Angelo on this point. He said that a statue ought to be rolled from the top of a mountain to the bottom before it was shown to the world. What remained after this experiment was alone worth keeping." Wilfulness of this type is to be deeply regretted.

VIII

Pursuing our investigations further, we are led to inquire: What is the difference between the originality of a poet and that of a discoverer in science? To materialise the question let us use the names of Shakespeare and Darwin, and ascertain, first of all, the nature of each originality, afterwards comparing and contrasting them until the essential difference is revealed. Shakespeare may be said to have found all the *raw material* for his poems and dramas in the world around him and in the records of past ages; his originality lay in the peculiarly individual manner in which he interpreted the knowledge he acquired, and the vigour and wealth of language in which he expressed it. These general terms set forth the chief facts. Darwin, on the other hand, set out to discover the mysteries of life in Nature. His originality lay in the elucidation of facts that had escaped other investigators bent on the same mission. We may say, therefore, that Darwin's discovery was the bringing to light of a fact already in existence.

[1] *Imitation in the Fine Arts.* 1837.

INTRODUCTION

The question now arises : In what way are the originalities alike and how are they different ? They are alike in this : that they interpret facts ; in Shakespeare's case the facts of human life in relation to feeling, knowledge and destiny ; in Darwin's case the facts of biology and the evolution of species. They are unlike in this : that Darwin's originality is purely a discovery of facts that were hidden, but existent ; Shakespeare's originality is a deeper thing—it is the creation of something new, new in the sense that it had no previous existence and was the offspring of his own personality. The blood circulated in our veins before Harvey announced the fact to a rather incredulous public ; gravity existed before Newton discovered its law ; and although imaginative genius was needed in order to bring these facts to light, the thought-product of the poet and artist is on a higher plane, because in the true sense it is more creative.

Originality, therefore, may be defined as the thought-characteristic of the individual who expresses himself and not another ; from which it follows that the more distinctive the individuality the higher will be the type of originality. An original mind is one which has a more than ordinary share in the joys of evolution, and in the felicity of furthering those processes of change that bring advantages, real and ideal.

IX

The outstanding fact about human individuality is its utter inscrutability, even to the individual himself. Men who have known each other for years, in business, at the club, on the golf-course, frequently find that their knowledge was, after all, confined to surface things ; for example, to political opinions, personal aversions and preferences, modes of looking at life, and methods of solving difficulties. Then there comes a day of great surprise when the John Smith who was supposed to be so cynical is discovered in the act of helping a man on to his feet—not directly, but through a second party. Smith's friends are amazed : they never knew he was " that sort of fellow."

ORIGINALITY

And yet a husband and a wife have celebrated a silver wedding without being able to claim that they knew each other; their individualities throughout a quarter of a century were partly hidden, and—to use the plaintive title of a once popular song—they are "Strangers Yet." Of course, in a hundred and one *ordinary* matters they *do* understand each other—especially the wife; but in the deeper, higher, finer, more subtle spheres of conscious life—No. All married people wear masks; they seldom tell each other all they think, all they know, all they desire, all they intend; but this does not mean that love is declining or respect failing; for the inscrutability of the self is merely part and parcel of the love-emotion—full and perfect knowledge might, indeed, make it an impossibility. Those people who are said to have " every thought in common " are no doubt united in a very close bond of sympathy, but each has thoughts not shared by the other; in fact, no man knows his own thoughts until circumstances reveal them to him.[1] We often surprise ourselves in good or evil manifestations: we did not know we had it in us. Really, there are two masks—first, the essential ego which screens itself from the analysis of our waking consciousness, and the mask that we put on when we meet other people. The mode in which the ego manifests itself is beyond scrutiny, hence analytical psychology is only an accommodating term; but the mask of social convention and of intellectual reserve is one that we make and wear deliberately.

We seldom show our true selves. If you doubt that state-

---

[1] Whitman expresses it thus:

"When I read the book, the biography famous,
And is this, then, (said I) what the author calls a man's life ?
And so, will someone when I am dead and gone write my life,
(As if any man really knew aught of my life ;
Why, even I myself, I often think, know little or nothing of my
    real life ;
Only a few hints—a few diffused faint clues and indirections,
I seek for my own use to trace out here)."

So also Ribot, who says: " La connaissance de nous-même n'est pas seulement difficile mais *impossible.*"—*La Vie Inconscient*, p. 69.

ment, take a sheet of paper and dare to write, as if for publication, all you honestly believe about your friends and enemies; all you believe about God and Churches; about women, about sex, about politics, about the newspapers, and about anything vital. Dare you do that? Before replying think of what is required: not surface " views," but what you believe in the depths of your heart. . . . Convention has too heavy a hand on us. To reveal our true inwardness would be to destroy social life. We should surprise the world by our narrowness, our prejudices, our ignorance, our cynicism; or by our unsuspected breadth of sympathy, our insight, and our boldness of policy. All of us would be found using Bellarmine's doctrine of mental reservation to the full. The professed Liberal next door is, at bottom, a Marxian Socialist; the Tory across the way is a Tory no deeper than his skin; the High Church vicar has left his heart in St Peter's, Rome; the bimetallist may be a monometallist underneath. The reader resents these criticisms? He may. But he, too, has his mask—not so pronounced or hypocritical, it may be, and yet he cannot afford to throw stones.

X

But let us see, if we can, how individuality originates. In its generic sense an individual is a unit separated from the mass.[1] A pebble is an individual separated from its parent rock; and the rock itself may also be an individual—a mountain separated from other mountains and named accordingly. Inorganic individuality, however, does not depend on size; for the diamond has significances that far outshine the mass of earth from which it is taken. In the animal world size and individuality are more closely allied.[2] In man these facts may be symbolical but no more than that.

---

[1] " Let us, however, again fix our attention on the essential feature of individuality. It is what distinguishes *this* from *that.* It is the balance of unlikeness which distinguishes this individual assemblage of processes and products from that other assemblage otherwise so closely alike."—Lloyd Morgan, *Instinct and Experience*, p. 174.

[2] Julian Huxley, *The Individual in the Animal Kingdom*, p. 5.

ORIGINALITY

Size, in the early ages of mankind, gave individuality to those who were fortunate enough to tower above their fellows in height and strength; but with the advance of mental power brain displaced brawn, and the man of pronounced individuality might be physically insignificant, for intelligence meant more than muscular strength to a world rapidly growing in civilisation. Individuality came to mean not only separation, but, more than ever before, separation with a difference. It was the something different that stamped one man as distinctive, and this is the rule to-day. Self-realisation is one of the sources of individuality, and to realise the self means, first, that there must be an abolition of blind and mechanical conformity to the laws that govern the many. Such nonconformity as this is quite commensurate with a meticulous obedience to the social code. Mrs Bloomer's invention and use of the garment that still bears her name was a display of individuality—a protest against the behaviour of the many; but in other respects she acknowledged and observed the decorum of the circles in which she moved. The life of the individual is not one thing and the life of the social group another : they are aspects of one life. But in 999 cases out of 1000 it happens that the group exerts the stronger influence; and the individual becomes a conformist in inward thought and outward deed. The speech, the dress, the religion, the party politics, the pleasures of his fellows he takes up one by one until his identity is lost ; he is typical of the community to which he belongs. Let some bold spirit enter the weaving sphere of industry, as did Arkwright, with revolutionary ideas, and he finds the most vigorous opposition. A new religion fares no better ; and the "love your enemy" notion is thrown to the winds as Christians fight for supremacy, burning one another at the stake as a proof that the martyr is wrong and the persecutor is right. The original man pays the price of violating the recognised order, except in cases where the public has felt the need of change such as that effected by some progressive mind. The price has often been death, a sufficiently grave warning to all minds of individual quality, living in a ruthless age, and yet eager for self-expression.

XI

Fortunately a larger toleration exists to-day, but the *spirit* of opposition to change is still operative.[1] A substitute for rubber that is as good as rubber would not only bring fortune to the inventor but a very considerable fame ; for this is an original discovery that we expect and hope for ; but let a man dare to propose leasehold marriage as did George Meredith and enemies multiply rapidly ; the clergy denounce him in pulpit and on platform, and the novelist's friends shake their heads sorrowfully ; their idol has had a weak moment. And yet Meredith simply detached his mind from all other minds and advocated a remedy for evils that are apparent to everybody : his weakness lay in not thinking what the majority of people think. But "the group as a psychical unit is *never creative*"[2] ; that is always the function of the individual—just as the Messiah created a new law as against the traditions of the elders. The group is generally repressive. New, in his *Life Wanderings in Eastern Africa*, says of the Wanika that "if a man dares to improve the style of his hut, to make a larger doorway than is customary ; if he should wear a finer or different style of dress from that of his fellows, he is instantly fined." We laugh. But, in London, instead of fining a woman who dares to be different we mob her in the street. Is not the savage custom *mutatis mutandis* more dignified than ours ? It may be more discouraging to innovators in thought, but it certainly manifests more control. Nevertheless, everywhere around us, despite educative influences of the highest kind, we have to contend for the rights of the minority, then for the rights of the individual.[3] Emerson truly said that society is a conspiracy against the independence of each of its members.

[1] Sir John Seeley in his *Ecce Homo* (p. 252) refers to the manner in which the majority of people receive the original man : he is "alarming, perplexing, fatiguing. They unite to crush the innovator." See also Nietzsche, *Dawn of Day*, p. 17, and Brandes' *Nietzsche*, p. 15.

[2] D G. Brinton, *The Basis of Social Relations*, p. 30.

[3] "There is nothing we have to fight for more strenuously than Individuality."—Havelock Ellis, *Impressions and Comments*, p. 195.

ORIGINALITY

XII

Let us recapitulate our findings in reference to originality. We affirmed that the popular verdict of " something new " was right and yet not right ; it was defective, as half-truths always are. Newness is relative—it cannot be otherwise, for past and present are an organic whole. And yet there are variations—real departures from the conventional ; new creations although not completely disconnected with the past. How do they come and why ? They are not plagiarisms, nor even higher imitations : what, then, is their origin ? We saw that it lay in the nature of individuality—the expression of the pure and unaffected self. As the self is inscrutable the inner source of originality may be described as inscrutable also. But, after all, it is no more than saying that mind itself is a mystery ; whereas the point at issue is the *nature* of originality. In its widest sense it is man's share in progress, his participation in a great world-scheme by bringing to light hidden truths, by becoming the channel of inspirational forces, and by adding to the conveniences of civilised life.

In order to carry out the programme which an inquiry into the nature of originality makes necessary we must study the nature of genius—that type of mind with which original thinking is most closely associated. We shall find that so far from being a matter of inbreathing it is mind working on its own higher planes, and thus has a natural history as well as natural laws of operation. This is the foundation fact : all the others rest upon it, and instead of restating them here we would ask the reader to inspect the extended analysis of contents from which he will see that it is possible to study the whole of the phenomena of originality by means of the accepted truths of psychology, biology, physical geography and sociology.

The addition of a section on Praxis was made in the hope that it would serve as a focus for the preceding sections, and perhaps also as a means of personal development.

SECTION I

THE NATURAL HISTORY OF GENIUS

CHAPTER I

CONSCIOUSNESS : SOME OF ITS CHARACTERISTICS AND IMPLICATIONS

I

IT has been said that there are three factors in every original conception or work : first, the material already in existence, and out of which the new product is made ; next, the original mind in action ; and finally, the new product itself. In the last resort, however, there is only one factor to be considered, and that is the second one : the operations of a highly individualised intelligence, covering the period of impregnation, gestation, and birth of the new idea. There are many types of original minds, but with minor differences they all obey the same laws. The experimental chemist who is using vast knowledge and far-seeing ability to discover a secret that will be of great service to humanity ; the mechanical inventor on the eve of a fine achievement ; the novelist approaching, with an emotion akin to fear, the creation of a striking plot ; the poet in the ecstasy of reducing a noble conception to words—these men possess one type of intellect, however different its manifestations ; and that intellect may be studied in its action quite apart from the material with which it is most intimately concerned, or the result, in whatever form it may be embodied. That which distinguishes the mind of unusual powers from the mind that is conventional or commonplace is its greater range of consciousness [1] ; hence many of our words used to describe

[1] Bosanquet would seem to be thinking of this idea of range when he says : " If a man has more power of comprehension and inclusion

19

the qualities of talent and genius are *spatial*. *Deep* thinking, *lofty* contemplation, and *breadth* of comprehension are cases in point ; and we have also the inspiration from *above*, the power of mental *penetration*, and the mind of great *compass*.

On the reverse side, a man of *circumscribed* intelligence is exactly what the adjective describes him to be : his range of consciousness is small, and the barriers effectually repel the attacks of new ideas, with the natural result that his ability never increases. The *narrow-minded* man is a similar individual : his range is *limited*.

One has only to reflect on the origin and grades of intelligence known to us in the world to realise the truth of these claims. Consider for a moment the numerous evidences of mind, or what we call mind, stretching from the answering movements of a telegraph plant to the thoughts and designs of man himself. The botanists claim that plants have intelligence and the psychologists claim they have not ; *?* responsible investigators affirm that the higher animals have reasoning powers and other investigators deny it. Into these disputes it is not necessary to go ; but everyone must admit that the wider the range of consciousness among animals, the greater is the ability they display to remember and to adapt themselves to new situations. Contrast, for instance, the utterly insignificant though none the less remarkable brain of an ant with that of a dog. How much does the ant know of the world, beyond the mechanical impulses which prompt it to play its dull and uninteresting *rôle* in a nest of earth ? If we may speak of its consciousness at all, it is a pitiably small affair when regarded in the light of that of the canine species, where there is a power to understand the changes in human conduct, and to respond to them with a knowing appreciation. To say that the constructive ability of a dog is not equal to that of an ant is to miss the essential point. An ant follows out what appears to be an elaborate system of life—not of choice but of

so that less is outside him, and that what is outside him is less outside him, his own unity and individuality is so far and for that reason not less, but greater. Consciousnesses are of all degrees of comprehension."—*The Principle of Individuality and Value*, p. 286.

necessity. Its "ability" is just as much a part of its mechanism as is its appetite. But a dog is able to enter into the details of its environment in a manner that is infinitely more comprehensive; and because its range of consciousness is wider its ability is greater.

II

We see the same fact in the growth of the human consciousness. If we ask a child of three to write an essay on Bimetallism we are immediately aware of an absurdity that is difficult to characterise. The child has a human mind, no doubt, but its development is still in the very embryonic stages; years must pass before its mind can grasp even the elements of a subject which to grown men is confessedly abstruse. And if we ask a young graduate of one of the newer universities, where Money is a more favoured subject than elsewhere, it *may* be that he will soon find the fundamentals beyond him—that is, he has not the necessary ability because the necessary facts and ideas are out of his range. On the reverse side we see how the declining ability of old men is determined by their increasing lack of appreciation; the circle of their interests is narrowed gradually; new ideas are outside their range of sympathy; in a word, the area of consciousness is reduced, carrying with it certain ineptitudes which, however natural, are undoubtedly restrictive. As Schopenhauer says: "There is then a sense in which . . . it is only in youth that a man lives with a full degree of consciousness, and that he is only half alive when he is old." [1]

In order to justify the definition just given of a mind with unusual powers it will be necessary to say what we mean by *consciousness*, and also in what sense we use the word *range*.

[1] *Counsels and Maxims*, p. 144. There is also an interesting passage in his *Wisdom of Life* (pp. 34-35) wherein he traces the various stages of conscious life ending with these words: "The highest product of Nature is the clearest degree of consciousness in which the world mirrors itself more plainly and completely than anywhere else."

ORIGINALITY

We shall have to invoke the aid of comparative psychology—
the science of intelligence as manifested in every kind of life;
we shall have to estimate the loss of ability due to diminished
interests, as seen in old age; indeed all the sources necessary
must be pressed into the service of elucidation, including all
that is reliable in recent researches into the subconscious.

III

What do we know about consciousness? We may truthfully claim to know something, but we do not know enough
to define it.[1] The attempt to define it has caused all the
trouble, and we are not surprised to read that Lewes, one
of the clearest of thinkers and writers, wished that the word
could be dropped out of use altogether. Let any man gather
together the quasi-definitions of consciousness propounded—
there is no other phrase more suitable — during the last
eighteen years, as Dr Schofield did for the years previous to
1892,[2] and he will see how little we have advanced; more
than that, he will see how little likely we are to advance.
The whole mass of psychological terminology badly needs
revision, but even a congress of experts could not define
consciousness; it could only narrow the meaning of the *word*,
and isolate it within better marked boundaries. Consciousness itself is a thing beyond analysis,[3] and therefore beyond
definition. Mark, not the *life* of consciousness—what takes
place *in* it—but the *state* we call consciousness, considered
apart from its associated activities. Any attempt to study
one's own consciousness will from the very commencement
have an element of vanity in it. The old objection still

[1] Prof. James, in speaking of "personal consciousness," says,
with a touch of sly humour: "Its meaning we know so long as no
one asks us to define it."—*Principles of Psychology*, vol. i., p. 225.

[2] *The Unconscious Mind*, p. 52 *passim*.

[3] "Consciousness itself . . . is an irreducible datum which
explanation obscures and analysis destroys. To try to find the
detailed elements of consciousness for the purpose of contrasting or
connecting them with the elements of the lower functions, is to lose
sight of consciousness itself and to consider its materials or its
product."—Boutroux, *The Contingency of the Laws of Nature*, p. 115.

stands : it is impossible during the same moment to be the observer and the thing observed.[1] The stream of consciousness cannot stop its course, turn back, analyse its origin, and survey its present condition, then go forward and estimate its destiny. It would then cease to be a stream. But surely (it will be said) there is such a thing as introspective or analytical psychology ? There is, and the results, plus those of the experimentalists, are highly impressive as a body of reasoned knowledge about the life of the mind. But our point is this : that no method can explain consciousness in a manner that enables us to define it. The true psychologist would be the last to make any such claim. Introspection on the old lines reached its limits a long time ago. Professor Case of Oxford, in a letter to *The Times* (26th May 1899), produced a long list of questions which had been discussed for ages without success. "Psychology," he said, "is a science full of involved problems, and of questions waiting for answers."[2] These failures are due to our ignorance of the nature of consciousness, owing to its essential inscrutability.

After the introspective school came the experimental school, led by Wundt. They have had a long and notable innings, and have achieved a good deal in the realm of sensation and perception and not a little as to the border-line between mind and body. But we have noticed that in recent years the experimentalist concludes a chapter of inquiry with a baffled feeling ; the discovery that seemed so near has receded into the distance, or the notion that promised a rare fertility has ended in barrenness. Kostyleff, in his *La Crise de la Psychologie Expérimentale* (1914), gives us a critical summary of the whole position, and it is not favourable to the future of experiment. Billia in his pamphlet, *Has the*

[1] "The mere act of observing the current phenomena of consciousness introduces a new element into consciousness which tends to disturb the processes going on. The observations should be oblique rather than direct : should be made not during, but immediately after, the appropriate experiences."—James, *Principles of Psychology*, vol. ii., p. 249.

[2] *E.g.*—What is Mind ? What is the origin of Knowledge ? The relation of the Mind to the body ?

ORIGINALITY

Psychological Laboratory proved Helpful? (1909), is even more negative. "The true laboratory of psychology," he says, "is nothing but consciousness." Admitting the great services of the experimenters, he affirms that a fundamental misapprehension remains : "the illusion of studying outside of consciousness a fact which takes place only within consciousness, and which outside of consciousness is not even conceivable." So also Jung, who contends that "modern experimental psychology is very far from being able to afford . . . any connected insight into the most vital psychic processes ; that is not its aim. . . . Hence it comes about that the inquirer after the secrets of the human soul learns rather less than nothing from experimental psychology." [1]

The newest school is that of Freud and Jung as seen in psycho-analysis. Into this we shall inquire presently ; meanwhile we may say at once that we do not expect *any* investigator to tell us what the mind *is*, although he may explain its working better than anybody else. Let us remember the words of Descartes : "Il est bon de comprendre clairement qu'il y a des choses que sont absolutement incomprehensibles " ; also Pascal's fine paradox : "La, on finit le raisonnement, commence la veritable certitude."

IV

It may be objected that there is no service rendered to knowledge in accentuating the great difficulties of its attainment ; and that this attitude is generally taken up by those who have no ability for investigation, and who try to cover their ignorance by denying the possibility of knowledge. There is a spice of truth in this criticism, and it is certainly more desirable to cultivate the spirit of inquiry than to damp its ardour. But facts are stubborn things. There were men of science in the last century who seemed to think we were on the highroad to a complete solution of life— Büchner used the phrase, "the mystery of the Universe solved "—but a period of humility set in and it is still growing ; there were also men—there are some still—who showed

[1] *Analytical Psychology*, p. 353.

a tendency to regard mind as an easy problem : a cell, a nerve, a sensation, a group of perceptions—and consciousness is accounted for ! Like the house-furnishing advertisement on the hoardings : "It's so simple " ! The tendency is always to pat ourselves on the back and say how much we know ; then a new discovery comes and moodily we bring our text-books up to date, parting grudgingly with our favourite theories. It is against this false spirit that we have ventured to protest. Of consciousness itself we know no more than men did in Greece two thousand years ago.

For instance, we have never yet found a psychologist who could define the difference between a Thought and a Feeling or between a Feeling and an act of Will ; indeed every teacher in explaining these words is anxious to assure us that the mind is a unity, and that there is Feeling and Thought in every act of Will, Will and Thought in every Feeling, and Feeling and Will in every Thought. Mind is thus set forth in almost exactly the same terms as the Godhead in theology ; God exists in three Persons—a unity in trinity and a trinity in unity. Similarly, the mind has three chief functions : to feel, to think, and to will ; but there are not three minds—only one. This gives rise to several reflections, the first of which is that even the *modes* in which consciousness manifests itself are, in the last resort, beyond analysis, so closely are they unified, and so easily do they, in working, shade off into each other. In other words, consciousness includes, at every moment, all that we mean by Feeling, Thought, and Will. We have tried too often to isolate these functions—to say, "This is altogether an Intellectual thing," or "This is a product of pure Emotion," or "There we see an act of almost pure Will." The result is that the study of consciousness has been sectionalised in such a manner as to neglect the work of the whole, *as a whole*.

There are activities of the mind which have not received the attention they deserve, mainly, we suppose, because they were not small conceptions, inviting meticulous analysis, but large conceptions involving more scope for imagination and judgment than for scientific measurement. The first is Plato's idea of "knowing," and the second is Newman's *Illative Sense.*

V

θεωρία—i.e. *theoria*—means a seeing, a beholding, followed by understanding ; an understanding made up of two elements, knowledge and vision. It is a look at life that embodies both science and philosophy ; it not only asks, What are phenomena ? but, What lies behind phenomena ? and Why ? And although it believes in logic and in reason, it believes just as much in *impression*, the direct message that phenomena gives to the soul. It is not only a thinking process but a method of mental vision.[1]

Professor Pillsbury has rightly pointed out that the real process in thinking, in the sense of reasoning a thing out, is one of problem-solving : to use his own words : " The occasion for the reasoning is a thwarted purpose." [2] In the attitude represented by the word θεωρία there is an entire lack of this element : it means, as already explained, a beholding, but not a beholding in which there is no thought, no mental comparison, no sense of contrast, no valuation ; these factors and many others are in their highest form of activity, mainly because they are working on a more co-operative basis than when the mind is engaged on work that is essentially logical or deliberately scientific. In that condition the whole focus is directed by means of the reason, using that word in its more logical associations. Mr A. D. Lindsay puts the whole matter into a sentence when he says that Plato " while always insisting on exact argument and care-

---

[1] Plato does not always use the same word, but the idea is the same. To him the highest form of thinking " is the comprehensive intuition of the man who sees all things as part of a system (ὁ συνοπτικος), realises that each part has its being in the whole and brings that system to bear on each thing."—G. S. Brett, *History of Psychology*, p. 82.

[2] Similarly Prof. Dewey says: " Demand for the solution of a perplexity is the steadying and guiding factor in the entire process of reflection."—*How We Think*, p. 11.

ful logical reasoning makes all reasoning depend finally on intellectual insight and vision which is immediate." [1]

Bergson is a philosopher whose teaching has gripped on a wide public : and the processes of intuition, to him, are as much a matter worthy of investigation as the purely logical processes ; nay, they are more worthy, for reason has not been a complete success in explaining life and phenomena. Commenting on a striking passage in *Creative Evolution* (pp. 862-868), Professor Cunningham says : "We need a new method of comprehension which will bring us into direct touch with the vital impetus. . . . Consciousness must turn from its natural bent and strive to *see* as well as understand, sympathise with, as well as construct, the universe which has produced it." [2] The proposed new method is really a modern application of Platonic vision. It was of Plato that Walter Pater said, "for him all gifts of sense and intelligence converge in one supreme faculty of theoretic vision, θεωρία, the imaginative reason." [3] Perhaps we might desire a difference in phraseology, though it be hardly respectful to a great master ; but the essence is there—θεωρία is the sum of all gifts of sense and intelligence, and not all its findings can be put into words, much less formulated into syllogisms.

VI

It is somewhat surprising that psychologists have of recent years paid so little attention to the implications of the

[1] *Five Dialogues of Plato bearing on Poetic Inspiration*, p. 9. Ackermann gives a more extended view, and adds : " It is doubtless difficult for us to imagine this, or to believe in the possibility of such a cognition, for the simple reason that we can only artificially form for ourselves a world-consciousness of this kind, while to Plato it was natural. For where the unity of the intellectual life is so divided, and sundered into activites so different and separate from each other, where the power of reflection is so completely severed from the maternal stock of the fulness of impression, and has attained such independent perfection and decided superiority among us, we can scarcely think of cognition as other than a purely immanent logical act of the understanding."—*The Christian Element in Plato*, p. 180.

[2] *The Philosophy of Bergson*, p. 27.

[3] *Plato and Platonism*, p. 127.

Illative Sense; possibly they have been too busy with experimental research. Some day, however, the doctrine may take a new lease of life, not in lowly circles, but in the very highest. The word Illative, according to the dictionary, means something pertaining to illation or inference, and the Illative Sense is defined as " that faculty of the human mind by which it forms a judgment upon the validity of an inference." The definition does not satisfy us, for the illative sense is not a " faculty "; and it is not clear whether the illation judges or estimates the validity of the inference, or whether it is a judgment consequent upon the inference. Newman himself does not seem to have given us a neat and formal definition in his *Grammar of Assent*, but Sir Leslie Stephen supplied the deficiency. To him the illative sense is " that by which the mind draws remote inferences without a conscious syllogistic process." [1] This brings us nearer, and we propose to offer the reader an illustration. Remembering that formal logic is a *test* of thinking, and not a process of discovering new ideas, or arriving at new conclusions, we will imagine that a London merchant, intent upon opening a branch of his business in Cardiff, is engaged in estimating the chances of success and the possibilities of failure. His cogitations centre in masses of figures, then pass to considerations of staff; he weighs the pros and cons of the new shop's position and its relation to the customers he has in view. The whole scheme involves many difficult calculations, so complicated, indeed, that no mathematician could symbolise the mental processes involved and no logician could syllogise them. Very well; how, then, does he come to a decision to act or not to act? By an estimate of probabilities, and that estimate is carried out by the illative sense. Newman illustrated his doctrine from Shakespearean criticism, but his exposition of method is of universal application, and that method is one of " the cumulation of probabilities, independent of each other, arising out of the nature and circumstances of the particular case which is under review; probabilities too fine to avail separately, too subtle and circuitous, to be

[1] *An Agnostic's Apology*, p. 205.

convertible into syllogisms."[1] But does the illative sense exist, or is it a figment of Newman's imagination? There is no doubt at all of its existence, simply because most people draw inferences without conscious logical effort : indeed it is one of the commonest forms of mental activity, employing the whole of our mental functions in a unified manner. That is really why we call attention to it at this stage of our inquiry. Sir Leslie Stephen, one of Newman's severest but fairest critics, admitted that the illative sense "undoubtedly corresponds to a real faculty or combination of faculties."[2] The language of this admission is not as exact as we should have liked it to be—the use of the word faculty, for instance—but we will take it as a confession that there may be more than one mental function at work during illation.

VII

The illative sense is strictly individual in its action. In Cardinal Newman's case it landed him in Roman Catholicism ; in Professor F. W. Newman's case it resulted in a form of theism. Why ? Because our illations depend on the nature of our temperament, our education, our environment, and our experience, but chiefly on temperament—that bodily setting which determines the tendencies of the mind and is partly responsible for the proportions of Thought, Feeling, and Will in our mental constitution. James Mill tried to make his son John a duplicate of himself, but John's proportion of Feeling was in excess of his father's, and he therefore illated differently—*i.e.* more emotionally. Böhme's illative sense, plus his experience, resulted in a system of theosophy ; Haeckel, with a narrow feeling-development, and an excess in the other directions, draws inferences of a very different kind. Thus we see the strange spectacle of men with great powers of intellect accepting superstitions as if they were truth — some superstitions being religious and others scientific ; we see men of equal ability diametrically opposed

[1] *Grammar of Assent*, p. 281.
[2] *An Agnostic's Apology*, p. 209.

in party politics; we see Tyndall scorning spiritualism and Crookes and Wallace believing in the reality of its phenomena; we see men of bright intelligence accepting Mrs Eddy's statement that disease is error, while other men, just as bright, smile incredulously; realists fight with idealists, Romanists with Protestants; art critics of some competence defend the new movements, whilst other critics, also competent, condemn them utterly. There must be some reason why highly developed and trained minds cannot agree on important issues; and we find it mostly in the unified action of our whole consciousness. It is not logic that decides; otherwise professors of logic would not disagree so passionately on free trade and tariff reform; our decisions respecting truth come from a blend of instinct, feeling, thought, and experience operating by means of the illative sense.

VIII

A further reflection is this: that the endeavour to find the nature of genius in a modification or expansion of Thought, Feeling, or Will is bound to be unsatisfactory, simply because the mind is a unity. There are times, no doubt, when one function will be preponderant, but at no time does either one of the three functions entirely occupy the field of consciousness. Schopenhauer said that "if the normal man consists of two-thirds Will, and one-third Intellect, the genius, on the contrary, has two-thirds Intellect and one-third Will."[1] Well, test this by an estimate of Napoleon and the inaccuracy is at once evident. He was a man of immense motive-power, and his Will was certainly in advance of his Intellect. Schopenhauer leaves no room for Feeling and all the finer issues of sensibility on which so much depends; and his attempt to measure ability arithmetically breaks down at once when we consider a genius outside the group of those whom he had in mind. But we have to admit that we often think in a manner that is unbalanced and unsound, because we give too much play to Feeling, to Thought, or to blind Impulse. Speaking of

[1] *The World as Will and Representation*, vol. iii., p. 140.

CONSCIOUSNESS

Robert Hugh Benson's conversion from Anglicanism to Romanism, Mr R. J. Campbell says: "Unless I am utterly mistaken, the intellect played almost no part in the tremendous decision which led him to submit to Rome." [1] This appears to be a reasonable judgment, but, after all, the mind that came to the conclusion referred to was Mgr Benson's not Mr Campbell's; and we have no right to say that the author of *The Dawn of All* changed his creed on account of "convictions" that represented, say, five-eighths Feeling, two-eighths Will, and only one-eighth Intellect. There can be no doubt whatever that with a mind of such sincerity the whole consciousness, governed by temperament, was involved in the decision, not in equal ratio of function, probably, but in the ratio of the man as Nature had made him. These guesses at mental proportional representation have academic, even practical, interest to some extent. Croce asks: "Was not the battle of Austerlitz also a work of thought, and the *Divine Comedy* also a work of Will?" [2] We can only reply in the affirmative, and reflect on the actuating motives of Germany in 1914 when the desire (feeling) of conquest, the carefully constructed (thought) plan of campaign, and the vigour of its prosecution (will) show the whole Teutonic soul at work. A French writer who has investigated the relationship between thought and action came to the conclusion that *penser: agir* are one form of energy—*i.e.* a unity. [3]

But what of an extraordinary gift in music, or memory-power? Does not this prove that even Nature itself indulges in irregularity by producing men with one power *in excelsis* and the others below the average level? That is not the point. We are discussing the interworking of the three functions of mind *whatever they are in their natural proportions*; and whilst the predominance of a special gift will control the direction of mental activity, it will not, and cannot, act in entire separation from the other functions; it merely takes the lead.

[1] *The Life of Monsignor Robert Hugh Benson.* By C. C. Martindale, S.J.

[2] *Philosophy of the Practical*, p. 7.

[3] *Le Reve et l'Action*, p. 359.

ORIGINALITY

IX

By *range* we mean, first, the possible reach of consciousness; its ability to encompass and to give approximate values to all kinds of phenomena. Next, we mean all that is implied in the activity of the subconsciousness, the range of which is as yet beyond our ken.

In reference to the first, we begin by saying that in its more elementary form it shows itself in the somewhat mechanical increase of knowledge—the storage of facts in the mind. A man who knows astronomy up to its advanced stages has a wider area of consciousness than the man who does not. We may add a knowledge of Greek to a knowledge of Hebrew, or supplement a study of language by a course in formal logic. But in its deeper meaning the word range, as used here, connotes a great deal more than additions to our store of information; it means a perception of unities amid diversities, a more or less emotional apprehension of wholes as distinct from parts. So instead of a sum in addition, adding fact to fact, Greek paradigms to Hebrew tenses, or the psychological powers of words to the forms of the syllogism, we realise their larger relationships to history and to human life. We become aware of the significance of things small and great.

Take an illustration. What are tears? The visible expression of strong inward emotion. Does that hasty definition tell us all about them? Yes; for the practical purposes of sympathy, presuming, for the moment, that the tears mean grief and not laughter. But ask the physiologist to answer the question, and he will discourse learnedly on the lachrymal glands and ducts showing how our tears are always flowing, and how grief, or laughter, diverts them from their natural channel through the two canaliculi to the nose. Ask the analyst: What are tears? and he will write down the formula [1] thus:

$$NaCl - H_2O$$

[1] Baltazar, one of Balzac's characters, says: "Ah! tears; I have analysed them; they contain a little phosphate of lime, chloride of sodium, mucin, and water." Perhaps Balzac did not seek scientific accuracy.

CONSCIOUSNESS

You may ask the cynic, the humorist, and a score of others to answer the question, and each will give his point of view, which in most cases is decided by temperament, occupation, and experience. We do not say that a man of knowledge may not be also a man of sympathy : we are merely drawing a distinction between information *about* a fact and our realisation of the fact itself. The man who first revealed the physiology and chemistry of tears rendered useful service to mankind, but the man with a greater range of feeling who said :

> "Tears from the depth of some divine despair
> Rise in the heart and gather to the eyes
> In looking on the happy Autumn-fields
> And thinking of the days that are no more "

contributed to the spiritual wealth of the world. His reach was in advance of the others. *They* told us of the immediate qualities of things : *he* told us of the thing in itself as it appealed to the whole consciousness ; he brought forth the finer essences.

X

The botanist looks at a flower with an eye to classification —its genus and species, its origin, its locality, its rarity. The poet, plucking it from the crannied wall, may know little of its natural history, but in his consciousness it is a thing that suggests thoughts that lie too deep for tears. Both are right ; indeed the botanist and poet may be one. But think of the difference between their points of view. To one the flower is a *specimen* ; to the other an *inspiration*. It is the poet, therefore, who has the finer reach of consciousness, for to him the visible has meanings that the poverty of speech renders difficult of utterance. He feels what he does not comprehend ; he senses what he does not know ; and sometimes he appears to recollect what he has not experienced.

There is a real sense in which the poet does not stand alone in this respect. Every man of mark has a specific ability which, translated into popular language, means that he sees more and sees farther than those around him; his range of consciousness is most extensive and intensive. He could not explain himself, however much he tried to do so; indeed, those manuals of the philosophy of Success wherein millionaires and other magnates show how they have made fortunes are full of misconceptions. The cynic says that it is not likely such men will part with their secrets for the price of a magazine article. The psychologist knows better. He says "they *cannot*, even if they would." The deepest secrets are always hidden, not only from the world but from the man who thinks he knows them. Who among us believes that the Port Sunlight business was developed mainly by steady application and perseverance? And yet this is what Lord Leverhulme would have us believe.[1] Of course every leader of note must try to explain himself to himself and to others: some strike the note of modesty, and a few become egotists; but the motive behind each is to avoid the belief in chance and to emphasise the relation of cause to consequence. We who have studied men in action know that even in matters of business the thinker who weighs matters carefully, even ponderously, is often mistaken in his laboured decisions; whilst the man who follows the first impulse of consciousness is more often right than wrong.[2] Here again we strike an analogy with the poet. "Thought by itself," says Leigh Hunt, "makes no poet at all. . . . Feeling, even destitute of conscious thought, stands a far better poetical chance; feeling being a sort of thought without the process of thinking—a grasper of the truth without seeing it. And what is very remarkable, feeling seldom makes the blunders that thought does."[3] Probably because in our feeling there is a large subconscious element.

[1] Three Addresses by Sir W. H. Lever, Bart.

[2] Speaking of Success, the late Dr Emil Reich said of the professional man that "the more and the better he thinks, the more he is likely to be successful in his profession." He adds significantly: "Not so the business man. The business man who thinks and argues much is lost."—*Success in Life*, pp. 280-281.

[3] *What is Poetry?* (Cook's edition), p. 66.

CONSCIOUSNESS

XI

The range of consciousness, then, is a phrase with a meaning which may serve to elucidate the problem of what constitutes differences in mental ability. There is not much help in the word itself: ability is ableness, the quality which denotes power to perform or to act. Undoubtedly this idea is at the basis of all kinds of ability. The lifting of a huge dumb-bell by a strong man is physical ability; the building of a bridge across a wide and deep ravine is engineering ability; the foretelling of an eclipse is mathematical ability: these men have certain powers of knowledge and action that produce results—they are *able* men. But there are obvious differences. The strong man may not be given to much thinking; his ability is purely muscular except so far as the accomplishment of new tasks is concerned. Into the feat of engineering there enters a union of theory and practice, while the astronomer's actions are confined very largely to intricate calculations on paper. The real question, therefore, is this: Is there not an ability that is purely intellectual—*i.e.* one in which Feeling and Will are at a minimum? We do not mean the difference between the Miltons who write great poems and the Miltons who are mute and inglorious; we mean the ability to reflect with sympathy and insight, even though no action follows, or in any sense is necessary. The only answer is a decided affirmative. A philosopher of distinction is bound to be a man of great intellectual power, and yet all the action that follows his thinking is confined to the writing of a book or the delivery of lectures. Kant is an interesting illustration.

For the sake of instructive contrast we will place Lord Leverhulme and Kant side by side. What is the difference between their kinds of intellectual ability? One is a master in the real world, the other a master in the idea world. Each has a wide range of consciousness, but not in the same direction. The professor deals with ideas; the business man with facts. The professor puts ideas into a closed atmosphere—like those delicate weighing machines covered

with glass—so that no disturbing breath of emotion may
lead his valuation astray; the business man, having no
patience with such finesse, takes the world as he finds it,
studies demand and supply, prices, transportation, and
accounts. But whilst the contrast between the two men
is thus evident the likenesses are not far to seek. The same
kind of brain-power is used albeit in different degrees and
for different ends. A Sandow or a Hackenschmidt can lift
a weight twenty times heavier than we can lift, but when we
have raised our puny weight we have used the same muscles
as theirs, under similar mental direction. The advantage
of superior weight is greatly on the side of the experts, but
both they and the weaklings use the same kind of bodily
energy. It is even so in the mental world. Ribot [1] has
proved conclusively that there is not one imagination for
the poet and one for the merchant or inventor. If a poet
forgets his umbrella he forgets it in the same way as the
ordinary person; and when the ordinary person has to
imagine a scheme for getting out of a difficulty, he uses the
same kind of imagination as a poet. An unpalatable truth,
doubtless, but still it is the truth. Shakespeare's brain was
a human brain, and so is that of the most inefficient one-act
playwright of the moment. The bard did not possess Feeling,
Thought, Will, and a fourth something which we call *genius*.
His mind worked according to the mental laws that govern
all minds; the difference between him and others lay in
one thing: his was a mind of almost infinite *compass*. The
average man has consciousness; Shakespeare had it to the
nth degree, so vast was its range, so susceptible its feelings,
and so profound its unity of conception.

XII

No psychologist has given a better definition of ability
than Sir Francis Galton. He says: "By natural ability I
mean those qualities of intellect and disposition which urge
and qualify a man to perform acts that lead to reputation.
I do not mean capacity without zeal, nor zeal without

[1] *The Creative Imagination.*

capacity, nor even a combination of both of them without an adequate power of doing a great deal of laborious work. But I mean a nature which, when left to itself, will, urged by an inherent stimulus, climb the path that leads to eminence." [1]   Here are three elements :

>(a) a consistent motive-power ;
>(b) good intellectual discernment, and
>(c) action.

They can be found well marked in any man of note where mental qualities are necessarily important : but let us not forget the place that Galton gives to Feeling as seen in the use of the words *disposition, urge, zeal,* and *inherent stimulus.* The first ability is emotional ability : the Feeling which, as Leigh Hunt said, makes fewer mistakes than Thought.   The next is mental perception : the means by which we collect, classify, and systematise what other sections of the mind give to us.   The third ability is action ability.

The history of genius and talent is an interesting picture of disproportions in these three abilities.   We have known at least one metaphysician who was so much out of touch with the Real and so much in touch with the Ideal that he could not earn a decent living.   Consciousness was out of focus.   Rousseau erred on the side of emotion, living for whole periods in a welter of tears, just as Swedenborg revelled in his self-hypnotised visions of another world. Lombroso, with a keen scent for the abnormal, hunted out all the disproportions he could find in literary and scientific biography ; and he concluded that genius was a form of insanity.   It was an easy conclusion, because disproportion is so obvious ; but why avoid such names as Plato and Aristotle, Shakespeare and Goethe ?   The greatest type of genius has never been one-sided ; its consciousness has never been out of touch with the facts of life, however much time it has spent in the world of ideas.

[1] *Hereditary Genius.*   Höffding says : " From antiquity downwards, psychology has laid the greatest stress upon the original bents of feeling which give the keynote to mental life, whatever line it may strike out."—*Outlines of Psychology,* p. 349.

ORIGINALITY

The Greek conceptions of directness, action, and harmony prevented any grievous errors in perspective : the poet must also be a warrior. As Mahaffy says: "The Greeks never thought of promoting a man for 'dead knowledge' but for his living grasp of science or of life."[1] Shakespeare wrote the greatest dramas of modern history, and yet, as a man of action, he organised a successful theatrical business; and in regard to details could "cavil to the ninth point of a hair." Goethe also was a practical man of the theatre; a philosopher, critic, and poet; and a scientific discoverer to boot. The geniuses of Feeling, of Thought, or of Action—*i.e.* considered as functioning mainly in these directions—are always the secondary geniuses, because consciousness has been abbreviated in important directions. That is why they felt so lonely. Intense subjectivity, without rational sympathies with others and without a sense of humour, comes to a head in the shape of self-consciousness; hence the egotism,[2] the feeling of solitude, the sense of antagonism seen in such a collection of testimonies as Morrill's *Self-Consciousness of Great Men* and Disraeli's *Characteristics of Men of Genius*. Genius in its finest manifestations is the outcome of consciousness as sensibility, reflection, and action. Schopenhauer, nearer the truth than in our previous quotation, defines it as "an eminently clear consciousness of things in general." He rightly places much emphasis on sensibility, stating that our mental powers are themselves forms of it. Jastrow confirms this by saying that each man "becomes the sum of his sensibilities and his world is bounded by the range of his appreciations."[3]

[1] *Old Greek Education*, p. 17.

[2] Coleridge said of himself: "You may not understand my system or any given part of it,—or, by a determined act of wilfulness, you may, even though perceiving a ray of light, reject it in anger or disgust : but this I will say—that if you once master it, or any part of it, you cannot hesitate to acknowledge it as the truth."—*Table Talk*, p. 248. Coleridge's system is a monument to the Unconstructed. His consciousness (or ability) was too limited on the side of action.

[3] *The Qualities of Men*, p. 5. Or, as Prof. J. M. Baldwin puts it: "To know that the greatest men on earth are men who think as

CONSCIOUSNESS

XIII

The fact is, all inward experiences and all external facts are known in a sense that is difficult to distinguish from the *mystical*. We *comprehend* little or nothing: everything is *apprehended*. It is not God alone who is unknowable. In the last resort everything is unknowable.[1] Is there one fact in science without its unknown side ? Even a child can puzzle a philosopher. George Eliot speaks somewhere of a juvenile who was told not to touch a wasp that was crawling up the window-pane, and this brought out the question, "Why ? "

"Because it will sting you."

"Why does it not sting the pane of glass ? "

"Because the glass has no nerves and it can't feel."

"Why do nerves feel ? " inquired the youngster, but the conversation was not continued. A keen question about anything, and—we enter the unknown. But is it the unknowable also ? Possibly, for every advance in knowledge does no more than push back the border-line of Agnosticism ; we have gained some practical information about a gas, or a metal, or the atmosphere : but the bases of the knowing process remain the same and our sense of the infinity of the Universe has been deepened. The more we know the more vast is the territory of the undisclosed ; and the greater our desire to conquer Nature the more feeble do our powers appear. As Professor Santayana puts it : "The resources of the mind are not commensurate with its ambitions."[2]

And yet it is with these powers that the best minds of the race, for untold ages, have essayed to interpret the mysteries of existence. It is a story of failure and partial

I do, but deeper, and see the real as I do, but clearer, who work to the goal that I do, but faster, and serve humanity as I do, but better— that may be an incitement to my humility, but it is also an inspiration to my life."—*Social and Ethical Interpretations*, p. 168.

[1] The kind of certainty that one objects to is seen in the following, from Dr Paul Carus, in *The Monist*, vol. i., p. 73:—" Memory is no mysterious power: it is the preservation of form in feeling organisms." Well, and what is *that* ?

[2] *Poetry and Religion*, p. 2.

success; and although many a man has been tempted to end his philosophising with the genial cynicism of Omar Khayyám, the cheering fact is that the majority still seek that they may find. Some day the progress of mankind, always marked by leaps and jerks, will take a forward movement for which past history offers no parallel. Meanwhile we are conscious of severe limitations. Even the exact things, the things which we thought were crystal in their clarity, seem to have uncertainties in them. Nothing, for instance, can be clearer, or more free from doubt, than that $1+1=2$. But we are told by authorities that although "one added to one makes two is abstractedly beneath controversy, it need not be true for the addition of concrete things. It is not true of two globules of mercury, for instance, nor for a couple of colliding stars." So it seems. Well may Sir Oliver Lodge conclude by saying: "Life can ridicule arithmetic."[1] The fact is, arithmetic and mathematics are mental conveniences for the purpose of adjusting phenomena to our consciousness. We have to remember that we owe the first elements of both sciences to the Pythagorean mystics,[2] and it does not follow because we can measure the parallax of a star or calculate the coming of a comet that mathematics is the primary certainty.

XIV

Then is the material world a delusion? No; it is a clearly defined experience, one of the immediacies of consciousness. We do not know *how* we know the trees, the flowers, and the

---

[1] *The Hibbert Journal*, Jan., 1912, article on "Balfour and Bergson," by Sir Oliver Lodge. Mr Bertrand Russell says, on another aspect of the subject, that "it was assumed as self-evident until Cantor and Dedekind established the opposite, that if, from any collection of things, some were taken away, the number of things left must always be less than the original number of things. This assumption, as a matter of fact, holds only of finite collections; and the rejection of it, where the infinite is concerned, has been shown to remove all the difficulties that had hitherto baffled human reason in the matter."—*Philosophical Essays*, pp. 27-28.

[2] Berkeley, *Mysticism in Mathematics*, p. 5.

sky; and it is merely playing with words to say that whilst *we* exist these objects only exist *as sensations and perceptions*,[1] having no external reality. But it is not our purpose to discuss the problem pro and con : we simply point out the almost mystical way in which philosophers and psychologists are compelled to describe things that are plain to consciousness but very difficult to put into words. They are not alone in this respect, for poets labour under the same difficulty when . they try to express the inexpressible. Mallarmé, indeed, regards the difficulty itself as a thing to be reverenced; and in his comments on *Le Mystère dans les Lettres*,[2] he will not so much as have things *named* : to name them is to drag them down into the known and the analysable.

Here, again, the reader may think we are solely bent upon displaying the impossible. We are doing no more than draw attention to the essential mystery of all experience. Take the words of two very different men and test them by your own knowledge of men and things. Says Anatole France : "I believe we shall never know exactly why a thing is beautiful."[3] Now, we put it to you as a problem : Do *you* know why a thing of beauty is beautiful ? The æsthetic philosophers and artists for centuries have debated the matter, and the library shelves groan with the weight of their findings, but nobody knows *exactly* why a thing is beautiful. Art is the most elusive of conceptions and yet it is one of the greatest of realities. We delight in it; we fill our galleries with new efforts and zealously visit those buildings which house the glories of the past; we have art criticisms in the Press every day and monthly journals of art keep us informed about the latest developments; and yet nobody has ever caught Beauty and confined it behind the bars of a definition. We should be distressed if this ever happened, for its elusiveness is the soul of its charm.

[1] The language of Prof. Lloyd Morgan is as near the truth as we can get : " The subject and object, involved in the sense impression, are like the colour or the scent of the rose, *distinguishable in thought*, but they are not *separable in experience.*"—*Comparative Psychology*, p. 309.

[2] *Divagations.* Paris, 1897.

[3] *Life and Letters*, Second Series, p. 176.

ORIGINALITY

XV

Take another confession—from Prof. Wm. James. "Intellectualism in the vicious sense," he says, "began when Socrates and Plato taught that what a thing really is, is told us by its *definition*."[1] If you doubt these words test them by an attempt to define some of the truths of your conscious life : *love, taste, right, soul, truth.* We use these words freely and understandingly, as if they presented no difficulty, but if some modern Socrates cared to cross-examine us and insist upon a definition we should soon be nonplussed, seeking refuge in the saying that we know the meaning but cannot phrase it. This used to be a confession of weakness. It is such no longer. For, however skilfully we attempt to define *truth* or *right*, it is admitted that some element of importance will be left out ; and usually the omission refers to that intangible something in thought which never comes within the range of language. Psychology, as a science, has achieved many gratifying successes, but it has not been a complete success—perhaps in the nature of things that is impossible. Researches in the world of mind have been conducted in the exclusive spirit of science, as if soul could be analysed ! There is a suggestive passage in Prof. Titchener's *Experimental Psychology of the Thought Processes* which indicates a welcome change of method. In speaking of his own ideas as to the conducting of inquiries he says : "I assume we are to attempt a psychology, and that psychology has here to pick its way between logic, or the theory of knowledge, on the one hand, and common sense on the other." Yes, and a good many psychologists have lost their way—not on the one hand, but on the other. Common sense as a guide to psychological truth is an excellent notion, and one of its functions will be to separate the indefinables and the unknowables. As Boutroux puts it : "All experimental finding is reduced, in the end, to confining within as close limits as possible the value of the measurable element of the phenomena. We never reach the exact point at

[1] *A Pluralistic Universe*, p. 218.

which the phenomenon really begins and ends." [1]   And it is always the beginnings and the endings everywhere that resist most resolutely our attempts at definition.   But things, in process, are really quite as resistant, for a phenomenon midway in its career can laugh at our efforts to discover its essence.   We find a few secrets and lay bare the method, but the thing in itself defies us.   It is well to recognise our limitations ; for dogmatism—that confidence which comes from a belief in our having secured the whole truth—is offensive whether it be the work of a reactionary theologian or of a cocksure scientist like Haeckel.   Prof. Schäfer has urged that "Vagueness, which used to be recognised as our great enemy, is now being enshrined as an idol to be worshipped."   Nothing of the kind.   All we want from men of science is a statement of the approximately known and unknown : it is no worship of vagueness to mark off the area of the undiscovered and frankly confess our utter ignorance of it.

XVI

But the range of consciousness includes the work of the subconscious.   There is no impropriety in speaking of the range of the subconscious, in spite of our ignorance of its nature and scope.   What we have in view is the whole sphere of mind, and mind includes the conscious and subconscious. The words themselves need not cause any difficulty : we may indeed adopt the phraseology of Sidis where he defines the subconscious as " mental states that have consciousness, but do not reach the personal consciousness " [2]—that is, the working itself is unknown and yet the results may manifest themselves to us.   Consequently any factor that affects the range of the conscious comes within our purview.

That there is a subconscious sphere is now almost universally recognised [3]; and, to use the language of Lipps, it is not so much a psychological problem as *the* problem of

---

[1] *The Contingency of the Laws of Nature*, pp. 27-28.

[2] *Normal and Abnormal Psychology*, p. 206.

[3] Münsterberg was an exception.   See his *General Psychology*, p. 27.

psychology. The first question that arises is this: How does the working of the conscious compare and contrast with the working of the subconscious? The answer is not an easy one, but the two spheres, so far as we can tell, appear to work in much the same way, with certain important differences. One is that the subconscious seems to act as a super-consultant and adviser to the conscious and, apparently, confines its activity to Thought and Feeling—Will is almost an absentee.[1] Here we come face to face with the most difficult problem of all—namely, the origin of the subconscious. Did it come *before* the conscious, or *after*? There is much to be said on behalf of the former contention. It would help us to explain the existence of infant prodigies, and of the early marks of genius in every direction. It would provide us with a hypothesis to account for the inward urge which, as Galton pointed out, is the first characteristic of natural ability. It would explain the unique achievements of men whose conscious minds have received little or no formal education. Besides, there is no *a priori* reason why in the subconscious sphere we should not have natural gifts— inborn facilities—just as we have in the conscious sphere. But every gift needs its objective experience, and no marvellous juvenile calculator could solve knotty problems mentally unless he had had some experience of figures and symbols. Hoffmann records an instructive case: "Vito Mangiamele, a shepherd boy of Sicily, was taken to Paris in 1837, when he was ten years old, and examined before the French Academy of Sciences by Arago, the famous astronomer. He put to the boy the following questions:— What is the cube root of 8,796,416? In half-a-minute Vito gave the correct answer 156. Another problem was the equation $x5 - 4x - 16779 = 0$. At first Vito answered 8: but

[1] It is too early to talk about "unconscious psychic processes" as "real entities" after the manner of Freud. He quotes Lipps, approvingly, who says: "The dominant factors of the psychic life are not represented by the contents of consciousness but by those psychic processes which are unconscious."— Freud, *Wit and its Relation to the Unconscious*, p. 227. If this means a dictatorship, set up without the authority of the conscious intelligence, it is another instance of a theorist squeezing his facts to suit his hypothesis.

afterwards changed it to 7 which is the true solution."[1]   Are we to be told that Vito solved these problems without ever having seen or known the multiplication table or the uses of x?   If so, then the age of "miracles" is still with us, and we shall be sceptics of the most pronounced type.   The more rational solution is that Vito had a facility for solving arithmetical and mathematical problems by subconscious processes, but that the elements of calculation were learned in the usual conscious manner.

XVII

But even if the subconscious is first in point of origin, and animal psychology lends support to that theory, there can be no doubt that for its *material* it depends on ordinary conscious activity; for we may see the day when the sub-conscious mind, of popular imagination, is proved to be the organised but unconscious memory-system of the individual self. The task that we fail to accomplish in our waking moments is accomplished by the subconscious whilst we sleep. In this way the ability of the subconscious is raised or depressed by the manner of life we live on the conscious plane; consequently it is not improper to speak of the education of the subconscious—indeed that kind of mental training in schools and colleges which leaves no room for individuality and spontaneity is defective simply because subconscious processes are crowded out. This is all the more to be regretted because these processes yield finer results than those which are conscious. Poincaré, in dis-cussing this fact, indulges in two hypotheses. His first hypothesis is that "the subliminal ego is in no way inferior to the conscious ego; it is not purely automatic; it is capable of discernment; it has tact and lightness of touch; it can select and it can divine. More than that, it can divine better than the conscious ego, since it succeeds where the latter fails. In a word is not the subliminal ego superior to the conscious ego?"[2] There are not two egos in the

---

[1] *Psychology and Common Life*, pp. 252-253.
[2] *Science and Method*, p. 57.

matter at all, for the mind is so definite a unity that even the semblance of separate conscious personalities does not destroy it. But there are two chambers of intelligence; in one the working is analysable to a large extent; in the other it is unconscious, nevertheless both chambers are in vital union. We confess to some regret, however, that Poincaré decided against the hypothesis just stated in favour of another, which argues that the æsthetic sensibilities decide the nature and scope of subconscious activities. To us the evidence that subconscious action is capable of greater achievements than conscious action is incontrovertible. As Prof. Dwelshauvers has said, in his *L'Inconscient*—the latest and most comprehensive book on the subject—nearly all inventiveness comes from unconscious mental operations.[1] There is a strange but very interesting illustration in the life of Charlotte Brontë. Readers of *Villette* will remember the vision consequent upon the narrator taking a drug in a dose of medicine; and the question arose as to how the writer obtained her ideas. "I asked her," says Mrs Gaskell, "whether she had ever taken opium, as the description of its effect was so exactly like what I had experienced. She replied that she had never, to her knowledge, taken a grain of it in any shape, but that she had followed the process which she always adopted when she had to describe anything which had not fallen within her own experience; she had thought intently on it for many and many a night before falling to sleep—wondering what it was like, or how it would be—till at length, sometimes after the progress of her story had been arrested at this one point for weeks, she wakened up in the morning with all clear before her, as if she had in reality gone through the experience, and then could describe it word for word, as it had happened." The *method* employed is the one that has been used from time immemorial: our forefathers always filled their minds with an urgent problem before going to sleep, experience having taught them that a solution might be expected one fine morning. But in the case of *Villette* the details of an opium

[1] *L'Inconscient*, by Georges Dwelshauvers, Professor in the University of Brussels. Paris, 1916.

vision are "found" or "invented" with striking accuracy; and if Mrs Gaskell's report be correct it suggests that the subconscious can perform some very wonderful works. Manifestly there must be limits, for no man, however well gifted subconsciously, could expect to rise one morning with the power to read Sanscrit, simply because he had resolved to read it. As in the case of Poincaré's discovery of functions, there must be some previous acquaintance with the subject. The date of *Villette* is 1853; the date of De Quincey's *Confessions of an Opium Eater* is 1821; so we may presume that Charlotte Brontë, recalling subconsciously the reading of the earlier book, was able to individualise her own conceptions of an opium vision. Of course we cannot prove that she had read De Quincey, but it is a reasonable supposition, and it does nothing to detract from the work of the subconscious; for, consciously, she at first felt herself incapable of writing the visions—her mind was a blank. But after a few weeks the whole thing "came"; and we all agree it was well worth the waiting.

The use of the phrase "range of consciousness" has, we hope, been made quite clear. It is the action of the whole mind in its conscious and subconscious spheres, and, as we see already, originality is due, mainly, to the interaction between these two spheres. We shall return to the subject again; meanwhile, we desire to show how the newer developments of psychology, consequent upon the failure, in part, of the older methods, throw light on the creative thought processes.

CHAPTER II

I

IF, then, the science of psychology, on its introspective and experimental sides, has reached what appear to be definite limits, or has come within sight of them, it is evident that a new method is desirable, not to say necessary—one that will enable us to approach the problem of mind from another point of view, and to approach it in the scientific spirit. Such a method is that of conceiving mind as a form of energy having more than a few analogies with physical energy. The study of psychology on this basis has already begun,[1] and, although its early results have, in some instances, the extravagances which one expects to see in the work of enthusiasts, the proved remainder is sufficiently encouraging to justify further efforts.

We are familiar with the law of the conservation of energy, and there is no need to enlarge upon it here, or to take into account its modern developments—*e.g.* the dissipation of energy. The bent bow, when released, transfers its force to the arrow, and the powder in the cartridge is transmuted into the trajectory of the bullet. These are stock illustrations. But when an attempt is made to establish an identity between physical and mental energy, not so much in essence as in mode of operation, a cry of alarm is raised. Theologians and idealists are afraid of materialism, and some of the materialists are afraid they will be charged with bad science. It is all a part of the eternal quarrel between

---

[1] We look upon M'Dougall's conception of psychology—*i.e. mental behaviour*—as one that is not only sound but progressive in the best sense. It is not a static mind that he analyses, but mind in action. And is there any other kind of mind ?

CONSCIOUSNESS AS A FORM OF ENERGY

Mind and Matter. Ostwald states the position neatly in these words :

"If, in the other pair of ideas, *Mind—Matter*, we substitute energy for the second member, then there results the pair *mind—energy*. In what relation do these two things stand to each other ; do they form an irreconcilable opposition or may they be unified ? This question has already been asked several times in other connections ; it has usually been determined in the negative sense. A careful consideration of all the arguments known to me, both *pro* and *contra*, has led me to conclude that it may be answered in the affirmative. *I deem it possible to subordinate to the idea of energy the totality of psychical phenomena.*" [1]

II

It is curious to note in what ways and for what reasons some thinkers object to the notion of the conservation of mental energy, and equally curious to observe how other thinkers appear to welcome the idea. Dr H. Wildon Carr affirms that "Energy in physical science is the conception of something that is measurable, something that undergoes change of form with quantitative identity.[2] To apply such a conception to mental activity is plainly impossible, and to apply it metaphorically is only confusing. In what sense, for instance, is the memory that forms part of my subconscious psychical life a latent energy, and what is this energy converted into when some association brings it to consciousness ? " [3] This ought not to be a difficult question for a

---

[1] Article on "The Philosophical Meaning of Energy," in *The International Quarterly* (Sept. 1903).

[2] Mr W. R. Boyce Gibson has offered a keen criticism of this alleged ability to measure physical energy. See *Personal Idealism*, pp. 151-154.

[3] *Mind*, July, 1914. See also Sidis (*Foundations of Normal and Abnormal Psychology*, p. 21), Lloyd Morgan (*Comparative Psychology*, p. 330), and Binet (*The Mind and the Brain*, p. 7). Binet, after saying that "Thought is not a movement and has nothing in common with

disciple of Bergson and his philosophy of *change*. But let us begin at the beginning. Mental energy, manifested in the varied activities of the mind as we know it, is the one kind of energy of which we are most assured ; we are infinitely more certain about its conservation and dissipation, from the dawn of consciousness to the approach of death, than we are of the energy in Nature, the existence of which is an inference, not a personal experience in the primary subjective sense. Indeed, it is only by mental energy that we become aware of the existence of energy in the natural world. That being so, why should it be impossible to seek some analogy between the two energies—if they *are* two—and where does the confusion come in ? Are not analogies helpful in the interpretation of facts that on the surface may seem to belong to different worlds ? Professor Jung is of this opinion and even suggests that mental energy, in the sense of original *desire*, is the same as Bergson's *elan vital*.[1] But older psychologists than Jung have found no contradiction in the idea of mental energy working on lines analogous to that of Nature ; and although Herbert Spencer is now regarded as somewhat out of date his deeply philosophic mind found its true work in the building up of comprehensive theories, consequently his views on such a problem are worthy of respect. He says : " Each manifestation of force can be interpreted only as the effect of some antecedent force ; no matter whether it be an organic action, an animal movement, a thought, or a feeling. Either bodily or mental energies, as well as inorganic ones are quantitatively correlated to certain energies expended in their production, and to certain other energies which they imitate ; or else nothing must become something

a movement," affirms (p. 175) that " Psychology is a science of matter—the science of a part of matter which has the property of pre-adaptation " !

[1] " All psychological phenomena can be considered as manifestations of energy, in the same way as all physical phenomena are already understood as energetic manifestations since Robert Mayer discovered the law of the conservation of energy . . . (which) . . . can be understood as vital energy in general, or as Bergson's *elan vital*."—*Analytical Psychology*, p. 231. See also Gore's *Art of Discovery*, pp. 127–128.

and something must become nothing." [1]   Such an argument cannot be evaded and evasion is never attempted except in the interests of a particular philosophic system.

But Dr Wildon Carr seems to lay stress upon the fact that physical energy can be measured, whereas mental energy cannot be measured.   True—in part—but the admission is not so damaging as it looks ; indeed the impossibility of measuring psychical energy may be some testimony to its essential superiority as a causative agency.   The impressive fact is that psychical energy exists.   Dr Carr asks us what a subconscious memory is converted into when some association brings it to consciousness.   Beyond saying that it is, for the moment, changed from a hidden to a revealed fact we are unable to answer, just as we are unable to say, in natural science, how a cause gives rise to an effect.   As to the subconscious being a form of latent energy, it is already a conviction on the part of some writers, notably Ribot, who says : " *L'Inconscient est un accumulateur d'energie* ; il amasse pour que la conscience puisse dépenser." [2]

III

Mental energy, contrasted with physical energy, is of a finer and much more subtle form ; indeed it is this difference which is responsible for the unwillingness to admit any suggestion of identity, or even to allow that there exists a true analogy of action.   Light and heat, as modes of motion have a counterpart in thought as a species of vibration : but a thought is the last word in refinement, compared with which a ray of light and a concentration of heat are crudities of the lowest order.   Let us take a thought and an action for

---

[1] *First Principles*, p. 205.   Boutroux says that the law of conservation " seems pre-supposed in every enquiry that tends to explain the states of consciousness, considered by themselves, in the way in which the physical phenomena are explained ; it is implied in every attempt of positive psychology."—*The Contingency of the Laws of Nature*, p. 136.

[2] *La Vie Inconsciente et les Mouvements*, p. 77.   See also Bergson's *Creative Evolution*, pp. 4-8.

analysis. A man says: "My watch has begun to play tricks with me, and soon it will be like that of our commissionnaire: when the hands point to a quarter past three he knows it is half-past eight! I think I ought to take my watch to the watchmaker, and I decide to do so. I therefore get my stick and hat, and off I go." Now the *actions* here referred to are, of course, physical, but their origin is mental; consequently mental energy precedes physical energy; indeed these two energies are bound together in a partnership of being and doing that cannot be dissolved without bringing both to grief; apart they cannot exist as separate energies. We can have no mind without a body; and yet the mind is always the senior partner and managing director.[1] When Goethe read Shakespeare he said: "I stood like one who blind from birth finds himself suddenly blest with sight by a beneficent Providence." Here is psychical energy working on an exalted plane. What caused it? Outwardly, the factors were the printed page and the organs of vision; inwardly, there was profound activity among the brain cells resulting in an enlargement of the sphere of consciousness. But the primary agent was the printed page, and without it this infinite expansion of feeling could not have taken place. Who, then, will venture to dogmatise about this process— some to state that all energies are one energy, and that although a book placed before the eyes of a dead man can produce no result, the result that was forthcoming in the case of Goethe is explainable by the mind's power of translating symbols into the realities of feeling—the very thing that calls for explanation; some to state that the exaltation referred to was merely the mind's use of a simple phenomenon —thus overlooking the question as to whether physical or psychical energy was the prior power; and some to state that Goethe's language was hyperbolical, expansion being a term totally inapplicable to mind as an entity—thereby forgetting that invisible things must be stated in the terms of the visible?

[1] The arguments brought forward by Prof. D. F. Harris, in his article on "Consciousness as a Cause of Neural Activity," seem to us unanswerable.—*Hibbert Journal*, January, 1913.

CONSCIOUSNESS AS A FORM OF ENERGY

IV

There is a phrase in common use by all psychologists : it is "the stream of consciousness." It means, of course, that mental energy is best conceived as *flowing*; we may control its direction, raise its temperature, increase its force by narrowing its banks, and in other ways affect its destiny, but in the long run our control is only partial. We did not originate the stream ; life and being were thrust upon us, so to speak, and although we can put an end to our existence, thereby defeating, temporarily, some purpose in the formation of which we have had no share, we realise we are free with only a limited freedom. We may look upon ourselves as persons totally separated from the blind energies around us, but finally we have to admit we are part and parcel of the whole scheme of life and death, and that our energies, however exalted, appear to have intimate relationships with the ebb and flow of energies on a lower level.

Let us examine the record of a day's conscious life. "First, the vague feelings that come at the moment of waking ; next the body thrill after a cold plunge, followed by a cheerfulness of mind and a keen readiness for the tasks of the day ; breakfast and the morning paper, then the morning's work and a light lunch ; afternoon interviews and business, also a visit to an old friend nearing death ; the evening social meal, then some form of recreation." We will imagine that on retiring, such a man resolves to trace the thoughts of the day, one by one, not to value them individually, but to study them as forms of mental energy. He finds that all thought appears to obey one law : making no difference between that concerning the mistakes of an invoice clerk and that concerning the death and final destiny of a good friend —eternal life or annihilation. In the first instance the thought was one of the frailty of youth and the annoyance to customers ; the second was exalted to a high degree, but to the mind it was simply—energy. He finds also that in the stream of consciousness there is much effort that is apparently aimless and wasteful. During the day, the deeds of which

we outlined, his mind was never unoccupied—at least not to
his knowledge, but he can now remember moments when he
"thought of nothing in particular"; there were swift impressions, intruding snatches of memory, fancies, notions
that meant nothing and ended in nothing. A mind may be
most highly trained, and it may belong to a man who believes
he never wastes a minute because he has always something
to do, and yet it is a mind that has its record of ideas and
half ideas, the mere effervescences of reflection that are
seemingly useless and whose presence in an ordered intellect
call for some explanation.[1] But, after all, is this wastage
real? Better still, is it wastage in any sense? It is not;
for the simple reason that the moment when consciousness
is not focused in the act of concentration, it disports itself
according to its nature and as affected by the influence of
immediate or remote associations. It can do no other. A
man of one thought, with a consciousness penned up, hemmed
in, and having no chance of quiet meanderings, becomes a
man insane.

V

Mind is a form of energy that is all the better for drill,
but it must have a period when it "stands at ease." And
this is not wastage; it is recuperation. We cannot safely
judge the brain by modern standards of efficiency any more
than we can apply them to the processes of nature. Are the
millions of acorns "wasted" because they do not become oak-
trees? And is not a measure of day-dreaming as soundly
psychological as a measure of concentration? In his doctrine
of the "second intellectual wind" the late Professor James
was misled by superficial analogies drawn from scientific
management in business, which seeks to use up every atom
of available energy in order to secure the highest possible
output. As an ideal it has certain merits, as we hope to
show, but it is not possible to treat brain power with such

[1] Prof. Boris Sidis, in a chapter on "The Chance Aspect of Life
and Mind" (*Normal and Abnormal Psychology*, pp. 97-100), says
they are *chance variations*, and that "*chance is at the heart of mental
life, not purpose.*"

methods as those applied to a machine. The output of a business can be analysed, measured, calculated, and graphed ; but we know too little of brain to treat it in the same way. What we do know, however, tells us that efficiency principles applied to mental energy will result in a brief miracle followed by a total collapse. Whatever control we can exercise over the stream of consciousness, there can be no doubt that it exercises a good deal of control on its own account, and mainly without our knowing it. From this fact spring our doctrines of the unconscious, the subconscious, the co-conscious, the subliminal, and all the rest of the terms used to denote a real something about which our knowledge is very dim. To speak of the subconscious *mind* is surely misleading. There is only one mind in each person ; some of its processes are conscious, others are beyond the fringe of consciousness ; occasionally bits of experience may in a sense be broken off from consciousness, and, sinking into the subconscious region, act prejudicially to reason and conduct ; but these admissions do not call for the hypothesis of a second mind : all operations of the mind are *one*.

This mental energy which works irrespective of our will and knowledge—like some of the hidden processes of the body[1]—calls for closer attention : it is the mind's power of self-movement. Reverting to the language of the psychologist we may express the idea thus : that the stream of consciousness is something of which we become aware because we are one with it ; that it flows on and on under our partial but not complete control : and that its exact relation to the ego or self is as yet undetermined. Does this enlighten us ? Not to any great extent. So, avoiding figures of speech, let us say that whilst we may be masters of our minds, our minds in a real sense are our masters, and in no section is this more apparent than in the subconscious life. True, the nature of that life depends on the nature of our voluntary thoughts and feelings, but no man can say : " Go to, I will dispense with subconscious activity." He cannot live the mental life without it ; nay, he cannot produce any result

[1] On this nothing could be more illuminating than Dr W. H. Gaskell's *The Involuntary Nervous System*.

of real merit without relying on subconscious thinking. For this reason the life that we live unconsciously ought to occupy a larger place in the programme of the psychologist. Too long have we given most of our attention to the statics of the mental world ; the time has come when we must find a place for every aspect of dynamic activity. We are not ungrateful for the curious work of the experimentalists who give us little curiosities like the Müller-Lyer illusion, or who . mapped out the sensitive areas of the skin on our bodies, or helped us in solving memory difficulties : what we say is that there are more important tasks than these, more important because, when even partially solved, they will have a direct bearing on human happiness and on the progress of original thought.

VI

Professors of psychology are often truly disappointing when they measure their vast knowledge and experience with the difficulties of adult intelligence. They have written excellent treatises on training the mind of children ; pitifully few, and those quite inadequate, for the young man between eighteen and thirty. We know of one case where an intelligent youth of twenty-three, a graduate, had allowed himself, to use his own phrase, to fall into the habit of mindwandering ; and when he applied to his professor for a remedy he was told to work out a few riders in Euclid every day. This advice has Locke behind it, but for all that it is pure quackery in the light of modern knowledge. Lack of concentration is a failure in the control of energy, and it has a definite cause. Only by careful investigation can that cause be laid bare. Such cases need skilful diagnosis, just as if the evil were a disease of the body ; and although a practical psychologist, like a practising physician, can quickly find the responsible factor, there is always the personal equation to be dealt with.

In developing our knowledge of subconscious mental energy, no writer or investigator has rendered more signal service than Professor Sigmund Freud of Vienna, although the drift of opinion seems to favour the better reasoned conclusions of Professor Jung of Zurich, in some senses a disciple of Freud. On the Continent and in America Freudian theories have received a good deal of attention; in England, comparatively little.[1] This is to be regretted because these theories, supported as they are by a number of demonstrations, are worthy of serious consideration; indeed they may ultimately become the centre of a new movement providing a vital conception as fruitful in psychology and mental physiology as natural selection was to science in the nineteenth century. Freud looks upon mind as energy working according to fixed laws for its expression. If this energy is not allowed to express itself naturally, in a suitable form of action, it is in danger of being repressed into a *complex*, causing much confusion in thought and conduct. It would take us too far afield to expound this doctrine in all its bearings, and it is not necessary; but it is necessary to give one or two illustrations of his practice in order to show its relation to the newer psychology, and open out the way to the one aspect that appeals to us in these pages—namely, the help which psycho-analysis may give in elucidating the problems of the creative mind. For originality, not Freudism, is our subject.

VII

A complex is defined as " a series of emotionally accentuated ideas in a repressed state.[2] A man with such a complex has passed through some crisis which, perhaps unknown to him, has left its mark in the shape of a group of operative ideas that affect him directly without his cognisance of the association. Here is an illustration. An elderly woman felt a strange and disturbing uneasiness whenever she met a red-

---

[1] In the long Bibliography at the end of Regis and Hesnard's *La Psycho-Analyse* there are only one or two British names.

[2] *Vide* Brill's *Psychanalysis*, also Pfister's *Die Psychanalytische Methode* (p. 132), who says: " I use the word complex to denote an accentuated and cohesive group of feelings which wholly has fallen into the Unconscious."

haired person. She was unable to say why. Needless to state, the experience caused her some mental anxiety, and this eventuated in treatment on Freudian principles. Psychoanalysis is a kind of cross-examination, the object being to discover the secret cause of the trouble—*e.g.* the origin of such an aversion as this woman felt. The expert believes that when he lights upon the complex it will be released and lose its power for further mischief. In the case under notice it was found that forty-eight years previously the woman had had a most unpleasant affair with a red-haired schoolmate, but so detached was the cause from the effect that for all those years the evil memory had reproduced itself distressingly on the conscious plane the while the operating factor was hidden in the subconscious and only revived by chance associations. To disinter the buried complex is to end its career, and when the sufferer realised the meaning of her aversion the sense of uneasiness departed.

Almost all our fears have a traceable origin. They are unfortunate transmutations of energy due to emotional crises. A man of thirty-three consulted a New York physician some years ago, the symptoms being a curious hatred of drugs and an unavoidable habit of washing his hands on every possible occasion. He was otherwise practically normal; but a spot on his coat created the fear that he might have touched it, and forthwith he washed his hands; and he would immediately wash them again if he thought that he had inadvertently touched a box of matches, sulphur and poisons being among his phobias. His complexes were duly traced. They arose chiefly out of repressions ending in moral crises of which the hand-washing was the cleansing symbol. Slow and persistent treatment on the mental method cured him completely in five months.[1] It would be possible to quote many other cases, but these must suffice; nor can we discuss them in any other of their aspects than their ultimate bearing on the mental processes of originality.

[1] Brill's *Psychanalysis*, pp. 131-136. Numerous other cases may be found in Freud's *Psycho-Pathology of Daily Life* and the same author's *On Dreams*.

CONSCIOUSNESS AS A FORM OF ENERGY

VIII

Psycho-analysis emphasises the obvious but often forgotten truth that *all mental history is continuous*. Even in psychiatry this truth has not had as much attention as it deserved. Causes have been sought in immediate circumstances and happenings rather than in those which were more remote, with the result that the mind, in some forms of disease, has not been understood because the method used was seriously at fault. But our own aim is to look at mental continuity in the light it casts on men of genius, talent and originality. Once more the conservation of energy is a dominating thought. In the life of the mind no energy is lost, no experience is forgotten, no crisis overlooked. The emotions of Goethe, as a boy, reappeared in the maturity of manhood ; changed, no doubt, but there they were ; and if one could analyse the real origin of *Faust* we should probably find that it began with the stimulus of interest created by Frau Goethe. The chance observations of Shakespeare's youth at Stratford, as well as his deeper experiences of love and hate, come to the surface in his great dramas. Tolstoi, when in Paris as a young man, witnessed a public execution which distressed him profoundly. Its effect at the moment was not formulated, but when years afterwards he re-read the New Testament, we can well imagine how it influenced him in the acceptance of the non-resistance of evil. Perhaps, too, it caused his antagonism to travel, for he affirmed that men and women should live in the place in which Providence had placed them.[1] We cannot look anywhere in the life of the mind without finding this continuity. A fine frenzy of exaltation originating in the exquisite rendering of a song, or of a pianoforte sonata, is not a lost experience ; the impressions, deep and powerful, find their way into the subconscious and appear again, transformed and enriched, when we are suddenly called upon to defend the morality of music, to make a great sacrifice, to sustain defeat with equanimity, to rise to our

[1] Evidently he modified his views before he died. See his *Diary* for 1897, where he takes a saner view.

opportunities, or to respond to the call for service. The utterances of genius are not secrets communicated to an otherwise ordinary intelligence by superior beings ; if that were so then our immortals are immortals no longer. Genius has its natural history, and all mental excellencies of whatever grade have an organic record. The mind is an economical arrangement ; it gathers up the fragments of experience so that nothing is lost ; and the picture, or poem, or book, or invention that startles us by reason of its brilliance could be traced, were we able, to the past life of a mind that works on continuous lines.

IX

Another reflection is this : *that there is a circulation of energy between the conscious and subconscious spheres.* We use this language until we can find something better ; meanwhile the notion is tolerably clear. There is a constant interchange between the two spheres ; of that we are certain, but of the *manner* of it we know little or nothing. Psychoanalysis promises some further light on the subject, and if the theory of complexes is ever demonstrated in a fashion that is convincing to the great majority of medical specialists and psychologists, then we shall be on the high road to further discoveries. A complex is evidently a clot of thought, and works mischief in the mental system like a clot of blood does in the body. In both cases circulation is impeded. Is that a cause or an effect ? Presumably a cause : a healthy relationship between the conscious and subconscious will tend to prevent the formation of complexes ; further, a well-regulated conscious mind must have its counterpart in organising the action of the subconscious.

It would appear as if we may adapt the words of St Paul, and say : "Howbeit that was not first which was subconscious but that which is conscious, and afterward that which is subconscious." Only in this way can we explain the existence of consummate ability. Men and women of small mental power have no wealth of conscious life to be passed on into the unconscious region—no insight, no range, no imagination—consequently the subconscious element is weak because it had not been supplied with material to be fashioned in its own way. In genius the relation between the two spheres must be one wherein the interchanges are many and continuous ; all conscious knowledge in general, and some knowledge in particular, will, in the subconscious sphere combine into new unities, ultimately to find a way into the conscious sphere in the form of inspirations. Hence the thoughts that " come " ; the bright idea that " strikes " us. We wonder whether an inspiration is the healthy aspect of that law which in its evil form issues in a complex ?

X

Freud's contribution to modern psychology cannot yet be determined, but he and his disciples are bound to leave their mark despite their love of system and their tendency to see in psycho-analysis the origin and cure of every mental ill. There can be no doubt that in some instances Freud has pressed his theories too far : witness his teaching that we forget a name or a fact because there has been something disagreeable connected with it. This is incorrect. Specialists in memory investigation know that the painfully experienced fact is the one that is unforgettable.[1] Do we forget the name of the man who borrowed fifty pounds for three months and who at the end of two years, after repeated applications for payment, coolly denies all liability ? Do we forget the cycling accident that caused the loss of a finger ?. Again, Freud sees sex everywhere : to him it is the sole causative, whereas, as often as not, it is the chief among other factors. We frankly admit that sexual influences are deeper and wider than previous physiologists and psychologists had imagined, but even Jung thinks that Freud has pressed these influences into a prominence that is not justified. Taking psycho-analysts as a body, however, we can only be thankful to them for presenting the mind anew to us as a group of

[1] Sidis says: " We do not forget our painful ideas. . . . Pain hammers experiences into the mind."—*Normal and Abnormal Psychology*, p. 202.

mental forces displaying their working in a manner as suggestive to the psychologist as it is to the student of mental
diseases. We agree with Kostyleff that psycho-analysis
has opened out a new era not only for psychiatry but for
psychology and the philosophic synthesis of our knowledge.[1]

[1] *Le Mécanisme Cérébrale de la Pensée*, p. 298. A critical estimate
of psycho-analysis is found in Regis and Hesnard's *La Psychoanalyse*.

CHAPTER III

I

BUT we have not yet reached the conclusion. Granting that genius, and all ability of the higher order, depends on the range of consciousness as previously laid down and defended, what is it that causes consciousness to extend its borders ? What is it that gives direction to this process ? And what is it that accelerates the speed of it ? At first blush these questions suggest that we have been content to introduce a synonym for genius, instead of saying what genius is ; and as the word genius has an importance of its own we will deal with it first of all. Hirsch, after examining about thirty definitions of the word, came to the conclusion that *no psychological meaning can be attached to it.* It is difficult to dispute this finding. "We can make out what a poetic genius is," he says, " what a performer of genius is, what a military genius is, what a scientific genius is, but to accept genius as a univocal term and attach one psychological definition to it, to any good purpose, is not to be done. Undoubtedly all men of genius have common traits ; but they are not traits characteristic of genius ; they are such as are possessed by other men and more or less by all men." [1] Genius means superlative excellence, usually an excellence connected with discovery or with creative activity ; but it also applies to remarkable skill in performance, especially of the interpretative kind. The common notion is that a man of great and impressive originality is one who has the ordinary man's mind, with Feeling, Thought and Will plus a distinct something called genius, just as a saint is a man possessed of the usual mental powers plus a halo. The genius is really

[1] *Genius and Degeneration*, p. 69.

63

a man in whom some power (or powers) is raised to a standard of working far in excess of that which is found in men of talent. But he has no " faculty " which might be called an "extra." Usually a genius is a genius in one direction—art, literature, poetry, engineering, military leadership—but there have been cases where genius has shown itself in two or more directions, notably in that of Leonardo da Vinci. We think of him first as an artist-genius, but he seems to have been quite as good a genius as a military engineer, and as a man of science generally. His biography is a bewildering account of originalities in pretty nearly everything ; and his workmanship, the drawings especially, is a wonder of neatness and accuracy. How shall we explain him ? By showing that his range of consciousness was not limited to art, but was equally extended in such different spheres as botany and bridge-building.

No ; we have not simply introduced a synonym for genius. We have tried to prove that genius is superlative excellence of thought or action in one direction—sometimes more than one. It is not a sort of mental sixth sense, or a clairvoyance of intellect : it is intellect as we know it raised to the highest degree in some particular form of expression.

II

A more serious question is that which has to do with the initial impulse—the inward urge that compels an increase in the range of consciousness, so characteristic of the original mind. The overpowering tendency to write, to paint, to construct, to trade for profit, to fight, to legislate—how do these tendencies arise ? We do not know. They seem to be qualities inborn, like the possession of a naturally strong memory or an aptitude for mathematics. Sir Francis Galton in discussing natural ability puts this emotional bias in the first place.[1] The mind has a glow, and the light points in a specific direction ; it will be art, law, medicine, divinity, trade, politics. But even men of average ability are not destitute of a native tendency ; they wish to do this or that

[1] *Inquiries into Human Faculty.*

because they feel they would *like* to do it ; and yet when contrasted with men of talent or genius the impulse of an ordinary man is no more than a species of curiosity : there is no power behind it, and therefore no growth, no enlargement, no fulness of conscious realisation. With genius it is different; the inward urge for knowledge and expression is masterful. "Original men," says Hamerton, "appear to be endowed with an almost ungovernable desire to find an outlet for their originality . . . all poets, artists, inventors, thinkers, are compelled to set forth their gifts." [1] Mr Hamerton is not as clear in this statement as he normally is, nor so happy ; for the ungovernable desire is but the first sign of genius, not its final outcome. But speaking from a wide knowledge of men and things he tells us in plain terms how deeply he has been impressed by the feeling-force which moves the thought-life of men of marked ability.

It is futile to try to find the origin of genius in the doctrine of inheritance. The parentage of Shakespeare casts little light on his own extraordinary gifts ; and his children appear to have had no more than average minds. They were short-lived, and Judith seems to have been quite illiterate. Love and marriage, so far as these concern great men and women, show that, on the whole, we cannot expect the laws of heredity to perpetuate the type ; it dies out almost as suddenly as it arose. A musical or mathematical gift that, to all appearances, has passed from father to son may be almost entirely a matter of development due to an atmosphere super-charged with definite suggestion. The youth, with his sensitive intellect, and actuated by filial love, unconsciously conceives a passion to follow in the parental footsteps. But this result is not forthcoming unless all the factors are present: there must be the capacity for feeling, the impulse towards expression ; and there must be a strong personal relationship between father and son.

Whichever way we look at the problem it is never soluble : for if genius is inherited why do we find it issuing from a totally undistinguished parentage ? And if it is due to training or environment, why have we been unable to develop

[1] *Thoughts About Art*, p. 199.

genius when and where required? The most reasonable answer to these questions is that we have not yet studied genius in a manner that is at all likely to disclose its secrets, or even a few of them. Since Professor Gerard's *An Essay on Genius*, published in 1774, this country has been content to issue studies of isolated aspects of the subject like Professor Sully's *Education of Men of Genius*—and foreign contributions have been too theoretical and not sufficiently physiological and psychological to extend our knowledge satisfactorily. What we want is a truly scientific analysis of mental origins and developments, and the right way to begin is to examine the *motive* forces. Until that has been accomplished we shall do no more than talk round the subject, leaving its essentials as mysterious as ever.

III

But there is one hypothesis so fruitful in suggestion that its credibility may be said to rise year by year: we refer to the interaction between the conscious and subconscious spheres of the mind. What impresses the observer of mental phenomena is the speed with which some operations are carried out—say, a decision on the part of a merchant to buy a £10,000 cargo, or the rapidity of a judge's appraisal of evidence, or the lightning quickness of a mathematician's calculation. These instances may be taken as almost normal, whereas in genius, the speed, though not increased, is made more significant by the results achieved—*e.g.* the immortal poem which appeared to come without effort, the fine generalisation that seemed to announce itself, and the music that simply floated into consciousness. Now the one point to be kept in view in discussing speed is this: that only one idea, concept, or notion can occupy the mind at any one moment. Here is an illustration. A man who knows many languages has a vocabulary of something like 500,000 words. How many words can he think of in a second? One—perhaps two. In a minute he may think of sixty—or more. But where are the other hundreds of thousands of words all this time? In the subconscious sphere. They appear when called upon, or when the laws of association so will it. Thus a man who is working mentally at high pressure, either writing or speaking, is calling forth ideas from the subconscious in one continuous stream[1]; and as fast as they appear and do their work they fall back into the subconscious. It is obvious, therefore, that excellence in writing, and, to a large extent, in speaking, depends on the stored material in the subconscious sphere and how it has been dealt with; on the ease with which, like a flash, the transfer of an idea can be made from the one sphere to the other; and, last of all, on the subtle changes that *may* take place during the moment of transfer. The diamond pre-exists in other and separated forms of matter before the crucible of Nature changes them into a new and higher value. It will be objected that to recall a fact from the unconscious sphere does not change it. No; but some facts recalled for the first time in a group, *and at the same moment,* sometimes fuse together into a new unity: and that way lies originality. We shall return to this thought later on; the aspect of it to which we would draw attention now is the supreme ease that marks the creation or production of distinctive work. The mind has two spheres, and, apparently, it is the right relationship between them that gives rise to high talent and genius.

IV

Let us appeal to analogy. There is a principle in science called the Principle of Least Action, and Mr P. E. B. Jourdain has expounded it with much scholarship and amplitude

[1] " In all thinking, whether successful or unsuccessful, there is an immense amount of subconscious activity going on; images, noetic schemes, acts of comparison, and experiment incessantly proceeding in that busy subterranean workshop. And there is no reason to doubt that every one of these subconscious mental acts, like every human act, has its own pleasure or pain, though it is only the feeling-tone resultant of a multitude of such acts that appears above the surface."—H. Sturt, M.A.; *The Principles of Understanding*, p. 152. Is it not in this transition from the subconscious to the conscious that we find the explanation of what Dewey calls " a leap in all thinking "? See *How We Think*, p. 26.

of detail. The one vital truth for us is that which he quotes
from Maupertuis : "When some change happens in Nature
the quantity of action necessary for this change is the smallest
possible." [1] With this idea before us we can begin to trace
the psychological analogy, and we cannot do better than
follow Ribot, at least in part, in his chapter on *Le Moindre
Effort en Psychologie.*[2] He begins by referring to Ferrero's
theory that "mental inertia is the law of the least effort,"
and which, in turn, is based upon Lombroso's theory of
misoneism.[3] We shall have something to say about these
theories afterwards ; let it be sufficient now to state that
Ribot and psychologists generally admit that there is in us
a *tendency* to the least effort.[4] This can be proved by an
analysis of our general conceptions. In our schooldays we
gleefully accepted from our fellows the knowledge of short
and easy methods of working arithmetical problems. The
economy in time and labour appealed to us as a most proper
thing in itself,[5] and, in addition, as a means of extending the
time for games and sports. On arriving at years of maturity
we still retained this admiration for achievements brought
about by the least expenditure of energy : that is why the
efficiency movement has made such rapid strides—it is in
harmony with nature. Long and tedious methods of labour
are not necessarily good in themselves although they may be
highly creditable as displays of sober industry. If the work

[1] *The Principle of Least Action*, p. 7.

[2] *La Vie Inconscient*, p. 117.

[3] This term means a repugnance to all innovations ; an objection
to new ideas.

[4] It is noticeable in little things as well as in the more important
things. For instance, we shorten names. Mr Kennedy Jones becomes K. J., not out of disrespect but because it is easier to designate
him. The tendency is to change breadth for narrowness and to
replace amplitude by a detail.

[5] Prof. Whitehead, in his *Introduction to Mathematics* (p. 61), gives
an example of time-saving symbols, adding: "This shows that by
the aid of symbolism we can make transitions in reasoning almost
mechanically by the eye, which otherwise would call into play the
higher faculties of the brain. Civilisation advances by extending
the number of important operations which we can perform without
thinking about them."[6]

performed can be done in half the time, more pleasantly, and with less exhaustion, then the longer and more tedious methods stand condemned as inefficient. Some people see in these contentions nothing more than an encouragement of the idle spirit. That is not true. The aim is Nature's— *i.e.* the least effort.* Of course there is sometimes a danger in the lack of occupation, but that is because such men and women have no inward resources ; they *have* to be employed, otherwise their time would not be well spent. Work, in that sense, is a concession to human weakness. We may deny the fact but we cannot gainsay it : a measure of idleness is still an ideal. Work may be divine, but the annual holiday is the true romance of the year ; economically it is the catch of the season. Paradise of old was a state of being in which there was no effort, and no perspiring days. An industrious German who had travelled every civilised country on the globe was asked for his most outstanding conception. "That all men loff lazee," was his reply. And the working man's idea of a gentleman's life is still that of a man who has no need to work.

V

Let us look at the matter from another standpoint. How does a pianist obtain the skill necessary to play Chopin to a delighted audience ? Well, first, he must have the music in himself ; next, he must practise on approved lines. In the early stages he will stumble, but as he works steadily, finally obtaining mastery over the instrument, the know-ledge of how to make the necessary movements becomes automatic : they belong to the subconscious and he does not think about them. Thus his one aim has been to play Chopin with the greatest ease in the mechanical sense, so that he may give all the more attention to interpretation. In other words, excellence lies in obedience to the law of the least effort.[1] The reason for this is, as stated by Professor

[1] " It has been set forth that mental energy is best conserved by cultivating automatisms and adhering to them. The movements of a skilled pianist, the writing of an expert stenographer, typewriting with the ' touch ' system at high speed, the expert accountant footing

Titchener, that "the more a piece of work is reduced to a matter of course, the more power has the mind to advance to further work,"[1] not merely as a saving of time but as an increase in power. These two are quite different although they may combine in one effort. For instance, we will contrast the principle of the greatest effort with that of the least effort. In counting 10,000 sovereigns the greatest effort would be to count the coins one by one and separate them into twenty-fives, fifties, and hundreds; the least effort would be to weigh them on the scales, seizing them by the handful, not isolating units by the finger-tip. Again, when you concentrate your attention on the solution of a problem, is it more meritorious to arrive at the solution in three hours than in three minutes? Certainly not, provided the solution has the same value in both cases. The palm belongs to the shorter and quicker method. Now in both these instances—the counting of coins and the solving of the problem—there is a time-saving, but is there an increase in power? Yes, in so far as the habit of acting on the least-action principle creates an ability to extend the sphere of its operation; less energy is consumed and consequently there is more to be used in other directions; and mental efficiency is brought nearer by reason of continually successful efforts.

Æsthetically, the least action stands on a higher level than the slower and more laborious style of working because the abbreviated method carries with it a pleasure that is all its own.[2] There is a finished excellence about it that evokes admiration. Nor is the moral quality absent. Salvation, according to theology, used to be obtained by keeping the

up long columns of figures at a rapid glance, the artist creating a complex object of meaning and beauty with a few rapid strokes of the brush, seem remarkable achievements yet performed with ease, grace and accuracy. . . . Nothing is done well until it is reduced to an automatic stage."—Prof. Seashore, *Psychology in Daily Life*, p. 89.

[1] *Primer of Psychology*, p. 81.

[2] " Our pleasure in straight lines or regular curves or symmetrical figures is not, however, entirely to be explained by the suggestion of pleasant movement. We must fall back on a fundamental principle of psychology, that *mental activity is pleasant in so far as it is successful*."—Valentine, *The Psychology of Beauty*, p. 48.

commandments and obeying the law. The life of the devout was one which called for a superabundance of effort : it was arduous in the extreme. Then came the Messiah, who abolished salvation by works and preached a gospel of faith and love. Love *fulfilled* the law.

VI

It was the principle of the least action once more, and it seized upon the rabbinical mind of Saul of Tarsus with all the force of a revelation : its originality, though hinted at in the Prophets, was startling in its simplicity and convincing power. Deliverance from sins had been pursued on the principle of the greatest effort—we see it in the record of self-torture, in penances, in meticulous obedience to trifling rules raised to the dignity of divine ordinances, and it is visible in all the arts of the ascetic and the Pharisee. When the new dispensation dawned action was reduced to its proper limits—the action, that and no more, which springs from a love relationship between the soul and God. The confusions and sufferings of Church history are due to struggles between the exponents of the greatest action and the least.

There is another sense in which the principle of the least action has a divine side. Repose, inertia, contemplation, superlative bliss by union with the Divine—all these notions of a future condition are notions of the actionless, and nearly every one of the heavens promulgated by the religions of more or less civilised peoples is a heaven of least action. The believer in reincarnation aims at a life which tends to dissociate him from material interests, and this, in turn, will tend to reduce the number of re-births, enabling him all the sooner to reach Nirvana, where existence is swallowed up in the Eternal. The heaven of the Christian is a state of *being*, not of *doing*; that of the Mohammedan is a state of sensuous enjoyment; in fact, whichever way we turn we are confronted with action *versus* inaction. It can only mean that we have kept back from our conception of the future life the very things which here have caused so much trouble : the wasted endeavour, the sorrowful mistake, the treading of the wrong road—in a word, we have regarded the perfect life as one in which action is at its minimum. Perhaps there is a deeper philosophy in work than we have yet fathomed, and that when Aristotle said, "We work in order that we may have leisure," [1] he voiced a principle that explains the nature of all our idealism so far as it concerns a future existence.

It will now be said : "Is there not a difference between using just the right amount of energy and not using any at all—as in a condition of inertia ? " Undoubtedly, and that is where Ferrero has gone too far. There is a sense in which mental inertia is a source of illumination, as we shall ultimately make plain when dealing with inspiration ; but that is only comparative inertia—giving up the pursuit of a particular conscious thought and turning to something else until subconscious action has discovered a desired solution. Complete inertia is an evil to be avoided ; it is a travesty of the real thing. Lombroso's *misoneism* [2] is a doubtful affair altogether. When the hand-loom weavers destroyed Arkwright's weaving machines, it was a bit of Lancashire and Yorkshire *misoneism* —an objection to progress. It was the law of inertia, a desire "to let things alone "—so we are told. But *was* it ? No ; it was an objection to new things which threatened the weavers' sense of security ; it was an act of self-preservation —mistaken, of course, but very different from inertia and indolence. The real *misoneism* is seen in a story told by the late Lord Avebury. When in the South Seas he engaged a Chief in conversation, and almost in the twinkling of an eye the Chief was asleep. The implication as to Lord Avebury's soporific talk is dispelled by what the Chief said when he "came to," ten minutes later. "Ideas make me so sleepy," he yawned.

VII

We are now in a better position to show how these apparently irrelevant notions are directly associated with the working of genius. We use the word genius to denote the very

[1] *Nic. Ethics*, x. 76.
[2] Fully explained and illustrated in his article on "Innovation and Inertia in the World of Psychology." See *Monist*, vol. i., p. 344.

acme of ease and success in any one direction; great results are obtained with the minimum of hard mental labour; briefly, genius is the least-action principle operating in the world of mind. But in what sense? In this: that all illumination is the outcome of the combined working of the conscious and subconscious spheres, and that, however long we may search for it the illumination always comes suddenly at the last—it flashes in upon us. A genius, therefore, is one who never agonises to enter the strait gate; the methods of observation and experiment of deep concentration, and slow and laborious reasoning[1] are dispensed with wherever possible, for they represent the principle of the greatest effort, and all his instincts lead him in the opposite direction. His belief that a spirit inspires him is pure fancy, but it is good descriptive psychology nevertheless. It means that intuitions—those fine leaps of the mind that reach the truth at a bound—are the very perfection of intellectual effort because they are so effortless. Now effort, as expressed in work and concentration spread over long periods, is the sign of a difficult communication between the subconscious and the conscious, just as the flash of intuition is a sign of the utmost readiness for transfer from one to the other. May we not then conclude that the nature of genius is found in some special relationship between the two spheres? Fundamentally, this is the theory of Myers, but Myers had an almost complete topography of the unconscious world, and with his subdivisions we have nothing to do. But his notion of intercommunion is essentially reasonable and highly probable; and, in our simpler form, is free from the objections which critics have urged against it.[2] Take the case of

---

[1] "Logic," says Mr A. J. Balfour, "has never shaken itself free from a certain pretentious futility: it always seems to be telling us, in language quite unnecessarily technical, what we understand much better before it was explained. It never helps to discover, though it may guarantee discovery; it never persuades though it may show that persuasion has been legitimate; it never aids the work of thought, it only acts as its auditor and accountant general."—*Theism and Humanism*, p. 175.

[2] "The Interpretation of Genius," a chapter in Prof. H. L. Stewart's *Questions of the Day in Philosophy and Psychology*, p. 97.

readiness in repartee. Are there not scores of us who know exactly what we *could* have said if only we had thought of it *at the time* ? What killing things we think of—all too late ! But why do we not think of them when they are wanted ? Because the connection between the conscious and the subconscious is not as facile as it might be. The connection is set up eventually, and the crushing reply, or the witty rejoinder, comes forth, apologetically, showing that we had ability to say the right thing but not at the right time. May not the right thing be the consciously reasoned thing ? No ; because there is no such fact as a consciously reasoned thing without subconscious help. Every moment there is a wireless between the two spheres, and a man or woman who is smart at repartee is one who can get a wireless from the subconscious almost before the conscious has Morsed the primary message. He—or she—employs the least action : we who failed worked the hardest and took the longest time.

VIII

To recapitulate. We began by defining the mind of unusual powers as one that is marked by a greater range of consciousness than is found in conventional minds, a suggestion of this truth being discovered in the use of spatial terms like *deep, lofty, breadth, penetration* and *compass* when applied to intelligence, and supported by the manner in which consciousness exists in various stages of animal and human life. Our analysis of consciousness, as a word and a fact, revealed an inability to fathom it ; and in spite of experiments and introspection the solution is as far off as it was two thousand years ago. We know the mind is a unity, functioning as Thought, Feeling, and Will, but even these modes of consciousness are, finally, found to be inscrutable. Hence Plato's use of θεωρία and Newman's doctrine of the *Illative Sense* approximate the truth as instances of consciousness working, not sectionally, but as a whole. The attempt to discover the secret of genius in an excess of any one mental function is a mistake : we cannot isolate one function and make it act out of union with the other two.

GENIUS AND THE SUBCONSCIOUS

Range means reach—the utmost possible limit of knowledge and appreciation. But we saw that whilst range of consciousness was increased by adding, say, a knowledge of Spanish to a knowedge of Italian, the range we speak of is more spiritual than that—like the difference between tears as a chemical product and as a representation of feelings beyond expression ; indeed this is the sort of difference that constitutes inequalities in mental ability. One man has " reach " in a direction to which other men are strangers. All men have consciousness, but ability means the extent of mental vision in some particular sphere, and ability is triune in form, as Galton pointed out ; there is first the motive power, then the discerning power, finally the power to act or work.

That we can only apprehend phenomena, not comprehend them, arises out of the complexity of consciousness itself : even the science of mathematics has to yield itself to life. The mystical nature of experience stands revealed : beauty is undefinable, indeed our efforts to define most things are only partly successful. And if psychologists cannot account for the chemistry of thought, they are not likely to be able to account for phenomena in a manner that is conclusive. This attitude we found to be necessary, however sceptical.

But our mental range is not complete without the subconscious sphere ; and after investigating this we saw that its activity was in many ways superior to that of the conscious sphere, being able to accomplish work impossible to the mind in its wakeful moments. The sum total of our reflections, thus far, may be expressed in these words : that the unusual mental ability which manifests itself in originality is not so much a super-development of Feeling, or Thought, or Will, but the work of consciousness as a whole, and as modified or increased by its range of action. This plea is supported by the essentially unknowable nature of all experience.

As further evidence of our contention we showed that mind was best conceived as a form of energy, especially as the methods of introspection and experiment had apparently reached their limits of success. The stream of consciousness is more than a figure of speech : it is mental activity as we know it. We did not originate the stream and our control over it is partial. Freud's services to psychology are important because he has dealt with mind as *energy*, and demonstrated some of his statements by successful experiments. His work brings out the continuity of mental history in a remarkable manner : no experience is lost. Herein we see how genius is indebted for its inspirations not to external agencies but to the working of internal mental laws, especially that law which has to do with the interaction between the conscious and subconscious spheres.

The question now arises as to what causes consciousness to increase its range in such a manner as to eventuate in originality. The initial impulse is undoubtedly inborn, and yet it does not depend on heredity. This is the real problem of genius. But the working of the mind of genius is not so difficult to understand. Its distinguishing characteristic is *ease of action* : whatever the effort, intense or otherwise, the brilliant idea always comes swiftly—it " flashes " in upon the consciousness. We found an analogy in the principle of least action—*i.e.* genius is the apex of success in the working of the mind because it represents achievement on the most economical basis, and therefore with the best æsthetic associations.

SECTION II

THE ORIGIN OF NEW IDEAS

CHAPTER I

INSPIRATION AS A NATURAL PROCESS

I

IT is highly probable that we shall never dispense with the word inspiration, but, speaking psychologically, it is used quite inaccurately. A new idea is not breathed into the mind from without by a Force, a Person, or an Influence; it is an origination within the boundaries of the human mental frontier, and a better word, though one less magical, would be *cerebration*. (An inspiration, considered in its historical associations, presupposes an agent who, or which, uses the human brain as a musician uses an instrument.) Wherein, then, lies the merit of such inspirations ? | It lies in the honour (we are told) of being chosen for this purpose, and there would seem to be an additional merit in having no individuality, also in cultivating the spirit of self-abnegation.[1] With this kind of inspiration we have nothing to do in these pages : it belongs to a sphere of its own. Our function is to discover, if we can, some of the origins of new ideas and to trace them through the elementary stages of their career. There are three factors involved : the physical, the mental, and the social. No one factor can be clearly separated from the others ; we can only discuss them as the psychologist would the threefold unity of the mind. The physical factor has to do with all those organs which in the interaction

---

[1] Plato states the old view thus: "For the authors of those great poems which we admire do not attain to excellence through the rules of any art, but . . . in a state of inspiration, and as it were *possessed* by a spirit not their own."—*Ion*, p. 6.

between mind and body, during health and disease, affect the number and quality of our thoughts. There are bodily conditions, as well as general environments, that promote fortunate trains of thought just as there are repressive conditions that either make thinking difficult or impart a quality to it that is pessimistic, cynical, taciturn. And where natural ability is considerable these good or bad conditions foster or destroy the moods that are conducive to inspiration and hence to originality. The second factor is *mental,* depending primarily for its efficiency on the state of the body and its general surroundings. When working in a manner that we may call happy, this factor renders the mind highly susceptible to external or internal stimuli ; and the two fused together with imaginative warmth often eventuate in a new combination of thoughts : in a word, an inspiration. The third factor is *social,* and has already been included in the description of the other two. It is represented in the widest sense by the effect of mind on mind, in whatever form the mind may manifest itself.

II

To discuss in greater detail the inter-working of these three factors it is necessary to ask and to attempt to answer this question : " In what way do ideas come to us ? " On the face of it, the question seems to be too simple to detain us very long ; moreover, the specific inquiry is as to how particularly good ideas, called inspirations, come to us. The broader question, however, will serve our purpose best, inasmuch as ideas that are superlatively excellent may be found to originate in the same manner as those of less importance, the difference being that the former are born when the brain is working at high pressure, and when all the necessary conditions are harmonious, whilst the latter fall into consciousness during its more prosy periods and when conditions are in no sense unusual. The method is not without objections, but it will justify itself in the end.

Ideas come to us from the external world through the medium of the five senses ; and from the internal world by means of reflection. The two cannot be dissociated, and the deciding element is the nature and depth of the response which external stimuli evoke in the observing mind. To Newton the apple was the symbol of a great law: to the market gardener it is a commercial affair; to the boy it suggests the idea of a feast. There are men and women who live amid scenes of wondrous natural beauty, but it is a beauty that seldom impresses them, and is in no sense a part of their consciousness. Genius, on the other hand, always shows and always has shown a keen impressionability to the facts of environment, both natural and human. Finsen, the celebrated Danish light-cure specialist, was one summer's day looking out of his study window. He saw a cat on the roof of a shed, stretching itself and luxuriating in the sun. It slept on, and Finsen watched it—almost aimlessly. Then he noticed that soon the shadow deepened and reached the cat; whereupon the tabby arose and went farther into the sun. Finsen was interested now, and he watched until he saw the act several times repeated. He came to the conclusion that light and heat were of some particular benefit to the animal; and that was the starting-point of his now famous work. Let us examine this case for a moment. First there is Finsen himself, a man with a keen mind acting by nature synthetically. Next, there is the shining sun; then the creeping shade and the sleeping cat. Probably scores of people have observed the same facts as those which were observed on this occasion: it may be that even Finsen had seen them before; but until this particular day arrived no one made the important *inference*. But in what sense does the new idea come from external stimulus? Only in this: that it supplied the raw material. It is mind acting synthetically that matters most. The cat might have acted its part on the roof of the shed every summer's day for ten years, but science would not have been furthered one iota unless an acute intelligence had been brought to bear upon the facts. The point is more important than it appears to be at first sight; indeed one is surprised to observe what confusion exists even among original thinkers.

ORIGINALITY

III

The late Dr Russel Wallace's letters provide an illustration. In one place he says that "ideas and beliefs are certainly not voluntary acts. They come to us—we hardly know *how* or *whence*." [1] A little later he refers to "the happy chance through which I became an independent originator of the doctrine of the survival of the fittest." The position he took up was this: that he worked industriously in biology and natural history, and that as a result the idea of natural selection "came" to him. But a few paragraphs before this he had answered the following question:—"Why did so many of the greatest intellects fail, while Darwin and myself hit upon the solution of the problem?" [2] And his answer is eminently satisfactory. Darwin and himself reached the same theory because they had a "curious series of correspondences both in mind and environment." First, they were ardent beetle hunters and beetles have an almost infinite number of forms. This created surprise and stimulated inquiry. Next, they had a great passion for collecting—*i.e.* an intense interest in the variety of living things. This interest, in Wallace's opinion, was to be "*the only one* which could lead us towards a solution of the problem of Species." The two men became travellers: they saw an immense number of varieties of life and began to trace changes. Finally both men read Malthus *On Population*, and in both cases it unified conceptions, reducing the many to one. The stages of the Darwin-Wallace originality are these: (*a*) knowledge of varieties here and in foreign countries; (*b*) observation of changes; and (*c*) the fusing of vast stores of facts into a whole, by the light of an analogy drawn from Malthus. Why, then, should Wallace speak of the thing as a happy *chance*, after so careful an explanation of his method? The truth is that, as in Finsen's case, Nature supplied the raw material, but the new thought arose in the interpretative mind after years of preparation.

[1] *Letters and Reminiscences*, vol. i., p. 117.
[2] *Ibid.*, p. 114.

INSPIRATION AS A NATURAL PROCESS

On a previous page we said that the deciding factor was in the nature and depth of the response which the mind makes to external stimuli. Wordsworth said of his first poem, the *Evening Walk*, that there was not an image in it that he had not drawn from his own observation of nature, and that he could point out the time and place where most of them were noticed. Clearly, this early habit can be seen with more striking results in his later work. The oak,

> " Its darkening bows and leaves in stronger lines "

is drawn from nature. "I recollect distinctly," he said, "where this first struck me. It was on the way between Hawkshead and Ambleside and gave me extreme pleasure. The moment was important in my poetical history, for I date from it my consciousness of the infinite variety of natural appearances which had been unnoticed by the poets of any age or country, so far as I was acquainted with them ; and I made the resolution to supply in some degree the deficiency." [1] Perhaps we do not quite endorse all that Wordsworth claims for himself in this respect, but there is no doubt his poetry affords us a fine study in the stimulus of nature, acting on a supersensitive imagination.[2] But Shakespeare is, of course, the classical instance of a deep and wide response to the effects of nature and civilisation. He was called myriad-minded because nothing escaped him ; and we have never read a more interesting chapter of literary history than that written by Prof. Halleck called "How Shakespeare's Senses Were Trained," [3] where we are shown in a few pages how much the bard owed to observation and

---

[1] *Authors at Work*, p. 291.

[2] Goethe strikes a modest note. " People are always talking of originality," he says, " but what does that mean ? As soon as we are born the world begins to act on us and this goes on to the end. And, after all, what can we call our own except energy, strength and will ? If I could give an account of all I owe to great predecessors and contemporaries, there would be but a small balance in my favour. . . . I by no means owe my works to my wisdom alone, but to a thousand things and persons around me that provided me with material."—*Conversations with Eckermann.*

[3] In *The Education of the Central Nervous System.*

how little to books. It is outside our purpose to reproduce the results of these analyses, to show him as an expert in the habits of bees or of tavern habitués; what we do wish to keep before the reader is this: that observation is only important as a means of supplying the raw material of thought. A woodman of 1589 would probably know all about the thirty-nine birds mentioned by Shakespeare, but he could not think and write of them as Shakespeare did: he had no mind for that purpose.

IV

It is certain, therefore, that the vital element in originality is the quality of mind which makes use of the material supplied by the senses; for, after all, even the things we see and hear, and which may impress us deeply and wonderfully, are internal conceptions. The idea that arises in the mind—whether from without, by vision, or within, by reflection—is a problem we have to solve; and we may repeat appositely the general question with which we commenced this section: *In what way do ideas come to us?* The only proper answer is: By the action of the laws of association. Those laws are the great trade routes of intellectual exchange, wherein things alike tend to coalesce and things unlike are made vivid by contrast. Ideas themselves are still a mystery: no psychology has ever yet fathomed them. But we believe that the *movements* of ideas are traceable, even those which are suddenly unified into other and new ideas. Both science and poetry afford interesting illustrations. "I have been speculating last night," said Charles Darwin to Horace Darwin, "what makes a man a discoverer of undiscovered things; and a most perplexing problem it is. Many men who are very clever—much cleverer than the discoverers—never originate anything. As far as I can conjecture the art consists in habitually searching the causes and meaning of everything that occurs." [1] This is only partially correct, for discovery is always something more than a strictly logical process, as Prof. E. B. Poulton pointed

[1] In *Emma Darwin.* See also Gore's *Art of Discovery,* pp. 45-48.

out long ago.[1] Of course objections were urged against such a plea, but they were urged half-heartedly, and Tyndall, on the one hand, and Ribot, on the other, have successfully established the claims of science to imagination and inspiration. And yet even now many people appear to agree with Shelley that "poetry is not like reasoning, a power to be exerted according to the determination of the will. A man cannot say 'I will compose poetry.' The greatest poet even cannot say it; for the mind in creation is as a fading coal, which some invisible influence, like an inconstant wind, awakens to transitory brightness."[2] To look for the origin of poetic illumination in a spirit outside the borders of intelligence has been the fashion, no doubt, but it is no more true than that we can "reason" whenever we exert the will to do so. Every man must have a god, and Shelley's was the belief in a god outside men who inspires poets. (To-day, however, as will be made evident in the pages to follow, inspiration calls for no greater factor than the mind in its conscious and subconscious activities. Even intuition is losing its mysteries, one by one. It used to be imagined that an intuition was "pure untaught knowledge," or signified "a cognition not determined by a previous cognition of the same object.") Did Colburn, the arithmetical boy prodigy, give square roots and cube roots at a moment's notice without a previous knowledge of figures, as figures ? Did Mozart compose without the slightest knowledge of musical notation, and play divinely the first time he set eyes on a piano ? Do we

---

[1] "It is a common error to suppose that the intellectual powers which make the poet or historian are essentially different from those which make the man of science. Powers of observation, however acute, could never make a scientific discoverer; for discovery requires the creative effort of the imagination. . . . Fertility of imagination is essential for that step from the less to the more perfectly known, which we call discovery. But fertility of imagination alone is insufficient for the highest achievements in poetry, history, or science; for in all these subjects the strictest self-criticism and the soundest judgment are necessary in order to ensure that the results are an advance in the direction of truth."—E. B. Poulton, *Charles Darwin and the Theory of Natural Selection*, p. 12.

[2] Shelley's *A Defence of Poetry* (Cook's Edition), p. 39.

not find that intuitions come from experience so richly unified that when a new situation presents itself illumination comes in a moment, and judgment is instantaneous? Memory, acting for the most part unconsciously, but with unusual efficiency, is the basis of our intuitions.[1] Instinctive likes and dislikes, immediate decisions when confronted with a new situation in business, are the spontaneous outcome of previous experience acting in a focus.

V

To reason a thing out is to turn to a collection of facts, to study their pros and cons, and to weigh them with a view to securing a preponderance on one side or another. The task is often laborious, and it shows intellect in its least attractive light; whereas in intuition we see the mind working on its highest levels; the process is rapid almost to instantaneity, but its rapidity is the sole difference dividing it from the slower method of reasoned argument.[2] The law of associa-

[1] John Stuart Mill, in a letter to Dr W. B. Carpenter, says: " I have long recognised as a fact that judgments really grounded on a long succession of small experiences mostly forgotten, or perhaps never brought out into distinct consciousness, often grow into the likeness of intuitive perceptions. I believe this to be the explanation of the intuitive insight thought to be characteristic of women; and of that which is often found in experienced practical persons who have not attended much to theory, nor been often called upon to explain the ground of their judgments. And I should agree with you that a mind which is fitted by constitution and habits to receive truly and retain well the impressions made by its passing experiences will often be safer in relying on its intuitive judgments, representative of the aggregate of its past experience, than on the influences that can be drawn from such facts or reasonings as can be distinctly called to mind at the moment."—*Mental Physiology*, p. 486.

" By intuition," says Bergson, "is meant the kind of *intellectual sympathy* by which one places oneself within an object in order to coincide with what is unique in it, and consequently inexpressible."—*Metaphysics*, p. 7.

[2] A writer in *The Monist* (April, 1916)—Mr H. J. Mulford—whilst arguing pretty much on the same basis as ourselves, puts intuition on a lower plane than reasoned thought. " It is merely reflex thought, without the value even of self-conscious thought " (p. 309).

tion, acting on the method of low pressure in one case and of high pressure in the other, explains the movement of ideas in both instances.

The more we are able to understand association the clearer will be our knowledge of all the mental processes involved in originality. We see it in those sudden advents of thoughts quite foreign to the subject in hand. You engage your attention and focus it on, say, the subject of *law* ; and after some time the stream of thinking is broken into by a sudden recollection—you are reminded of a man whose name has not entered your mind for perhaps ten years. Why does it do so now? You say you cannot tell. True—not for the moment ; but if you think back slowly you will most likely find that the words law and *fugitive* are associated, and that Fuge, the name of the long-forgotten person, did not come into consciousness by chance, but by law, the law of association—this time as similarity in sound.[1] We often say a thought " came " to us, just as Wordsworth conceived when he said :

> " Think you, 'mid this mighty sum
> Of things for ever speaking
> That nothing of itself will come
> And we must still be seeking ? "

and we have encouraged ourselves in believing that readymade thoughts and fine inspirations sometimes come to us from a spiritual world outside us. To deny it would be to fall into the dogmatic habit we condemn in these pages ; but we *can* say it is highly improbable, even when telepathy is admitted. The sudden and mysterious " comings " are true enough, especially with men of genius, but these comings, if they could be studied closely, would be found to have a

This is the cart before the horse, and Mr Mulford should henceforth avoid any spontaneous notion. Carson (in his *Mathematical Education*, chapter on " Intuitions ") says: " Intuitions are on the same footing as primary assumptions concerning gravitation. They differ from these in that they are formed unconsciously as a result of universal experience rather than conscious experiment."

[1] An excellent and up-to-date investigation of association generally is found in Prof. Felix Arnold's *Psychology of Association* (U.S.A.).

natural history in the mental world to which they belong. Inspiration is that familiarly favourable moment when the factors of thought—*i.e.* external stimuli and internal response —are in true *rapport* with each other. We cannot affirm that there is a *law* of inspiration, but we know some of the *conditions,* some of the bodily and mental states accompanying mentally creative activity, and these we shall now study *in extenso.* If a law is a mode of operation then we may rightly speak of these conditions as laws of inspiration.

CHAPTER II

THE LAWS OF INSPIRATION

I

A. One of the primary conditions of inspiration is *that a period of close inquiry and reflection should be followed either by a change of subject or a period of mental inactivity.* After producing evidence in support of this law we shall endeavour to explain its underlying causes. Haydn said : "When my work does not advance I retire into the oratory with my rosary and say an *Ave*; immediately ideas come to me."[1] Here, a change of subject was sufficient to arouse dormant notions, and one wonders whether the result would have been the same if Haydn had turned to painting or botany. Later, we shall hazard a guess as to why a sudden transfer of interest to a new emotional association can establish a desired connection in a sphere where direct effort was unsuccessful. It is almost as if a telephone subscriber, failing to get the number he wanted, deliberately rang up somebody else, and immediately got into touch with the first number asked for.

Another illustration is found in the life of Berlioz. He desired to compose a song, with chorus, for the *Cinq Mai* of Beranger, but was pulled up short by the refrain :

> " *Pauvre soldat, je reverrai la France,*
> *La main d'un fils me fermera les yeux.*"

He tried it again and again—but in vain. He gave it up in despair. Two years afterwards he was bathing in the Tiber, and on rising from a dive he found himself humming the musical phrase so long sought in vain.[2] The length of

---

[1] Lombroso, *Man of Genius*, p. 19.

[2] Paulhan, *Psychologie de l'Invention*, p. 24. Prof. Jastrow gives a number of cases in his book on *The Subconscious*. "Hamilton evolved the intricate conception of the invention of quaternions while walking

time between the original effort and the final issue is extra-
ordinarily long, and one would like to cross-examine the composer as to how many times during the two years his
thoughts reverted to the refrain ; or whether he had forgotten
it altogether.   But even as it stands the case is one that
illustrates the law of suspended conscious action.

II

We will now turn to the case supplied by the late Professor
Henri Poincaré.   It is rather long, but its interest is so great
that the length of its recital may be forgiven us.   For a
fortnight Poincaré had been attempting to prove that there
could not be any function analogous to Fuchsian functions.
One night it chanced that he took a cup of black coffee (quite
unusual for him) and he worked at his problem through the
night, being unable to sleep.   In the morning he had established the existence of one class of Fuchsian functions and
verified them.   Guided by an analogy to elliptical functions,
he desired to represent the new functions by the quotient
of 2 series. · He found eventually what he called Theta-
Fuchsian.   A geological conference at this moment neces-
sitated a journey to Constances, and his mathematics were
forgotten in the incidents of travel.   But on entering the
brake at Constances it quite suddenly came into his head
that the transformations he had used to define Fuchsian
functions were identical with those of non-Euclidean geometry.
On returning to Caen he verified this idea satisfactorily.   He
then began to study arithmetical questions, but without
apparent result, and having no suspicion that they were
connected with his previous researches.   His failures annoyed

with Lady Hamilton in the streets of Dublin, the flash of discovery
coming to him just as he was approaching the Brougham Bridge.
Mozart had the aria of the beautiful quintette in *The Magic Flute*
come to him while playing a game of billiards, and seemed prepared
for such occasional influxes of musical ideas by carrying a notebook
for their instant record. . . . Prof. Kukulé tells how he saw the
atoms dancing about in mid-air in conformity with his theory of
atomic grouping, while riding on top of a London bus " (p. 95).

him, and he went to the seaside for a time, forgetting the matter entirely. One day whilst out walking, the idea came to him suddenly, concisely, and with certainty, that arithmetical transformations of indefinite, ternary and quadratic forms are identical with those of non-Euclidean geometry. He returned to Caen and verified this as he had verified the other; indeed he worked the notion out to its final issues, establishing all of them except one, the solution of which came suddenly as before whilst engaged in serving his time as a soldier.

These and other instances impressed upon Poincaré the belief that sudden illuminations point to "a long course of previous unconscious work." They are "never produced except after some days of voluntary efforts which appeared absolutely fruitless." [1] This contention is supported in a letter written by Clark Maxwell. "I set Prof. Thomson a proposition which I had been working at for a long time. He sent me 18 pages of letter of suggestions about it, none of which would work; but on Jan. 8, in the railway from Largs, he got the way to it." [2] We might fill pages with such evidences of the law under discussion, not only from the realms of music and mathematics but from every walk of life. The nature of the subject matter of thought does not affect the working of the law. Thomas Aquinas, called from his studies of heresy to dine with the King of France, entered into the social atmosphere of the occasion, completely oblivious of books and theories. But a long-sought-for argument suddenly dawned upon him, and banging the table with his fist, he exclaimed, with delightful irrelevance: "That is conclusive against the Manicheans." Sir Walter Scott, faced with an unsolved difficulty during the day, always looked to the morning for a solution; indeed he came to rely on his early morning thoughts. "I lie *simmering* over things," he said, and if a search in working hours failed to reveal the wanted idea he would say, "Never mind, I shall have it at

---

[1] *Science and Hypothesis*, p. 24. The reader, like ourselves, may not be able to follow these mathematical details, but he will be able to understand the psychological argument.

[2] *Life of J. Clark Maxwell*, p. 104.

seven o'clock to-morrow morning."[1] Charlotte Brontë
was not so confident of an early access of ideas. Mrs Gaskell
tells us that sometimes weeks or even months elapsed before
she felt that she had anything to add to that portion of her
story which was already written.

III

We promised to hazard a guess as to the reason why a
change of subject, or a period of mental inactivity, was
followed by an inspiration in such cases as those referred to.
The solution must be sought, first of all, in the inability of
the will to control the more remote functions of the mind,
one of which is the transition from the unconscious to the
conscious. Mr Arthur Lynch[2] has provided a suitable illustration in the account he has given of trying to recall a forgotten word. He had quoted the sentence : "The labour we
delight in lessens pain," and had immediately recognised that
"lessens" was wrong. He tried to recall the right word—
that is, he *willed* it to come—but was not successful, so
he turned his attention to other studies. Suddenly—these
things are always sudden—he remembered the right quotation : "The labour we delight in *physics* pain." Will-
power was not able to evoke this result at the desired moment,
the reason being that time is required to obtain the right
connection when a wrong one has been set up—like the wrong
number in the telephone call office. It may be objected
that there is a difference between the process of recalling a
lost word and that of inventing an original idea. But is there
such a difference ? The lost word is remembered when the
needed associations are found, and the original idea is forthcoming for the same reason ; moreover, the *modus operandi*
is the same in both cases—*i.e. think of something else* : to
reach A you commence to walk towards B. The real question,
apart from the limits of Will, is : Why should prolonged
concentration appear to be a failure and deliberate mind-

---

[1] Pebody, *Authors at Work*, p. 67.
[2] *Psychology : A New System*, vol. i., pp. 255-256.

wandering a success? If there is a target, why do we hit it by aiming at another object?[1]

IV

The answers to these questions will eventually be found in the part which the subconscious plays in thinking generally—*i.e.* the thinking that calls for more than merely surface reflection. The reason why Poincaré could not at once obtain the desired result lay in the fact that the subconscious action needed time for the completion of its work; and that as soon as it was complete the result, being marked *urgent*, was at once communicated to the conscious sphere, abruptly and suddenly, just as a local call is interrupted by a trunk call. The time element, therefore, is of the utmost significance; for although there are some matters concerning which subconscious action is immediate, as in intuitions, there are others, usually connected with new knowledge, where the result cannot be willed: we have to wait until it "comes," and it comes when it is ready, not before. Thus, this cessation of concentration, and this turning to other things, are not associated in what we might call an organic way; the main item of the operation is to give up strenuous effort. The nature of the mental occupation taken up afterwards is not so important as is apparent.

The speed with which an inspiration is evoked varies with the individual and with the subject matter in which he is interested. Usually a man of science is slow to discover the secrets of Nature; the poet seldom has to wait so long— inspiration is to him an experience so vivid that he can almost imagine he hears a voice dictating the lines one by one. William Blake, in speaking of his *Milton and Jerusalem*, said:

[1] Souriau disagrees. When trying hard to recall a name, instead of waiting until it "comes" to us, "we are restricting our minds from finding it through wider associations. A man is looking for something. He will find it more quickly by letting his eyes wander over the ground than by looking through a magnifying glass, inch by inch."—*Théorie de l'Invention*. Yes; but the method is not to seek at all: we turn away and think of something else quite different from "the wider associations" he mentions.

ORIGINALITY

"I have written the poem from immediate dictation, twelve or sometimes twenty or thirty lines at a time, without pre-meditation, and even against my will. The time it has taken in writing was thus rendered non-existent, and an immense poem exists which seems to be the labour of a long life, all produced without labour or study." [1] An exaggerated account, doubtless, but one that shows the speed of mental creation during a period of frenzy. How different was it with La Rochefoucauld, who is said to have spent fifteen years on his famous *Maxims*, re-writing and re-polishing some of them thirty times before they satisfied him. And how different also is the case of Darwin, slowly gathering facts, record-ing them, classifying them, organising them with a view to a larger unity, the idea of which eludes him until he has read Malthus's *On Population*. These three instances enable us to understand why the word inspiration has been refused as inapplicable to any type of work that is at all mechanical and laborious.

The poet's inspiration has an ease, an elevation and a manner—so it is said—that suggests a divine inbreathing : La Rochefoucauld and Darwin are reckoned as dignified plodders. We do not accept these verdicts to-day. We know, for instance, how Tennyson constructed his *In Memoriam* ; we know how other poets revised their work, cutting here and enlarging there ; and we know how our literary stylists agonised to find the one word or phrase that better than any other would embody their thoughts. Pater's erasures and substituted phrases resulted in physical as well as mental exhaustion ; and Flaubert was ready to work himself into a fever whilst searching for the *mot* that would magically conjure up the idea in the reader's mind. [2] As a matter of fact this labour is but the preliminary to the sudden illumination : thus it fulfils the law. If it did not, what could we say of Napier's logarithms, the working out of which took twenty long years of arduous labour, and

---

[1] *Letters of William Blake.*

[2] This is vividly brought out by the five renderings, beginning : "Ainsi vu d'en haut."—See *Recueil de Morceaux Choisis d'Auteurs Français.* London, 1909.

concerning which Lord Moulton, a competent judge, said that the whole conception came like a bolt from the blue, so remarkable was its originality. No previous work led up to it, and nothing had foreshadowed or heralded its approach.[1] Working and waiting, in constant repetition, gives inspiration a personal history. As Dostoievsky says in one of his *Letters* : " It is the fate of all first books to be altered over and over again. I don't know whether Chateaubriand's *Atala* was his first book, but I do know he rewrote it seventeen times. Pushkin did the same with quite short poems. Gogol used to polish away at his wonderful works for two years at a time." [2]

V

Poincaré, commenting on his own experiences, was inclined to accept the notion that only a portion of our unconscious thoughts is invited to cross the threshold into the consciousness itself ; and that only those unconscious thoughts succeed in making the transition which directly or indirectly affect our sensibility. This seems to be a French rendering of Sir Francis Galton's " Antechamber of Consciousness," [3] and there is no doubt that it touches upon the one fact which may give us the explanation, so far as it is possible to have one.

Success in thinking depends on three things : first, " a large attendance in the antechamber "—the subconscious ; next, the absence of ideas alien to the topic under consideration ; and, finally, " the justness of the logical mechanism that issues the summons." [4] The result is that " the mind frequently does good work without the slightest exertion."

[1] In an address at the Napier Tercentenary Celebrations at Edinburgh.

[2] *Letters*, p. 23.

[3] " When I am engaged in trying to think anything out, the process of doing so appears to be this: the ideas that lie at any moment within my full consciousness seem to attract of their own accord the most appropriate out of a number of other ideas that are lying close at hand, but imperfectly within the range of my consciousness." —*Inquiries into Human Faculty*, p. 146.

[4] *Ibid.*, p. 146.

ORIGINALITY

This can only be explained by the fortunate relationship which, in all people occasionally, and in men of genius more often and more fully, is established between unconscious and conscious mental activity. Such a relationship cannot be in its origin a matter of education or discipline; it must be an inheritance—a gift of the gods: and, however much attention may be devoted, under competent oversight, to the training of unconscious activity, by conscious means, the fact remains that the transitions from one sphere to the other are mostly dependent on native facility. Nevertheless, results of a notable kind have been achieved on the lines of slow development.

VI

A review of the last few paragraphs brings into light again the often forgotten impotence of the will to control the whole of our mental forces.[1] The disposition of the day is to glorify the will as if it were well nigh omnipotent; whereas, even in so insignificant an occurrence as the forgetting of a name, not all the will-power of which we are capable can enable us to recall the missing word; for *association*, not *force*, is the secret of recollection. The more annoyed we become because the word eludes us, and the more emphatically we resolve to find it quickly, the longer will be our search, because a strong combination of feeling and will block the way. Then something happens to divert our attention: our minds are occupied by other thoughts, and, suddenly, the name leaps into consciousness. Why? The way was clear. Previous effort had set up a tendency to connect two associations together, the connection between which had become weak, but energy was expended uselessly in trying to force matters to a speedy result and the tendency was restrained from its fulfilment. At last the misspent energy was re-controlled and used in a normal manner; the energy behind the set-up tendency got its chance; the connection was established and with a little shock the forgotten

[1] Mr Graham Wallas has some interesting notes on what the will *can* do in Chapter X. of *The Great Society*.

name announced itself. That which is not in consciousness at a given moment, and which refuses a summons to appear from the ante-chamber, cannot be compelled to appear until the right association has been found. For this, time is required; and the attention must be diverted.

The same law holds good, apparently, in regard to *any* transition from the subconscious to the conscious. Even men of genius cannot command the presence of brilliantly original ideas, and it would seem as if deep concentration of a prolonged character is a psychological error. The true method, according to Poincaré, is to work diligently for a period, then to turn to a new source of interest. In this connection one recalls a striking comment from the pen of another Frenchman : "Since I studied nothing I have learnt much. It is indeed in our leisurely strolls that our great intellectual and moral discoveries are made." [1] And, lest the reader should imagine that the author of *Sylvestre Bonnard* is not to be trusted in so serious and exact a reflection, we will refer to still another Frenchman : René Descartes. Professor Mahaffy says of him that he slept a great deal, "and particularly recommends idleness as necessary to the production of good work." [2] Idleness, in sensible proportions, gives the subconscious mind its opportunity; close work, on the other hand, with its constant absorption of eye and brain, monopolises the whole area of the waking mental life, allowing few opportunities for transitions from the subconscious to the conscious.

VII

Let the reader but remember what he knows of biography, especially that of poets, novelists, essayists, painters, and musicians, and he will see that the vagaries of the artistic temperament take on the semblance of rationality. Their lackadaisical habits, their eccentricities in part, their

[1] *Life and Letters* (Second Series), p. 116. There is another saying, attributed to Tellier : "The best employed time is that which one loses." See Hamerton's *Intellectual Life*, p. 369.

[2] *Descartes*, p. 138.

irrelevancies, their bohemianism and their fits of laziness were part and parcel of their intellectual method; unconsciously they obeyed a psychological law which demands change, leisure, and partial day-dreaming if the best results are to be forthcoming. There is a sense in which strenuous mental effort to arrive at a scientific solution, or to phrase a haunting line in poetry, is profoundly unpsychological—unless relief is sought in recreation or idleness. The subconscious must have time to exercise its creative power. Wallace often said he was lazy. "His idleness," says one who knew him, "was his way of describing his long musings, waiting the bidding of her whom God inspires—Truth, who often hides her face from the clouded eyes of man. For hours, days, weeks, he was disinclined to work.[1] He felt no constraining impulse, his attention was relaxed or engaged upon a novel, or his seeds, or the plan of a new house, which always excited his interest. Then, apparently suddenly, whilst in one of his day-dreams, or in a fever (as at Ternate, to recall the historical episode when the theory of Natural Selection struck him), an explanation, a theory, a discovery, the plan of a new book came to him like a flash of light, and with the plan the material, the arguments, the illustrations; the words came tumbling over one another in his brain, and as suddenly his idleness vanished."[2]

The truth that lies in such misquoted definitions as "Genius is an infinite capacity for taking pains"[3] is still there, but it is not even a half truth: it is a one-third truth. We see it in the tremendous industry that follows an inspiration; but the notion that "taking pains"—in other words, hard work—can produce originality of the most distinctive kind is nonsense.[4] Even Matthew Arnold contradicted

---

[1] The philosophy of work, as a human activity, contains some interesting, and rather difficult problems. A few of them (the natural history of work, for instance) are dealt with in Leo Sera's *On the Track of Life*, chapter entitled "Work and Morals."

[2] *Letters and Reminiscences*, vol. ii., p. 242.

[3] Carlyle said: "Genius (which means transcendent capacity of taking trouble, first of all)."—*Frederick the Great*, vol. i., Book IV., chap. iii.

[4] See also Türck, *The Man of Genius*, pp. 455-456.

himself on this point. "Genius is mainly an affair of energy," he tells us in his essay on *The Literary Influence of Academies*, but in his *Note Books* (pp. 5-6) we find the qualities thus tabulated :

"The three tokens of genius ; extraordinary understanding, extraordinary conduct, and extraordinary exertion.

"The three things that improve genius : proper exertion, frequent exertion, and successful exertion.

"The three things that support genius : prosperity, social acquaintance, and applause."

Pater in his *Renaissance* comments on Leonardo's many-sidedness—a quality that disposed him to an effort which sometimes made itself visible—" as in those heavy German foreheads—too heavy and German for perfect beauty. . . . What an anticipation of modern Germany, for instance, in that debate on the question whether sculpture or painting is the nobler art ! " But the Italian painter does not work all day and every day for the illuminating vision ; he " will never work till the happy moment comes—that moment of *bien-être* which to imaginative men is the moment of invention. On this he waits with perfect patience ; other moments are but a preparation, or after-taste of it." [1]

VIII

Virtuosi like Josef Hofmann, Kreisler, Paderewski, and Godowsky have stated that they do not "work " in the manner in which an admiring public is often led to believe.[2] Hofmann when asked how much he practised, smiled as he said : "Not nearly so much as the newspapers would like to have me. Often not for a week. Often not more than an hour and never when I am incapable of absolute concentration." Kreisler affirmed that musicians were positively superstitious about practice : ". . . this grinding and dulling of the mind, as well as the sense, for hours at a time ! It seems to me little short of insanity . . . I can't practise for

---

[1] *The Renaissance*, pp. 117-118.
[2] *The Literary Digest*, 18th Dec. 1915.

more than one hour at a time. . . . I can play five hours at a time, but to practise . . . ! ''

Perhaps idleness, as a virtue, is a conception not easily admitted, in view of the doctrine that all work is sacred. But are modern ideas of the value of work necessarily true in every detail ? That they are true in regard to the discipline of character may be taken for granted, but, for intellectual progress, absorption in routine, or any form of inquiry without the advantages of variation, is clearly a mistake.[1] A wise thinker, keen on any kind of discovery, never wearies himself to exhaustion by pursuing one line of investigation to the exclusion of every other, unceasingly, unrestingly ; he knows that after careful work he can safely leave the subconscious activities to contribute their share to the final solution. Prof. William James, in one of his lectures to teachers, says that a friend of his, anxious to succeed in a particular direction, always thought about something else—with good results. The Professor does not doubt the statement, but he seems to regard it as unusual and freakish. Sustained concentration, in some cases at least, will "groove" the mind and unfit it for that spontaneity on which we rely for the truly individual quality of thought ; and even though Newton is said to have discovered the law of gravitation by "thinking about it " there is no evidence to show that he worked at this problem until he solved it—giving no attention to Biblical prophecy, astrology, and other light subjects.

Work ? Perhaps the present century will not pass without revising some of our notions on the relationship between leisure and progress. In America, where work is a vocation and a destiny, there is published a translation of Paul Lafargue's book on the right to be lazy.[2] In England the pamphlet does not seem to be known, but the idea is familiar, the socialists having preached it for a good many years past. It is a bit of socialism we should like to see in full realisation, just as we hope to see other bits sink into the nethermost abyss. And this plea for leisure need not revolt the soul of

[1] See the interesting chapter on '' Routine and Genius '' in Hight's *Unity of Will*.

[2] *The Right to be Lazy.*

Jew or Christian, for they both cherish the story of the Garden of Eden. Before Adam fell he was a gentleman of light occupation,[1] and yet this state is held out to us as the first and perfect condition of God-created man. But when Adam "fell," and the curse was pronounced upon him, he found that he and his seed had been sentenced to hard labour for life. What then is the true conception of Paradise?[2] The truth is that the modern era of industrial and commercial expansion, a world-embracing phenomenon, has blinded us to the need of leisure, not only for one class, but for all classes. And even when the leisure has been found, it discovers us so exhausted mentally with the monotonies of labour that we have been glad to participate in forms of recreation which do not foster real advance in the things that matter. The leisure we desiderate is the quiet species, not the fifty-mile rush to a seaside resort, followed by unhygienic methods of eating and drinking that culminate in the fag of week-ending.

IX

The conclusion, therefore, is that there must be *work* and *waiting*. If it is a mental law that concentration must not be prolonged when good results are sought for, it is also a mental law that inspirations depend on a certain amount of disciplined labour. \Napoleon believed that battles were won by means of sudden inspirations on the field—mental excitement being the generating power, and the previously acquired knowledge of strategy, tactics, men, material, and terrain, the substance. ∫The chances are that an untutored Napoleon would have had no inspirations at all. Joly has it that "whenever a man, in concentrating his faculties on a matter of importance, conceives an idea which surprises him by the magnitude of its results, we say that he has been inspired; but it will be difficult to aver that a man has ever

[1] "Original persons have also for the most part been the namers of things," says Nietzsche.—*Joyful Wisdom*, pp. 207-208.
[2] The indignity—and dignity—of labour, so ably argued in Prof. Veblen's *Theory of the Leisure Class*, is, of course, not within our purview.

been inspired in an art other than that which he understands and practises continually, and for which he has a natural inclination." [1]

\ Observation and experiment are the keywords of the scientific method, but for years now we have realised that the poet and the artist, the man of science and even the man of business, are of imagination akin./ Tennyson, on his knees, peering into the depths of a bubbling spring in order that he may know its every aspect, is a scientific observer; he becomes an experimentalist when he essays to embody his vision in words—not succeeding at first, perhaps; the inspiration comes after effort. [2] Madame Curie, in search of radium, and Selfridge in search of new commercial conquests, exhibit the same stages in their progress: a close study of the facts concerned, an effort towards realisation, a few set-backs, then, finally, the desired result. So the brain worker in any field of operation may now logically place himself side by side with the artist—*i.e.* observe, strive, and wait for his inspiration. \On this point Professor Lloyd Morgan remarks that "it is idle to expect through the application of rules of scientific procedure to attain scientific insight; for the man of science, in so far as he is creative, is an artist. /\One can only say to him, as one would say to other artists: Saturate yourself through and through with your subject and with all that bears, or may bear upon it, and *wait.* If the flash of insight comes, treasure it, and then patiently work it out in all its bearings, remembering that no art product is made convincing without labour. *Then* you may apply your rules of scientific method, with profit and advantage. And if it does not come, still *wait.*" [3] Maeterlinck's *Life of the Bee* is a suggestive combination of science and the poetic spirit. Moreover, his methods are those which we have proved to be truly psychological. He believes in work plus meditation—a

[1] *Psychologie des Grands Hommes*, p. 232.

[2] Byron, in *The Bride of Abydos*, first wrote: "Mind on her life and music on her face." In the next draft it was: "The mind of music breathing in her face." Finally it was: "The mind, the music breathing from her face."

[3] *Comparative Psychology*, p. 307. The waiting should, of course, be *expectant.* To wait hopelessly is to hinder the desired result.

meditation that allows the mind to go its own way, superficial attention being given to the life around — nature, social doings, the process of daily experience. "When one is able to follow Maeterlinck's experience, step by step," says his wife, "one gets a revelation of the formidable *rôle* played by the unconscious in our spirits. His work is not the result of a mental intention only ; it emanates from a force which is in perpetual movement, always awake, which acts unknown to him, outside of him, and seems to take on a human voice in order to dictate those profound pages which he has written about the share which this very unconsciousness has in our thoughts." [1]

A final hypothesis as to the reason why waiting must follow working is found in the law of intellectual rhythm ; but as this has considerable importance for other reasons it may be wise to study it separately.

X

B. *Inspiration is governed by the process of Intellectual Rhythm.*

We confess to some confusion when we are asked to define this law, but of the fact itself we are quite certain : the mind has its periods of expansion and contraction—the systole and the diastole of its heart. In one of its aspects Mrs Meynell has described the moral outcome of the process. "Periodicity," she says, "rules over the mental experience of man according to the path of the orbit of his thoughts. . . . Happiness is not a matter of events ; it depends on the tides of the mind." [2] Hope and fear, exaltation and depression —these are part of every human lot ; only the gods go free. The world of spiritual things in its entirety—and apparently the world of material things also—is subject to this law. Coleridge, speaking of the moral law of polarity, remarks that "when the maximum of one tendency has been attained

---

[1] "Maeterlinck's Methods of Life and Work." See *Contemporary Review*, November, 1910.

[2] *The Rhythm of Life*, p. 1.

there is no gradual decrease, but a direct transition to its minimum, till the opposite tendency has attained its maximum; and then you see another corresponding revulsion. With the Restoration came in all at once the mechanico-corpuscular philosophy, which, with the increase of manufactures, trade and arts, made everything in philosophy, religion and poetry objective; till, at length, attachment to mere external worldliness and forms got to its maximum—when out burst the French Revolution; and with it everything became immediately subjective, without any object at all." [1]

XI

And as to strictly material issues rhythm clearly governs the welfare of our investments [2] which are tabulated according to their highest and lowest. The ebb and flow may be different here from what they are there; here a lingering ebb and there a fuller flowing, but the fact remains : we are creatures of a world in which rhythm rules. Then how does this affect originality ? It causes periods, long or short, of dullness and infertility just as readily as it causes periods of lively imagination when ideas bubble up from the depths. We all know these periods—the gloom of the stagnant days

[1] *Table Talk*, p. 149. Similarly Falckenberg says : " The Greek view of the world is as classic as the plastic art of Phidias and the epic of Homer ; the Christian, as eternally valid as the architecture of the Middle Ages ; the modern, as irrefutable as Goethe's poetry and the music of Beethoven. The views of the world which proceed from the spirits of different ages as products of the general development of culture, are not so much thoughts as rhythms in thinking, not theories but modes of intuition saturated with feelings of worth.' —*History of Modern Philosophy*.

[2] " Thus far in our survey we observe that the commercial rhythms of which we have been treating, undergo a continual rise and fall. The lowest points at which iron is sold ; the time at which the least number of immigrants arrive in the country ; the time when the railroad building is the least active ; the time when stocks reach their lowest points ; the times when failures are the most numerous ; these times, with but minor difference, occur together."—R. H. Smith, *The Science of Business*. New York.

and the bounding joy of those that are creative. We disagree with Mrs Meynell when she says that "man—except the elect—is hardly aware of periodicity . . . the individual man never learns it fully, or learns it too late." We are not of the elect, and yet we know periodicity only too well; but if Mrs Meynell means that we never study the tides of the mind, and that we make the mistake of trying to create ideas during the ebb instead of the flow, we agree. The unfortunate part is that duty often calls upon us to produce good work when good work is psychologically impossible, and then . . . ?

Nevertheless, the use of observation and experiment in the study of mental rhythm should have practical value of the highest kind. When important work is before us it is a manifest advantage to know the times, seasons, and circumstances when experience and experiment have assured us we may expect the best results. To blunder along unscientifically, not knowing these things, is to waste energy and to achieve only a modicum of the excellence that might otherwise be forthcoming.

We now turn to the other question—namely, whether the law of rhythm, as now understood, casts any light on the reason why *waiting* follows *working*, apart from those reasons already adduced. We think it does. All illumination is the outcome of the alternate action of the conscious and the subconscious. We may not agree altogether with Souriau that originality is never the result of pure reflection, but we can agree to this extent, that the forward movement of reflection seldom succeeds in arriving at a solution; persistency in thinking in a continuous line is rarely effective. The explanation seems to be that only by a rhythmical movement can the wealth of mental associations, conscious and subconscious, be drawn within the required radius.

XII

C. A further condition of inspiration, closely related to the first, is this: *that the new idea is partly dependent for its birth on the action of the right external stimulus.* These stimuli may be classified as primary and secondary, the first consisting of those things seen and heard which apply the spark to a train of thought that has previously been prepared in the brain ; the second class is composed of objects, positiòns, or general surroundings which foster the creative mood. When Rousseau was walking from Paris to Vincennes one hot summer's day, to ask about Diderot, then in prison, he chanced to see in a newspaper, which he had picked up at the roadside, a notice of a theme propounded by the Dijon Academy. *Si le retablissement des Sciences et des Arts a contribué à èpurer les mœurs.* " If anything ever resembled a sudden inspiration," he writes to Monsieur de Malesherbes, " it was the movement that began in me as I read this. All at once I felt myself dazzled by a thousand sparkling lights ; crowds of vivid ideas thronged into my mind with a force and confusion that threw me into an unspeakable agitation . . . a violent palpitation oppressed me. . . . I sank under one of the trees in the avenue and passed half-an-hour there." One is surprised he did not weep also—his emotionalism often took that form, unless, as is likely, he always exaggerated— but, as an instance of the right external stimulus, nothing could better serve our purpose. The average genius generally receives *one* thought by way of a sudden inspiration : Rousseau received a crowd of them—or was it that one great idea flashed through his mind and he immediately began to formulate a series of inferences ? We cannot tell. But of one thing we are certain : if Rousseau had not been thinking previously on the lines of the theme referred to, the newspaper item would not have made the same impression on him. We only respond to a stimulus for which the mind has had an adequate preparation. That is why the great men of one age are always indebted to the great men of previous ages.[1] All inspiration, of course, does not come in the same

---

[1] A group of such instances has been made by Dr C. J. Whitby in his *Makers of Men*. " Goethe was profoundly influenced by the genius of Shakespeare ; Scott owed a strong impulse to poetry to his translation of *Goetz von Berlichingen* ; Flaubert's realism was largely based on sympathy with his father's enthusiasm for science ;

way and from only one source, but the instances quoted and those to follow—somewhat familiar, we confess—prove that the most direct stimulus for a poet [1] or for a scientist is other poetry and other science.

XIII

When Byron had conceived the idea of his *Sardanapalus* —the germ was discovered in Juvenal's description of Otho —he proceeded to develop it in a manner of which he gives a somewhat detailed account in his *Diary*.

Jan. 13, 1821.—*Saturday.* Sketched the outline and *drams. pers.* of an intended tragedy of *Sardanapalus* which I have for some time meditated. Took the names from Diodorus Siculus (I know the history of Sardanapalus, and have known it since I was twelve years old) ; and read over a passage in the ninth volume octavo of Mitford's *Greece*, where he rather vindicates the memory of this last of the Assyrians.

Jan. 14, 1821. Turned over Seneca's tragedies. Wrote the opening lines of the intended tragedy of *Sardanapalus*. Rode out some miles into the forest. Misty and rainy. Returned—dined—and wrote some more of my tragedy. Read Diodorus Siculus—turned over Seneca, and some other books. Wrote some more of the tragedy. Took a glass of grog. . . .

Feb. 15, 1821. Last night finished the first act of *Sardanapalus*. . . .

Galileo owed many suggestions to the study of Leonardo's MSS. ; Harvey's life-long interest in the problem of circulation was directly inspired by his intimacy with Fabricius ; Leibnitz was profoundly influenced by the study of Bacon ; Kant, by the study of Hume ; Darwin, by the example of Henslow and the generalisation of Malthus ; Jesus, by the teachings of Hillel, Isaiah, Daniel and John the Baptist ; Marcus Aurelius, by his admiration of the Emperor Antoninus," etc. (p. 286).

[1] Pindar says: " Poet from poet learns his art both now and of old."—Quoted in Butcher's *Harvard Lectures on Greek Subjects*, p. 139.

ORIGINALITY

Ravenna, May 28, 1821. Since my last of the 26th and 25th I have dashed off my fifth act. . . . But now comes the copying over, which may prove heavy work—heavy to the writer as to the reader.[1]

Here the stimulus comes from various quarters : Diodorus Siculus, Mitford's *Greece*, but chiefly from the tragedies of Seneca. The reading of such authors focuses attention in such a way as to create *atmosphere* : this, in its turn, brings the *mood* in which there is ease of recollection and a surprising facility in forming associations leading to unity of conception. George Eliot said that she might admit all Rousseau's erroneous views, and yet " it would not be less true that Rousseau's genius has sent the electric thrill through my intellectual and moral frame, which has awakened me to new perceptions— and which has made man and nature a fresh world of thought and feeling to me ; not by teaching me any new belief. It is simply that the rushing mighty wind of his inspiration has so quickened my faculties that I have been able to shape more definitely for myself ideas which had previously dwelt in dim *Ahnungen* in my soul." [2]

XIV

These examples have their counterpart in the life of every man whose vocation requires fertility of idea : he needs something to stimulate his invention, and he usually finds it in work of an analogous character—which he purposely seeks. But very often the right stimulus comes unsought. Life is one vast field of hetero-suggestion, not merely in the invitations to buy the goods of those who sell, or in the tendency to imitate social customs, or to conform to public opinion, but in the variety of ideas that assail us. These ideas are often of a fugitive character, but their effectiveness is not necessarily impaired on that account. The right stimulus may come as we read the newspaper, talk with a friend, walk the street, or motor through the country. Only the man

[1] Pebody's *Authors at Work*, p. 264.
[2] *Life of George Eliot*, vol. i., p. 199.

with more than average sensitiveness to external impressions responds to the unsought stimuli that bring inspiration.

The stimuli classified as secondary were defined as those composed of objects, positions, or general surroundings which foster the creative mood. Ibsen used to keep a number of little images on his writing desk : they helped him in the work of composition, he said, but declined to say *how*, adding : "That is my secret." Similarly, Kant used a certain tower, visible from his study window, as a sort of mental focus for thinking out his categories ; and when, in the course of time, some trees grew up and hid the tower, he wrote to the City Council asking them to cut down the trees so that he might once more see the tower, *and think*. The story goes that the City Fathers complied. Buffon's eccentricities are well known, the chief among which was his inability to think to good purpose except in full dress. Shelley found that munching bread was helpful in composing, just as Addison and Sheridan liked to have a bottle of wine handy, and Schiller a flask of Old Rhenish—also rotten apples in his desk. Gautier said : "It is only the smell of printer's ink that can make me move." Dr Johnson needed a purring cat, and orange peel and tea within reach. Jokai could not write unless he had violet ink : black and blue ink would make work impossible—it had to be either violet ink or a lead pencil. Thomas Hardy, prior to beginning work, always removes his boots or slippers.[1] Charles Lamb's sister says that Elia could do nothing in a room with bare and white-washed walls ; that was the kind of room in which Stevenson could work to advantage. The contrasts in habit are as striking as it is possible to imagine ; for whilst Rousseau liked to think out his pages bare-headed in the sun, Bossuet preferred to work in a cold room, his head wrapped in furs ; and Zola pulled down the blinds at midday because he found more stimulus in artificial light. Ribot remarks that "some require motor excitation ; they work only when walking or else prepare for work by physical exercise."[2] And yet there are others who, like Milton, Descartes,

[1] Most of these details are found in Erichsen's *Methods of Authors*.
[2] *The Creative Imagination*, p. 73.

ORIGINALITY

Leibnitz, and Rossini, find the horizontal position more advantageous.[1]

To the average man, especially the practical man of business, or the city lawyer, these facts are mere oddities of character and have nothing whatever to do with fostering the mood in which poets, dramatists and others discover their best thoughts. But we cannot say so much as that. Immediate surroundings have a great deal to do with mental processes : witness the healthy and muscular farmer who, seldom if ever away from home, cannot sleep in a strange room. His consciousness needs a certain accustomed environment just as his body requires a position that must be " just so " ; otherwise sleep will not come. The eccentricities of the writing fraternity are proverbial ; they have a long and curious history and we are compelled to admit that, so far from being artificialities or affectations, they are a real part of the psychology of composition. The banker who has discovered that to walk from Charing Cross to the City (whenever he has a problem to solve) is to see daylight on a difficult situation, can be assured that his case is no different from that of poet and *littérateur* : he has set up a well-marked topographical association between difficulty and solution.

XV

D. A closer study of the advent of new ideas proves that *the employment of analogy, consciously or unconsciously, is a creative method.* Before we give this method the attention it deserves it may be well to show its relationship to knowledge *per se*. Bain defines knowledge as the consciousness we have of the *difference from and agreement with—i.e.* when surveying phenomena, and especially phenomena new to us, we can only know one thing from another by marks of agreement and difference.[2]

This position still holds good as a statement of our ex-

[1] *The Influence of Bodily Posture on Mental Activities*, by E. E. Jones, Ph.D.
[2] *The Senses and the Intellect*, p. 335. 1894.

perience—the way in which external facts are understood by us. If, then, analogy occupies so important a place in the scheme of the mind's activity, there is all the more reason to suppose that further knowledge as well as new ideas have no small connection with the same method of understanding.

This is the method : our minds gather ideas from experience. These ideas are classified, and a standard is set up for each class. New facts are known mainly by their difference from facts previously known, but the discovery in most cases arises out of some points of similarity. Likeness and difference are governing mental operations : we cannot even imagine the alleged inhabitants of the planet Mars without thinking of them in human terms—i.e. their points of agreement and disagreement with ourselves. There are thirty-six varieties of haddocks, and only a Billingsgate expert can identify them : this he does by knowing to a nicety their resemblances and differences.

XVI

It follows, therefore, that until all the possible analogies have been perceived and all the possible contrasts catalogued there is a whole world of discoveries yet to be exploited ; and instead of saying there is no new thing under the sun we rather ought to be impressed by the narrowness of our knowledge. Analogy has played a great part in science, in philosophy, and in art : and it is suggestive to note that nearly all our great problems are concerned with facts for which we can find no analogy—e.g. consciousness, and the origin and destiny of life. Instead our mysteries are those of beginnings and endings—or the border lines which at once unite and divide one kingdom of nature from another. Genius has always been marked by its keen perception of analogy,[1] and Professor

[1] Carveth Read, in an interesting article on " The Functions of Relations in Thought," says that genius consists in an unusual power of " thought by analogy," but adds that " the sensitiveness to analogy . . . must (it seems to me) be supported by extraordinary power of registering experiences."—*British Journal of Psychology*, vol. iv.,

ORIGINALITY

James endeavoured to draw a distinction between those who merely *notice* the analogy and those who *obey* it. Perhaps we had better quote his own words : " According to our view, there are two stages in reasoned thought, one where similarity merely *operates* to call up cognate thoughts, and another farther stage when the bond of identity between the cognate thoughts is *noticed* ; so *minds of genius may be divided into two main sorts, those who notice the bond and those who merely obey it.* The first are the abstract reasoners, properly so called, the men of science and philosophers—the analysts, in a word ; the latter are the poets, the critics, the artists—in a word, the men of intuitions." [1] Then do not the poets notice the analogy when they obey it ? It is no verbal quibble to ask such a question. What Professor James meant, no doubt, was the difference between the working of analogy in one mind—say the poet's, and another mind, say that of a physicist. In the one case there is no deliberate search ; in the other there is. But both must notice the analogy and both must obey it. The one more easily thinks and talks in figures of speech because his subjects are more varied in character ; but the other, within the limits severely imposed upon him by the nature of his investigations, has just as keen an eye for the advantage of analogy. Professor James himself would have admitted that Fechner thought on the method of analogy as richly as any poet.[2]

XVII

The fact is, analogy is a necessary mode of all our thinking, and genius is often another name for the power to see similarities in phenomena, natural or mental, that have hitherto been undetected. Mr Havelock Ellis has brought this out clearly in his *Impressions and Comments*. " It was a fine and

1911. Ackermann points out that one of the two constituents of Plato's system is: " Analogy explains the totality of things."—*The Christian Element in Plato*, p. 171.

[1] *Principles of Psychology*, vol. ii., p. 361.

[2] See his study of Fechner in *A Pluralistic Universe*: " Fechner's great instrument for vivifying the daylight view is analogy " (p. 150).

deep saying of Aristotle," he says, " that the greatest thing by far is to be master of metaphor. This is the mark of genius, for, said he, it implies an intuitive perception of similarity in dissimilars. All the great thinkers have been masters of metaphor because all vivid thinking must be in images and the philosopher whose metaphors are blurred and diluted is one whose thinking is blurred and diluted. Thus it comes about that the thinkers who survive are the thinkers who wrote well and are most nearly poets. All great thinkers are great masters of metaphor because all thinking of any kind must be by analogy." [1] A host of illustrations springs to the mind immediately. Boole traced the analogy between logic and algebra, just as Descartes had previously shown the likeness between algebra and geometry. So soon as light and radiant heat are found to have similarities newer discoveries immediately follow. Faraday found the rotation of the plane of a beam of polarised light by a magnet, and at once Wartmann found that a beam of polarised heat rays was similarly affected. [2] Modern knowledge is replete with similar illustrations. Igo Etrich, the inventor of the Taube flying machine, got his idea whilst in India, where he noticed that the seed of the zanonia, a kind of Indian vine, was practically a natural aeroplane. It has curved crescent wings, slightly turned up at the tips. The seed proper is placed in the centre of this vegetable " plane " in the position of a pilot in a monoplane, thus giving it balance ; and although Taubes are now superseded the wing principle is still considered sound and reliable. [3]

XVIII

In things medical analogy has had and will continue to have the same range of application. Dr Forbes Ross, observing the knotted outgrowths on the trees in his orchard,

[1] *Impressions and Comments*, pp. 81-82. See also Max Müller's article on "Metaphor as a Mode of Abstraction," in *The Fortnightly Review* (1886).
[2] Gore, *Art of Discovery*, p. 329.
[3] Article in *The Evening News*, 1st Feb. 1915.

was led to ask himself why the trees in the forest so seldom had these growths, for he thought he detected a departure from normal health in these ugly developments : he began to think of them as tree-cancers. The conclusion at which he ultimately arrived was that they were caused by the absence of potassium in the soil. This absence was explained by the fact that in orchards all the leaves are usually swept away, and the grass is either eaten by cattle or cut for hay. The potash thus removed, the trees develop excrescences and outgrowths, their limbs wither, and the fruit becomes lop-sided. In the forests, on the other hand, where the potash is given back to the soil, the trees remain perfect for hundreds of years. And just as potassium is absent from cultivated orchards, which develop a form of cancer, so it is sometimes largely absent from the water we drink and the food we eat. Dr Forbes Ross concluded that potassium would be a remedy for this frightful disease, and he claimed that experiment proved his argument. Medical authorities may dispute his theories and doubt his evidence, but they cannot deny the rightness of his method.

But take a very different illustration of analogy. Mr T. A. Cook has written a remarkable book called *The Curves of Life*, about which we shall have more to say in another place. Mr Cook's study of spiral formations in nature, science, art—everywhere, in fact—may be best understood in the light of his own words : "Just as Newton began by postulating Perfect Motion and thence explained the working of the solar system, so it may be possible to postulate Perfect Growth (by means of a logarithmic spiral) and thence arrive at some law ruling the forms of organic objects as gravitation is held to prevail in the physical world." We should not like to say that Mr Cook has satisfied his readers, but those readers are very grateful to him for the twenty years he spent in the study of curves as seen in his entertaining chapters. Speaking for ourselves, we think it would be wiser to postulate nothing. Follow ordinary methods of inductive inquiry. Already enough material has been gathered to show that the curve is a fundamental with a secret in its grasp ; and one day we may have a thrill. But what is it that is so strongly appealing in such books as *The Curves of Life*? It is what Bain called "the fetch of similarity." There is something in us that compels a love of analogy. We see it in the long life of such treatises as Butler's *Analogy*, Bagehot's *Physics and Politics*, and even Drummond's *Natural Law in the Spiritual World*.

XIX

We see it also in displays of wit and humour. When Sir James Barrie was asked by an enterprising editor to give some account of his methods of work, he wrote, in reply :

Journalism			*Fiction*			
2 pipes	.	1 hour	8 pipes	.	.	1 oz.
2 hours	.	1 idea	7 oz. .	.	.	1 week
1 idea .	.	3 paragraphs	2 weeks	.	.	1 chapter
3 paragraphs	1 leader		20 chapters .	.	1 nib	
			2 nibs	.	.	1 novel

Similarly, Mr Stephen Leacock's "Lodging House Euclid" is a statement of the vicissitudes of the boarder in terms of postulates and definitions. We reproduce three :

A landlady is a parallelogram—or other plain, oblong, irregular figure which cannot be described, and is *equal* to *anything*.

.   .   .   .

The bedclothes of a lodging-house bed, though produced ever so far both ways, will never meet.

.   .   .   .

If there shall be two lodgers in the same flat, and the amount of *side* of one be equal to the amount of *side* of the other—each to each—and the *wrangle* between one lodger and the landlady be equal to the wrangle between the landlady and the other lodger, then shall the *weekly bills* of the two lodgers be *equal*—also each to each ; for if not, let one bill be the *greater*—then the other bill is *less than it might have been*, which is *absurd*.

H   113

The gratified feeling that arises as we read these sparkling even though forced analogies can only spring from a sentimental regard for unity of idea. When Mr Lloyd George was advocating his land policy, a wag wrote to the papers to say that as he owned a piece of ground in Brookwood Cemetery, six feet by three, for which he had no use at the moment, he would present it free of charge on condition that the Chancellor would *enter into immediate occupation*. It was the sort of joke that diners retailed to each other at the clubs, and the reason why friend and foe alike enjoyed it was, of course, its pointed analogy of conception. The same may be said of the story of Wendell Phillips when he was on a lecturing tour in Ohio. Tackled as an abolitionist by some clergymen, the following dialogue took place. Said one of the parsons :

"Are you Mr Phillips ? "

"I am."

"Are you trying to free the niggers ? "

"Yes ; I am an abolitionist."

"Well, why do you preach your doctrines up here ? Why don't you go over into Kentucky ? "

"Excuse me, are you a preacher ? "

"I am."

"Are you trying to save souls from hell ? "

"Yes ; that is my business."

"Well, why don't you go there ? "[1]

XX

There is a phrase used by De Quincey which is worthy of reproduction. It is: "An electric aptitude for seizing analogies." He had often been complimented on his marvellous memory, and the compliments offended him ; for he

---

[1] Quoted in Brill's *Psychanalysis*—chapter on "Freud's Theory of Wit." Schoolboy "howlers" are often the outcome of mistaken analogies due to sound. "The King was not to order taxis without the consent of Parliament." "Henry VIII. was very fat, besides being a Nonconformist." "People often lose their consciences when they are ill."

believed that it was not memory that gave him power so
much as "the far higher power of an electric aptitude for
seizing analogies, and by means of these aerial pontoons
passing over like lightning from one topic to another." [1]
The quickness with which analogies are perceived, recorded,
and used, is certainly some guide to mental ability.[2] But the
perception need not be speedy in order to possess worth.
What could be better than this from Ribot : "All imaginative metaphysics have a dynamic basis, *e.g.* Platonic *Ideas*,
Leibnitz's *Monadology*, the *Nature Philosophy* of Schelling,
Schopenhauer's *Will* and Hartmann's *Unconscious*." [3] In
a section on the mind's love of unity, Sir William Hamilton
gives us the secret of our liking of analogies.[4] It is our
effort to reduce the many to the one, and it is one of the causes
of philosophy itself. If a man should ask for a method that,
applied diligently and intelligently, would lead to promising
results, he could not do better than cease to view his problem
as an isolated fact, but as one having analogous facts in other
spheres, a study of which cannot but throw a suggestive light
on the main issue.

Like memory, or a turn for mathematics, the sense of
analogy is, more frequently than not, a gift ; but this does
not mean that a low range of power cannot be developed into
a higher. An eye for analogies can be trained like a nose for
news—maybe not up to the standard of an inborn gift, but
up to the pitch of skill and quickness that at first seems
improbable.

XXI

E. Another law of inspiration is this : *that when the mind
is bent on a discovery, or otherwise set upon the realisation of*

[1] *Autobiography*, vol. i.
[2] Jevons indeed looked upon it as the true measure of intellect.
"There is a rare property of mind which consists in penetrating the
disguise of variety and seizing the common elements of sameness ;
and it is this property which furnishes the true measure of intellect."
—*Principles of Science*, vol. i., p. 5.
[3] *The Creative Imagination*, pp. 253-254.
[4] *Metaphysics*, vol. i., p. 67.

*an idea, its energies may suddenly be side-tracked by a concep-
tion with few relationships to the immediate purpose ; or it
may make what is called a chance discovery of a totally different
nature.*

An interesting illustration is found in the history of photog-
raphy. Niepce had taken several strides towards discovery
but he died before achieving his purpose and Daguerre continued his experiments. He found an under-exposed plate in
a cupboard, and was surprised to note that the picture had
been developed. Presuming that the cupboard had something to do with it, although it was empty, he tried various
experiments, and always with the same result. Ideas of
" sorcery " assailed him ! Then he noticed in a corner of the
cupboard a capsule full of mercury, a metal that emits steam
at an ordinary temperature. He supposed that this steam
had developed the plates. To make sure he put an under-
exposed plate in a perfectly dark room, making sure no picture
was visible on the plate. He exposed this to the vapour of
mercury, and then, as he looked, the picture appeared on the
plate. Daguerre had made one of the great discoveries of
the century.[1] It would be possible to provide large numbers
of such illustrations in science, and in commerce, but they
have the one common quality which Daguerre's experiments
contain—namely, the unexpected, the accidental—or, as some
persist in saying, knowledge by *chance*.[2] Now chance is a
very large subject, with many ramifications, and we can deal
with only one : its relationship to new ideas. What is that
relationship ? So far as we can judge, it is one of law, for,
as Hume said : " What the vulgar call chance is nothing but
a secret and concealed cause." [3] Whewell, in arguing against
the notion of chance as it existed in his day, declares that
" in whatever manner facts may be presented to the notice of
a discoverer they can never become the materials of exact
knowledge except they find his mind already provided with
precise and suitable conceptions by which they may be

[1] Paulhan, *Psychologie de l'Invention.*
[2] Gore's *Art of Discovery* (p. 224) contains a number of good
instances. See also R. A. Gregory's *Discovery.*
[3] *Treatise on Human Nature*, Book III.

analysed and connected."[1]   This rightly places the emphasis
on the knowledge and mental acumen of the discoverer.   It
is true that he discovered something which he did not set out
to discover, but had he not been the man he was he would
never have noticed the phenomena which, on further investigation, led up to a new fact ; and without a use of the
scientific method the new fact would have continued its
undiscovered career.

XXII

The question naturally arises : Can we predict mental
phenomena ? and it is a most reasonable question, in spite of
the fact that it asks more than is justified by the position we
have taken up.   Mental processes observe the laws that rule
our conscious and subconscious life, but until those laws are
fully known there will be a margin of experience where law
is untraceable.   That, however, does not prove the absence
of law.   If the Prince of Wales is in town we may meet him
in *The Mall*, but if we do not meet him it does not prove that
meeting him is an impossibility.   If a student of history is
doing research work at the Record Office we cannot predict
that he will discover some new items about Shakespeare's
life at Stratford, but we can predict that if he sees a remote
allusion to these items in a volume of law cases, he will have
both the impulse and the ability to follow the clues step by
step to the last issue.   This may seem a small and un-
important claim to make, but in reality it is a great truth.
It means that if all the alleged accidental discoveries could
be analysed, we should find the familiar laws of association
would explain every one of them.   When d'Orbigny saw a
peasant woman spit on a hot iron to test its heat, and noticed
that the " spit " flew off the iron before it could evaporate, he
got the right idea for solving phenomena in connection with
volcanic eruptions.   An accidental discovery ?   Certainly

[1] *Novum Organon Renovatum*, p. 47.   Prof. Karl Pearson, in his
Grammar of Science, says: "What we are to understand by a chance
distribution is one in accordance with law, and one, the nature of
which can, for all practical purposes, be closely predicted."[1]

not—at any rate not in the sense that chance is itself a cause, and that we must wait until the god of chance has the whim to put discovery in our way.[1] The kind of prediction we can make in the mental world is indicated by the laws of thought generally. We cannot say what notes an organist will use when improvising, but we can say—when we know the performer and his mood—in what direction his impulse will take him, and with what power and finish he will express his feelings and ideas.

XXIII

Paulhan offers some interesting illustrations of the way in which writers during the prosecution of their work will *deviate* from their original purpose.[2] But their very deviations show conformity to law. Who of those who knew Alphonse Daudet in the flesh, or who know him only as a writer, will be surprised that he allowed a visit to a sanatorium to affect the development of one of his characters ? Speaking of a much-criticised episode in *Numa Roumestau*— the death of Hortense le Quesnay—Paulhan says that an accident in the life of the author caused its insertion. " Why consumptive ? Why this death so sentimental and romantic, this facile allurement of the emotions of the reader ? Because " (Daudet continues) " one is not master of one's work ; because during its gestation an idea takes possession and haunts one. Whilst I was working at Numa I was taken to Allevard . . ."—and then he gives a picture of consumptive humanity in all stages of suffering, adding that " one of them thrust herself into my book in spite of myself, bringing her

[1] Prof. E. Mach says: " But granting that the most important inventions are brought to man's notice accidentally and in ways that are beyond his foresight, yet it does not follow that accident alone is sufficient to produce an invention. . . . In all such cases the inventor is obliged *to take note* of the new fact, he must discover and grasp its advantageous feature, and must have the power to turn that feature to account in the realisation of his purpose."
—" Accident in Invention and Discovery," *The Monist*, vol. vi., p. 166.
[2] *Psychologie de l'Invention*, chap. iii.

melancholy train into the beautiful pastoral setting." Was the insertion, then, a literary blemish? The critics must judge as to that : to Daudet it was the right and happy thing to do, just as it was proper on the part of Victor Hugo to insert a mass of archæological. detail in his *Notre Dame*. There have been men of genius who have raised the unexpected into a principle of guidance—Musset, for instance. He reproached Scribe for the regularity and even balance of his work. "When Scribe," he said, "commences a piece, an act, or a scene, he always knows how it will start, how it will go, and how it will end. There is undoubtedly the merit of the straight line which gives great solidarity to all he writes. But there is also a need of suppleness and imagination. He is too logical : he never loses his head. I, on the contrary, midway in a scene, or a piece of poetry, find that I must suddenly change the plan . . . I had started for Machiel, and I arrive at Constantinople." [1] There is no doubt a charm in such mental adventures ; we go out, not knowing where or how, and expecting to meet the unexpected, so to speak ; but even so we shall only meet and recognise that which is in accordance with the inward self. As Maeterlinck puts it : "Do not forget that nothing happens to us that is not of the same nature as ourselves. . . . Climb the mountain or go down into the village, travel to the ends of the world, or take a walk round the house, you will meet only yourself on the paths of chance." This is the law which governs the mental process of accidental inspiration.

XXIV

F. The most important condition of inspiration has been reserved for final treatment. It is both simple and brief : *Think for Yourself.* In one sense this is implied in every form of mental activity. Even in reading the thoughts of another we are testing the writer's opinions and estimating their value. But to think for oneself in the special sense

[1] Paulhan, chap. ii. Sourian says: "It rarely happens that the ideas we find are precisely those we have been seeking. . . . We find our ideas most often by digression."—*Théorie de l'Invention.*

here referred to is to approach a problem without the assistance that may be drawn from books or other sources. Gibbon's method has some bearing on the practice. Before sitting down to read a new book, he first of all cross-examined himself on the subject of the book, to ascertain the extent of his knowledge and to discover how far his opinions had been formed. Naturally, this presupposed some previous knowledge of the subject, obtained in the usual way; but as a means of developing the spirit of challenge to, as well as appreciation of, a new writer—nothing could be better. Still, it belongs more to the ethics of reading than to the psychology of inspiration. What, then, do we mean by urging a man to think for himself? We mean that he shall discover the problems of life before they are disclosed to him by authors of books or by some other form of discourse. These problems are infinite in variety and we do not refer specially to any one genus or species : a problem may be the origin of life or the mystery of sleep. Take the latter as a familiar example. What happens when a man desires to solve this mystery? He generally commences what is called a course of reading. He devours book after book : makes voluminous notes ; studies his own dreams and the dreams of his friends ; and at the end of a year, if you ask him how he is getting on, you find that his talk is all about what this Professor says, what Marie de Maneicene says, and what a profound mystery this apparently simple matter has become. He has made the mistake of mastering the literature of sleep ; he ought first to have studied the subject by the unaided light of his own intelligence. "But," you object, "would this be any good unless he happens to have, naturally, a very acute mind ?" Well, it is the only possible way of bringing out any originality he may possess. Besides, it is the method of all truly original investigators. He may ask himself a simple question, as : Why is sleep necessary? and after turning it over in his mind, may decide that it is one of the primal rhythms of physical nature, and that, looked at mentally, it is like daylight and action to the subconscious world. When he comes to study what others have thought he may find some of his most valued ideas are old and hoary-headed ;

and that other ideas of which he hoped much have been severely criticised; but, as often as not, it happens that there is a residue of theories which possess original merit— *i.e.* thinking for himself has brought inspiration. This is no fancy picture of the mental life; it is a happening that could be repeated over and over again if men and women would but avoid the wrong method. That method consists in leaning upon others, and in conning what others have said and done.

XXV

To some people the idea of telling an uneducated man to think for himself savours of absurdity; they would argue that a man must first know *how* to think before he is advised to think for himself. We disagree entirely. Every man can think for himself: training shows him how to improve in this respect.[1] And in many instances he trains himself in the school of experience. Some of the most original men in business have owed little to the schools and much to individual effort, relying solely on their own intellections. The ideas which came to them, and which they carried out with fortunate results, were the offspring of the final law of inspiration. Indeed this notion that only a highly educated man can, or ought to be allowed to, think for himself is pathetic in its ignorance; it is just as wrong as the other idea—namely, that no sort of education or training can improve the powers of reflection. But let us go more deeply into the matter. Why is it that to think for oneself is the final law of inspiration—the one royal road to ideas if so be that such a road exists? It is because *our own* ideas can come in no other way. We do not say that to get a new idea by reading a book or studying an advertisement is not thinking for oneself, but we shall admit we have had some assistance. The kind of reflection under review is one where such assistance is all but dispensed with, and where we rely almost entirely on

---

[1] "A being who could not think without training could never be trained to think; one may have to learn to think *well*, but not to think."—Dewey, *How We Think*, p. 29.

ourselves for the original impetus and for its future development.

XXVI

The natural tendency among the majority of people is to think by proxy : we lean upon others, or we follow in their footsteps. Now the opposite method—that of thinking for oneself—is not only highly educative, but it is, as already stated, the one way to originality. On that everybody is agreed—it is too obvious to be denied. The untaught man, however, unless he has a strong emotive temperament urging him forward to action, does not know how to begin. Let us suppose he is in business and is anxious to strike out in a new direction. He needs special information on certain points, but does not know how to get it ; and instead of thinking out ways and means of his own he relies on tit-bits of knowledge he can pick up here and there. In the final issue he builds his new venture on foundations laid by other men, not on his own foundations. Let us suppose, further, that a friend, eager to stimulate independent thought, gives him a copy of Schopenhauer's *On Thinking for Oneself*[1] and Lord Coleridge's essay on *Thinking for Ourselves*.[2] Will these enlighten him ? Only to the extent of telling him what *not* to do. Their whole influence is rather moral than intellectual. The fact is, nobody can tell us how to think for ourselves, except in this almost unnecessary rule : that before consulting other opinions we should make a strong effort to form our own. To do that we generally need a knowledge of the facts involved, and these are seldom obtained without a search in which books figure conspicuously. But there are many facts which we should do well to collect for ourselves ; and in economics this is particularly true. Political economy was called the dismal science because it was at first the product of *thought*. Professors approached it from their own standpoint instead of from the standpoint of social and industrial phenomena. The first qualification of a social reformer is to know by personal experience the evils he would remedy.

[1] In *The Art of Literature*.
[2] *New Review*, July, 1890.

THE LAWS OF INSPIRATION

A professor of Political Economy may discourse learnedly on rent, but he is not likely to touch the bottom of the subject until he has known men and women in pathetic difficulties with their landlords. The unsatisfactory nature of much of our modern education is traceable to its academic nature, which means that it is in some respects out of touch with reality. The failure of the academic mind in practical politics is nothing short of tragic. Such men are the apostles of a scholastic tradition ; they never think for themselves in a truly radical manner, for it would involve a loss of caste and constitute an offence to the precedents which guide them.

XXVII

That there is a good deal of what may be termed hidden originality is a truth well known to men who have gained the confidence of their fellows. We have met men who on the surface looked and talked like the bumpkins of popular humour ; but in expansive moments, when the stranger has become a friend, they have outlined a striking improvement in an agricultural instrument, or suggested a much-needed modification in the work of butter-making. "Why not patent these ideas ? " we have asked. The answer was not slow to come. " Ted Nicol patented *his*—he's a mile across there —and the London agent charged him ten pounds and Ted got nothing. I'm a country man, I know, but ideas is expensive —eh ? " Perhaps a better Patent Office and a reformed agency system will come with the new regime. But not only in things material but spiritual do we find hidden originality. Get into the confidence of men in town or country, who appear to be quite average men, and you will sometimes find they have evolved for themselves a system of the universe, crude in its logic, perhaps, but not unintelligent in its perceptions. This applies to mysticism, especially, where subjective experience is the sole end and aim[1] : but it occasionally applies to things more mundane, even the most practical things. In the depths of the country, miles from what we call civilisation,

[1] This side of consciousness has been dealt with by Miss E. Underhill. See her " The Mystic as a Creative Artist,'' in *Quest* for July, 1913.

we have listened to a man, dressed in shabby clothes, discoursing on the theory that in certain stages of heat the fireman's hose simply added fuel to the flames. The argument was conducted with fervour and with many references to the laws of physics; it was not convincing, and yet no one of us vanquished him. He veered off later into a discussion on ἐξουσία which he said had six distinct meanings; and although a self-taught man he would "back himself against Liddell and Scott's Lexicon any day." The session—for it was nothing less than that—closed by the statement of a theory that every man and woman ought to know the day of death. He knew his, and had prepared accordingly. "How *can* we know?" he was asked. "Just ask in the. Silence," he replied, "and it will be given you in the watches of the night." A strange man he was, somewhat avoided by his neighbours, half-unconscious of his originality, and a little annoyed that his views should be so sceptically received.

The reader may declare that the world does not want any village eccentricities. Probably not. But we want the atmosphere of freedom, in which any man is at liberty to declare such new ideas as come to him. His fellows are certain to criticise them adversely at first; but if there is any value in the ideas their advantage will be realised, whereas in a cynical atmosphere the ideas remain unspoken. We also want social machinery whereby mental ability of all kinds is not allowed to be fruitless. A Clearing House for Ideas, not as a Government Department—God forbid—but as a profit-making concern, would be a gain to every department of the community.

CHAPTER III

I

THE inspiration of ideas brought about by artificial means is a subject of no mean magnitude, and in these pages we can do no more than touch the fringe of it. Strictly speaking, some of the phenomena do not belong to the artificial sphere at all; they are natural in their origin and effects; but as they are more easily dealt with in this section, on account of their association with poisons and drugs, that must be our excuse for their appearance out of place.

Disorders like gout infuse a toxin into the blood that at certain times gives the patient a brain so clear and penetrating that he is thus far more advantaged by his suffering than hindered by it. When do those times occur? When the poison locates itself in a joint of the foot and draws the rest of the toxin in that direction. But if there be no location, and the toxin distributes itself throughout the system then the brain receives its share, and intense irritability is the result. Medical writers are not quite certain as to why this result is what they claim it to be; the mere layman imagines that blood minus toxin is better for anything than blood plus toxin. And yet there are strange happenings that go to support the very opposite view. For instance, William Sharp says of Heine, who suffered from a painful malady, that "as the body died the mind more gloriously effloresced, like the fantastic flower of Borneo, which displays its richest blooms as the stem rots at the root. New ideas, fresh impulses, creative instincts arose within him; his mental horizon widened, the atmosphere became rarefied . . . it was during the last three years of suffering that the genius of the poet reached its climacteric."

ORIGINALITY

Dr Reed has instituted a striking contrast between two periods in the life of Robert Louis Stevenson. At Hyères, "after a terrible hæmorrhage he fell a victim to sciatica and was temporarily blind from ophthalmia. All light was excluded on account of his eyes and his right arm was bandaged to his side on account of the hæmorrhage." This would be enough to place any ordinary man out of the running for anything except enforced patience, but, "to circumvent fate he had a large board covered with paper laid across his bed, and on this, or on a large slate, he wrote out with his left hand most of the poems in *The Child's Garden of Verses.*" Pulmonary complaints notably harmonise with optimistic feelings, and there would appear to be an accentuation of the action of all the vital centres, resulting in an increased stimulation of the brain. This fact is abundantly illustrated in the case of J. A. Symonds.

II

But to return to R.L.S. At Vailima his health rapidly improved, and the tubercular trouble was arrested; and although this was better in one way it was a disadvantage in another, for he seems to have lost the stimulus of disease. Writing to Baxter, he says: "I am come to a dead stop. I never can remember how bad I have been before, but at any rate I am bad enough just now; I mean as to literature; in health I am well and strong. I take it I shall be six months before I shall be heard of again." The contrast is certainly striking, but the specific influence of disease on the creative powers of the mind is as yet speculative. ⟨ Nevertheless the drift of opinion seems to be that in some cases bodily ills and fine thinking are in the relationship of cause and effect.⟩

Drug-taking as a means of securing intellectual elevation is a practice that is happily dying out—at any rate among workers. We read our De Quincey, and the details of bibulous authors in the past, with a sense of history rather than of modern practices. The cocaine habit and other similar forms of seeking momentary elation are not part of literature or of business; they belong to the general practitioner and the mental expert.

III

Inspiration is of two kinds : (*a*) natural, and (*b*) artificial. The natural kind is that which is brought about by the activity of the mind, apart from any physical agencies specially introduced for the purpose of stimulation; the artificial kind is that which is brought about by the use of drugs like alcohol, opium, haschish, and cocaine, wherein the nervous excitement of the body has a direct effect on feelings, on thought, and on consciousness generally, resulting in mental states that are unusual, or abnormal. The bodily and mental characteristics of natural inspiration have been the subject of close study for many years past, and in the paragraphs that follow, we desire to exclude from consideration all the phenomena of Hindu Concentration, Hebrew Prophetism, Greek Divination and Modern Spiritualism; they belong to the history of religions rather than to the Psychology of Inspiration.[1] Their intention is not to discover new ideas but to obtain divine knowledge for inward enlightenment and for external guidance. Hence, they are outside our purview. What we have to consider, chiefly, is the process of originative thought in its physical and mental accompaniments. The physical signs, other than those referred to in a previous section, are very few indeed. If a man is walking when an

[1] In some cases they are literary or artistic. For instance, Coomaraswamy, an Indian writer of high repute, says: " The artist who desires to receive inspiration for any new work must proceed to a solitary place after bathing his body and putting on new or newly washed garments. Then he must perform the sevenfold office beginning with the invocations of the hosts of Buddhas and Bodhisattoas in the open space before him. He must offer to them real or imaginary flowers and end with a dedication of the secret he thus acquires, to the welfare of all beings. Then the artist must realise in thought the four infinite qualities: Love, Compassion, Sympathy, Same-sightedness . . . only when the mental image of the figure descried is clearly seen does the artist begin to model or to paint."—*Orpheus* for June, 1910.

inspiration overtakes him, he shows a tendency to slacken his pace, or else he stops suddenly.[1] But when he resumes his walk he finds an increased blood pressure; speed is accelerated. Mental excitement has reacted on the body.

IV

This exaltation of feeling is the first and most noticeable feature of an inspired experience, and there are cases where the physical accompaniments are depressive. De Musset said: "Invention annoys me and makes me tremble. Execution, always too slow for my wish, makes my heart beat awfully, and, weeping and keeping myself from crying aloud, I am delivered of an idea that is intoxicating me, but of which I am mortally ashamed and disgusted next morning."[2] Similarly, Alfieri says: "That part of composition which I have called creation is a fever, and during its access one feels nothing else." Again: "The whole day I pondered, as I always do as soon as the fever by means of which I begin and carry through a work, seizes me I know not how?"[3] Lombroso has collected some curious instances of exalted feeling with their physical concomitancies[4] on much the same lines, but his purpose somewhat vitiates the fairness with which he tries to deal with them. The nervous system of the thinker is the deciding factor in saying what position his body will assume during inspired moments and what will be the peculiar manifestations of his mind. We do not know how Aristotle and Plato, Shakespeare and Goethe acted when moved by the conception of their finest thoughts. Perhaps they would have said no more than this: that they "enjoyed the excitement of origination."[5] Certainly it must be admitted that the eccentricities of such men as those to whom Lombroso refers are not the necessary

---

[1] " But as they walked, Socrates, engaged in some deep contemplation, slackened his pace."—Plato, *Banquet*, p. 20.
[2] See Ribot's *The Creative Imagination*, p. 52.
[3] See Hirsch's *Genius and Degeneration*, p. 96.
[4] *The Man of Genius*, p. 22.
[5] See *Life of Walter Bagehot*, p. 32.

accompaniments of inspiration; but it would seem as if musicians, poets, and artists—in that order—are more outwardly affected by their conception of new ideas than men who specialise in other forms of invention. For instance, a thoughtful writer, both critic and composer, remarks : " Every composer has endured weeks of torture owing to the persistence, on the edge of his mind, of a tune which he cannot define clearly. He is unable to ' visualise ' distinctly." [1] Allow a little for exaggeration, and sufficient remains to show that in some cases the creative mood has nervous components that are almost distressing. Nevertheless, have there been no modern composers and poets, who have given the world great creations, and who, in conceiving them, did not pass through nervous crises of any kind ? Mendelssohn among musicians, and Tennyson and Browning among poets, appear to have been physically and mentally normal during the creative period. Indeed, this question is like the question of the relationship between genius and insanity ; and as we find the greatest of all geniuses were not insane, we can leave the eccentricities of the secondary geniuses to the medical psychologist.

V

An instance of another and quieter kind of inspiration is found in the life of George Eliot. Lewes said to her one day : " You must write a story." She did not take kindly to the suggestion.

"I deferred . . . after my usual fashion. But one morning as I was thinking what should be the subject of my first story my thoughts merged themselves into a dreamy doze, and I imagined myself writing a story of which the title was *The Sad Fortunes of the Rev. Amos Barton.* I was soon wide awake and told G." [2]

Another feature of the inspired moment is its profound mental detachment : an ability to abstract the attention from immediate surroundings and to concentrate it on the

---

[1] W. Wallace, *The Musical Faculty*, p. 95.
[2] *Life of George Eliot*, vol. i., p. 415.

subject. The extent to which this kind of concentration is possible may be doubted by many, but in that species of originality which depends on following a train of thought leading ultimately to a great discovery there is a possibility of abstract attention which can at least be imagined if not described. The stories that have come down to us about Sir Isaac Newton are not highly improbable; rather the opposite.[1] Absent-mindedness simply means that the thinker is only partly conscious of the things of sense, but deeply conscious of the thoughts he is thinking. To him thoughts are the most real things in the world; in fact, they seem to take on the attributes of matter and produce results accordingly. "When I was describing the poisoning of Emma Bovary," said Flaubert, "I had so strong *a taste of arsenic in my mouth*, I was myself so far poisoned that I had two consecutive fits of indigestion . . . real indigestion." Here, as always, the personal equation governs everything; a genius, as chemist, could concentrate on arsenic, even in a most dramatic poisoning case, without getting the taste of arsenic in his mouth. But Flaubert was particularly liable to suffer from what we may call an advanced form of identity with the subject of his thought. In a letter to Madame X., written two hours before dawn, he gives an account of the terrible physical and mental sensations he suffered whilst describing the adventures of Madame Bovary: "dizziness, pain in his heart, unspeakable lassitude . . . he has to open the window and breathe the cool air; his groans bring his housekeeper into the room." These unpleasant manifestations arose out of his sense of oneness with the people and things of his imagination. He says: "I have ridden with them in a forest on an autumn afternoon, under the falling leaves, and I was the horses, the leaves, the wind, the words they spoke, and the red sun which made them half close their eyelids . . . with love."[2]

---

[1] A number of cases may be found in Carpenter's *Mental Physiology*, pp. 544-549.

[2] Paulhan, *Le Psychologie de l'Invention*.

VI

Novelists are accustomed to identify themselves with their characters but it is not necessary to suffer bodily pains on that account. Dickens, Thackeray, George Eliot, Thomas Hardy, Meredith—these are not names that suggest agony in composition—and yet their creations are highly individualised, like that of Madame Bovary.

Some of the reflex influences of abstraction, especially where the individual is of a highly strung nature, are worthy of notice. One of them is *clairaudience—i.e.* thoughts become audible. The case of Blake has already been referred to. Nietzsche appears to have had a similar experience although not so continuous. In a private letter, presumably to Brandes, he says *Thus Spake Zarathustra* was conceived chapter by chapter during long walks, "with a feeling of inspiration, as though each sentence had been shouted in my ear." [1] It may be argued that this feeling must be regarded as a symptom of advanced nervous trouble, the hearing of "voices" being looked upon by medical men as evidence of a derangement, and to this finding we shall offer no objection. Both these men ultimately became insane. But there are geniuses who have had these audible thoughts without losing their reason, even temporarily.

Nevertheless the experience is not healthy, not only because the nerve currents are disturbed, but because the individual himself is in danger of developing delusions in matters of everyday life. Taine says that Balzac, at the house of Madame Gay, was describing with animation a fine white horse he intended to present to Sandeau. So deeply did the intention possess him, and so vivid was the realisation of the projected transfer, that some days later on meeting Sandeau he asked him how he liked the horse! It was the first time Sandeau had heard any reference to the matter.

The right kind of identity is not one that is mystic in the wrong way, but which is spiritual—*i.e.* a love interest that yields full knowledge and insight, yet preserves the proper relationship of subject and object.

[1] Georg Brandes, *Nietzsche*.

SECTION III

BIOLOGICAL FACTORS

CHAPTER I

AGE AND ORIGINALITY

I

THE man of average intelligence produces his best work, or yields his best service, between twenty and forty. After forty his powers begin to decline. This is not a necessary decline; it is not an inevitable outcome of his age[1]; his brain power loses its elasticity because as a rule he takes no pains to develop it or even to preserve it. The man who is a shade or two above the average is determined that the fatal forties shall not find him relaxing his efforts; and it is effort that keeps him mentally fit when other men of the same age begin to lose grip. A reason for effort is the desideratum of tens of thousands of people in the middle years of life.

But the question that concerns us here is this: during what period of years does the original mind produce its best work? To answer such a question satisfactorily calls for a scientific study of the biography of genius. A promising beginning was made by Sir Francis Galton, Professor Sully, and others, and recently by W. A. Dorland in his interesting little book entitled _The Age of Mental Virility_, wherein he has collected a mass of biographical data, which, when thrown into statistical

---

[1] Schopenhauer argued that "on passing his fortieth year, any man of the slightest power of mind,—any man, that is, who has more than the sorry share of intellect with which Nature has endowed five-sixths of mankind—will hardly fail to show some trace of misanthropy."— _Counsels and Maxims_, p. 136.

form, proves that the average years of mental fecundity
are from twenty-four to fifty.[1] After fifty energy is consumed not so much in opening out new fields of thoughts or
action as in prosecuting the purposed originalities of previous
years. Cases where great achievements have been accomplished after mid-life are to be explained by the work of preceding decades, just as Goethe, issuing his *Faust* when he was
quite an old man, offered the world a token of genius which
had taken him well nigh half-a-century to mature. Thus the
plea that " because old age, in the past, has produced some
of the world's classics, we may therefore expect great things
from the grey heads of the present," is, to say the least,
rather misleading. Originality after fifty or sixty is not so
much the outcome of an ability that has been developed since
the fiftieth year was passed as the result of the deep and
wide sensuous life, the reflective power, and hard work of
young manhood ; in fact, the essential idea of a classic work
may have been originated at thirty-five and yet remain
unpublished until sixty-five : what of Kant's famous
Critique and Cervantes' *Don Quixote* published when the
author was fifty-seven ? *The Descent of Man* was published
when Darwin was sixty-two ; *Robinson Crusoe* when Defoe
was fifty-eight. Samuel Richardson, as an eighteenth-
century novelist, and William de Morgan, as a nineteenth-
century novelist, are instances of men who " blossomed late,"
but it is not, after all, the lateness that is the significant
fact. It is in Richardson's case the long years spent in a
silent study of feminine motives, and, in de Morgan's, the
union of keen observation with acute reflection, applied
to the life of a social period, not for one decade but for
several. Every originality has a history, and the date of its
appearance is not an exact guide to the present ability of its

[1] Professor Sully examined 287 cases of what may be called supreme
genius, and found that out of 258 cases, 101, or nearly two-fifths,
obtained their first considerable success before twenty-five ; and
155—in all about three-fifths—before thirty. But he also found that
31 cases, or nearly one-eighth of the whole, did not attain their
distinction until after forty. And among these were names of the
highest eminence.—" Genius and Precocity.": See *Nineteenth Century*,
June, 1886.

author. The initial conception may go far back to those days when fine frenzies were more numerous than they are in maturer years, the intermediate period being spent in those testings, emendations, corrections, and enlargements with which the works of genius are usually associated.

II

The reason why fifty is the usual outside age limit to original thought is quite obvious ; the bodily powers begin to fail, imperceptibly, perhaps, but none the less really, and the mental powers follow suit. Physical resistance to weariness and disease loses some of its force ; the blood is minus the electric qualities which it once possessed ; there is a growing disposition to take things " easy " ; *action* has less impulse behind it. On the mental side there are corresponding changes [1] ; the mind shows a tendency to look on the past, and to consider the lessons of the journey ; receptivity diminishes because the circle of intellectual interests narrows itself gradually ; a subtle tired feeling insinuates itself into the very centre of consciousness, and it is felt that the insoluble problems which youth believed would be easily solved *some* day are more than ever beyond solution. Such men are quite willing to let others break their powers on the granite walls of the Ultimate. The one-time vivacity is replaced by a desire for quiet contemplation—in a word, body and mind *begin* to seek repose and the glory of conquest has a diminishing appeal. There is no exact age for the oncoming of this condition ; it may arrive at fifty, at fifty-five, at sixty-five, at seventy-five ; in special instances, like Gladstone's or Dr James Martineau's, it may not have arrived at eighty.

At sixty-five Edmond De Goncourt wrote in his *Diary* : " I am at the end of my intellectual life. I can still understand, and even imagine construction, but I have no more strength left for execution ! " [2] We may justly doubt

[1] Max Nordau presents a strong picture of these disabilities—too strong, perhaps—in his *Meaning of History*, pp. 240-241.

[2] *Journal* (Nelson's edition), p. 330.

whether this is a true account of his mental condition. If understanding, and power to imagine, were still retained he could not legitimately speak of the end of his intellectual life. Inability to act, to execute, is not a sign of mental decay, otherwise Amiel's keen intellect was dying whilst he was yet in his twenties. He was naturally a *spectator*, hence his sense of failure, his self-criticism, his pathetic effort to cultivate human impulses. But his intellectual life was brilliant; indeed, apparent failure turned out to be his method of success. Now De Goncourt's thinking was thinking for action's sake—for beauty and for truth. He was a symmetrist, not a hermit philosopher; he believed in an all-round life, not in semi-monastic seclusion. But at sixty-five bodily weakness reacted mentally; the desire to do things began slowly to die and he became *un contemplateur*.

The youth of genius and of high talent has a different story to tell. At twenty-four or twenty-five, and for many a year afterwards, ambition is a vital force; existence has cohesion, enthusiasm, purpose. Everything has its colour, and that colour is welcome whether it be red rose or sepia. At twenty-five a young man has often lost his "young" illusions, and learned much by painful experience, but, if anything, his motive power has grown notwithstanding, and it has better skill in focus. Ideas are clear and vivid, and they exist in close association with the motor centres. Over all is the dominating sense of the future, its allurements being such that the inward urge towards discovery and achievement has no difficulty in maintaining itself at white heat. Here then is no holding back, no desire for calm repose, no retrospective memories; it is life, movement, aspiration, conquest. And this is the great period of mental fertility, when the world has been enriched by the advent of poems that have become classics, romances that will never die, paintings that are priceless, and inventions that have permanently advanced our civilisation.

In early and mature manhood the laws of association work in a manner that allows for possible *creative* action, and this action comes from the glow of feeling and interest; in later years, and in old age, association simply reproduces the past *without addition* ; memory works mechanically, not creatively ; ideas have lost their tendency to coalesce into new unities. The cause must be found in the lower degree of physical and mental vitality.

CHAPTER II

I

ARISING out of the general question of age, just concluded, is that of the sex element in its effect on creative thought. The subject would appear to be quite an easy one to deal with, mainly on account of certain obvious analogies—*e.g.* that the average years of sexual life correspond to the average years of original thinking—from twenty-four to fifty. Even so, the analogy is not very close, for the average sexual life commences earlier than twenty-four and concludes later than fifty. Further, the intimate nature of the subject occasions several difficulties, the chief one being the lack of authentic information in many cases when such information is highly necessary to true research.

We may begin at the beginning by stating two fundamental facts : (1) that the real commencement of the productive mental life synchronises with puberty ; it is the time when imagination and emotion assert themselves and seek new objects and new forms ; (2) that in old age the loss of generative power is accompanied by the loss of mentally creative power.[1]

This does not mean any more than that the genesis and exodus of the sexual impulse are timed to the genesis and exodus of the more creative element in thinking. It does not mean that creative activity on the physical plane will be followed by creative activity on the mental plane, or vice versa ; but it does mean that the two kinds of activity have more to do with each other than we have been accustomed to imagine. Even if Freud has overstated the case, we may reasonably endorse Jung's contention that

[1] See Ribot, *The Creative Imagination*, p. 76.

138

SEX AND ORIGINALITY

" despite all the indignant assertions to the contrary, the problem and conflicts of love are of fundamental importance to humanity, and with increasingly careful study, it comes out even more clearly that the love life is of immensely greater importance than the individual suspects." [1]

Spencer was of the opinion that in the organic world what we call beauty is somehow dependent upon the sexual relation ; and he instances the colours and odours of flowers, and the plumage and songs of birds, as the media of this relationship. He adds : " And the trite observation that the element of beauty which grows out of the sexual relation is so predominant in æsthetic products—in music, in the drama, in fiction, in poetry—gains a new meaning when we see how deep down in organic nature this connection extends." [2]

II

On the other hand, if we study the history of asceticism we shall not find many of its pages illuminated by the evidences of brilliant originality; rather the reverse. The main function of the religious celibate was to preserve, as pure and undefiled as possible, the truths discovered or revealed by others—a habit of mind which in itself was not calculated to promote independent thinking, unless it had the stimulus of comparison and contrast, either Platonic or Aristotelean. The monks who moved the world in which they lived were those who either cut themselves adrift from ascetic policy or very lightly identified themselves with it : Luther, Loyola, Rabelais, Charron. True, St Francis and Savonarola exercised a deep influence in their day, but the former, like St Augustine, had already lived the life of the senses ; besides, their contribution to thought has nothing very striking in it ; both were moral rather than intellectual forces.

To fight against nature is to fight against oneself. That is a general truth we cannot doubt ; but to affirm that a repression of sex may eventuate in a repression of originality is a statement that calls for explanation. All we can say

[1] *Analytical Psychology*, p. 364.
[2] *Principles of Biology*, vol. ii., pp. 252-253.

with confidence is that the natural procedure of love and marriage is good hygiene for both body and mind, and that this is borne out by a study of the lives of men of genius. Of Kant, Nietzsche, and Leonardo da Vinci we know little except that outwardly they were celibates; of Schopenhauer we know more, and yet his life would appear to have been practically loveless. Notwithstanding this he is one of the shining lights of German philosophy, perhaps the most brilliant of all the system makers of the Fatherland. If love and marriage, or love alone, were an absolute necessity for original thought, then these, and others whose cases could be outlined, must be considered as exceptions, an admission that would tend to destroy the argument.

But if asceticism exercised a restrictive effect on intellectual growth a greater freedom of life, even licence, promoted original thought. Lord Morley has affirmed that "private depravity and political debasement went with one of the most brilliant intellectual awakenings in the history of the world."[1] Yes; "went with it"—that is, the connection was associational rather than fully causal. It is not necessary to believe, on the one hand, that a period of loose morality will be marked by a lack of originality, or that, on the other hand, a period of circumspect life will show itself in dazzling discoveries. Other factors enter into the process. The ascetic mind is seldom a fertile mind because it places its values in the unattained glory of another world, free from bodily contacts and temptations. Therefore, instead of delighting in the things of this life it shows a tendency to bemoan them; and, bemoaning them, it dulls the edge and quickness of perception; it sees the worth of this life only as a preparation for a future life. There follows, naturally, a lack of interest in material things and this begets an otherworldliness that bars the possibility of creative thought.

Now the men and women of the Renaissance looked upon creation in the light of the book of Genesis: "And behold it was very good." Even the body with its passions was not a bad thing, for it was part of God's own creation; the lust of the eye resulted in fine paintings; the pride of life was

[1] *Machiavelli*, p. 17.

manifest in elaborate clothes, in great equipage, and in ornate dwellings. It was surely better, they said, to acquiesce in life and make a good thing of it than to mortify it, to crucify it and live gloomily for an uncertain existence in a merely possible world to come. Into the theology and ethics of these views we are not called upon to enter, but we can see at once how much more natural it was to have a marvellous mental fertility during the Renaissance than during the ascetic epochs. Originality of thought and action betokens deep absorption in life, and all its implications, and this the Renaissance period possessed to the full; whereas those men and women who sought seclusion, as a means of finding salvation, developed a mental narrowness that effectually prevented both freedom and advance; albeit they sometimes developed the milder virtues to a high degree. Their cry was: "Love not the world," and it was met by another: "Love the world," or, in the words of Rabelais: "Abandon yourself to Nature's truths, and let nothing in this world be unknown to you."

III

Love, licit and illicit, exercises a specific influence on thought, acting mainly as a dynamic. Burns never wanted to write poetry until he fell in love. Love awakens the mind to the possibility of new experiences: it is a stimulus to all that lies hidden and awaiting expression. Consequently, we may expect to find that the lives of men and women of genius are not destitute of the love element; we know, indeed, that in many instances this element, if not in excess, was often pronounced. Only in a few cases does it appear to be absent entirely—but, of course, we have no exact information to guide us. George Eliot was a student, a translator, and a critic until—after what seems to have been a little love skirmish with Herbert Spencer—she met George Henry Lewes. Her union with him was the beginning of the work that is distinctively original. How much of Swift's masterly creations is due to the influence of Stella and Vanessa—the loved and loving—of his women associates? Did Cowper owe nothing of his inspiration to Mrs Unwin, and later to Lady Austin and Lady Hesketh ? We might go through the whole of literary history and couple names together in a love association—maybe what is called Platonic, as Dante and Beatrice ; or social, as Dr Johnson and Mrs Thrale ; or irregular, as Shelley and Mary Godwin.

We do not mean to imply that love, in one of these associations, is absolutely necessary to the full expression of genius or great talent ; candour compels us to admit that to all appearances there have been loveless men and women who are to be classed with those just mentioned ; and in some cases, the best work would appear to have been produced before love and marriage. Our aim is to elucidate a comprehensive fact by showing that the physical function of sex, and the love connected with it, has a definite relation to creative mental processes ; and that a severe and intense asceticism is therefore not likely to promote original thought. For the most part history supports this contention ; celibate communities, whilst preserving good traditions and rendering conspicuous social services, have been intellectually stationary. On the other hand, periods of freedom, like the Renaissance, following the naturalism of the Greeks, have been marked by great intellectual eminence, even though for want of *sophrosune* they ultimately came to grief. Nevertheless the service which asceticism renders to the individual must not be overlooked. Self-denial, which means repression, is a good ; and it is significant that Nietzsche, the great exponent of the holiness of instinct and of the glory of expression, did not hesitate to naturalise the ascetic tendency, a tendency which in his opinion the Church had spoilt. Instead of self-denial, he wished for self-strengthening ; a gymnastic of the will.[1] And we may here say that the psychology of Freud and Jung does not seem to have dealt satisfactorily, as yet, with this type of repression. If repression, as a species of action, be as dangerous as these teachers appear to believe, then the history of humanity

---

[1] " People have scarcely got the courage yet to bring to light the natural utility and necessity of asceticism for the purpose of *the education of the will.*"—*The Will to Power*, vol. ii., p. 336.

ought to be far more strewn with mental wreckage than it has been.[1]

IV

Much has been written about the comparative strength of the masculine and the feminine mind, the sum total of which has been that, speaking generally, the brain power of woman is not equal to that of man. With this broad question we have no concern in these pages ; but we may very reasonably ask whether the charge of a lack of originality has any serious basis. If we take the great names of history we find that those of women, as contrasted with those of men, are exceedingly small in number. Woman's contribution to literature, art, science, and philosophy during the past two thousand years is not one that would lead us to suppose she possesses the inward urge to self-expression in the same degree as man evidently does ; and this absence of originality throughout the centuries has led to the belief that the feminine mind has no instinct for progress ; it is essentially conservative. But the fact that there have been women whose work was superlatively good must be taken as an indication that there are no intrinsic disqualifications in the feminine brain, as a brain[2] ; and although it would be too much to say that what one woman has done other women can do, yet the cause of their lack of originality in the past

[1] Prof. E. B. Holt, in his *The Freudian Wish*, does not seem to have expounded this advantageous repression. Prof. Dearborn, in his *Influence of Joy*, and speaking both as a physiologist and a psychologist, says: "Many of these motives for restraint have brought about habits which are in effect instincts, and so numerous are these that in civilised lands it is uncommon to find any emotion expressed in the case of adults in that perfection of naturalness which elsewhere and among wild animals regularly obtains."[1]

[2] Prof. Romanes says, in his essay on *Mental Differences between Men and Women*, that under the most favourable conditions as to culture, and supposing the mind of man to remain stationary, it must take women many centuries to produce the missing five ounces of the female brain. This is saying a good deal more than the facts will legitimately bear.

should be sought in other directions than that of differences in brain structure or tendencies.

, Have not sociological historians proved that in the early days of communal life woman's inventiveness was responsible for the development of the home accessories of budding civilisation ?

There may or may not have been a Matriarchate on the scale suggested by certain responsible writers, but it is fairly well established that at one time women occupied a higher place in the life of the community *mutatis mutandis* than they do to-day; and this was on account of their ability to originate and control. Of course the sphere in those days was restricted; it was homekeeping and motherhood. There is still the same narrowness about it; but where women have had sufficient leisure, freedom and detachment, as in the case of Madame Curie, for other kinds of work, they have sometimes done brilliantly.[1]

V

The one original difference between the masculine and feminine mind is too much lost sight of ; a woman's brain is quick to know and to decide on everything that furthers her interests as a woman, a wife, and a mother. Thus at an early age woman's mental facility is in excess of man's ; she has sown and reaped many crops of ideas long before man has even seen the land or begun to plough it. That is why a quite young woman often feels that men much older than herself are really " such children." [2] But the same woman

---

[1] In America there are a good many women in professions and businesses who by sheer ability and industry have proved their power to do the work of men, even men of the highest qualifications. Miss A. M. Durkin, as a contractor, has built some of New York's sky-scrapers ; Mrs A. H. Taylor has a mail order business worth a quarter of a million. Other women in other occupations earn from £600 to £10,000 a year.

[2] In Kipling's " The Garden of Eden " (*Soldiers Three*, p. 180), Captain Gadsby objects to his young wife talking about his marrying again. Mrs Gadsby says: " Never, never, never tell your wife

will probably feel that a boy of twenty-three, just graduated from his university, completely eclipses her in knowledge, and is on that account an individual who wins her high regard. There can be no doubt that in the earlier and formative years the feminine intellect has an agility that is superior to the masculine type; but this agility is functional; it has to do with woman's mission in the world rather than with knowledge itself. Consequently women who devote their lives to celibacy and to intellectual plans of an exclusive and absorbing character are, in most instances, playing against instinct. The feminine mind is made for intuitive flashes of insight rather than slow and ponderous investigation, for music and literature rather than research in neurology or philosophy. That there are instances which give the lie to these judgments we cheerfully admit, but the fewness of such cases must be taken into account. One would have thought that among the many woman doctors we could have found a respectable number of original investigators whose work had culminated in great and important discoveries, but neither in medicine nor in science do we hear of numerous cases of striking originality, even though we do hear of an increase in the graduate lists of the highest classes. The fact is, women are as yet too much obsessed with the self-consciousness of their sex. Rosa Bonheur, a woman of the world and undoubtedly a great painter, was not free from it. "Have you not noticed," she asks, "that women, much more so than men, do not as they approach the end, let their artistic work fall below their highest level? Look at George Sand and so many others; their best productions are their latest." [1] We venture to say that an immensely strong case could be made out for the very reverse of this plea, but that is not our point. It is in the self-conscious sex element. As much as to say: "I am a woman and in my work I have to show that women's work is as good as, if not better than, that of

anything that you do not wish her to remember and think over all her life." The Captain replies: "By Jove, how do *you* know that?" Mrs Gadsby answers: "I don't . . . but I feel that I know so much, oh, so very much more than you, dearest."

[1] *Reminiscences of Rosa Bonheur*, pp. 377-378.

men." Strictly speaking, it is sex antagonism, and it may exist in half-a-dozen different forms ; but, whatever the form, it is bound, in proportion to its intensity, to exercise a repressive influence on those finer activities of mind that lead to originality. Rosa Bonheur was a woman of several loves, and her unconventional but not unsocial life saved her from any permanent mischief in this direction, despite occasional outbreaks against masculine dominancy ; but in its cruder and more violent forms sex antagonism is a potent cause of the comparative failure, mentally speaking, of progressive women. We are not surprised that the anti-man section among the suffragettes is intellectually inferior to the other sections.

Any mind which is made up in this way :

$\frac{1}{4}$ Sympathies
$\frac{3}{4}$ Antipathies

is certain to stagnate.

Sex antagonism is anti-biological to begin with ; there is an unhealthiness somewhere that calls for serious attention. Then it is anti-social ; it strikes at the first basis of race progress in limiting the growth of population ; finally, it is anti-psychological ; it prevents the finest and subtlest activities of the intellect. But when women cease to be sex conscious, and when, as a consequence, they can investigate life with mental detachment, we see no reason why, in conjunction with the necessary favourable conditions, they should not achieve an impressive record of originalities.

SECTION IV
HINDRANCES TO ORIGINALITY

CHAPTER I

THE SENSE OF THE PAST

I

WE should define a hindrance, in this connection, as that which prejudices mental growth and self-realisation; it may be a natural lack of ability, or it may be a subjection of ability in the interests of a creed or a principle; it may arise from the defective organisation of the State, or out of the undue pressure exerted upon the individual by a group.[1] Consider for a moment the effect of our *sense of history*—by which we mean our sense of obligation to, and dependence upon, the past, not only politically but in every other sense. If we desire to justify ourselves when challenged, we do so, as often as not, by an appeal to history. Now the record of history is a babel of opinions; it always has been and it always will be. The first difficulty centres in the question: "*What happened?*" and whilst we can boast of a fair number of important certainties, the wrangle about the thousand and one disputed points is interminable. The second difficulty centres in the question: "*Why?*" and

---

[1] "The public, collectively, is abundantly ready to impose, not only its generally narrow views of its interests, but its abstract opinions and even its tastes, as laws binding on individuals. And our present civilisation tends so strongly to make the power of persons acting in masses the only substantial power in society that there never was more necessity for surrounding individual independence of thought, speech and conduct, with the most powerful defences in order to maintain that originality of mind and individuality of character which are the only source of any real progress."—J. S. Mill, *Principles of Political Economy*, vol. ii.

here there is more discord than ever ; each writer has his pet theory of *causes*. The third unruly element is made up of the historians' *opinions* about events, and their views of the light thus cast on the present.[1] One consequence is that the imagination of the world is bound by its subjection to the historical record ; the religious devotee swears by, and trusts to, ideals that have come down to him from the ages ; unscrupulous princes like Bismarck and the leaders of modern Prussia follow a crude interpretation of Machiavelli, believing him to be the embodiment of political wisdom ; and working men object to new machines that will reduce the number of employees—history and common-sense (they say) are against such inventions.[2] We cannot stay to discuss the right and wrong of these particular attitudes ; we refer to them simply to show that in religion, in politics, and economics we, for good or evil, turn our eyes to the doings of past centuries, believing we shall find guidance there that is superior to anything obtainable here and now.[3] Needless to say, this is the wrong method, because past conditions can never be the same as those in which we live to-day. But after all, that is a historian's question ; ours is the effect which this habit of turning one's back on the present is bound to have on the output of originality.

II

Consider an example—Lord Bacon, one of the most original men of all time. How did he regard history ? He tells us in *The Advancement of Learning*, and we will quote the whole

[1] Max Nordau says : "The real meaning of history . . . is . . . the manifestation of the life force of mankind in an ascending scale of human adaptation to nature."—*The Meaning of History*, p. 371. Not very illuminating.

[2] Disraeli's chapter on " Domestic Novelties at first condemned " is an entertaining study of this sort of prejudice.

[3] Dr Beattie Crozier, one of our most independent students of history, has well said, that "while History *accounts* for the present, it does not really *explain* it ; and while it enables us in a way to *anticipate* the Future it does not help us to guide or direct it."—*Civilisation and Progress*, p. 22.

section, where the argument is on the comparative merits of antiquity and novelty.

"Surely the advice of the prophet is the true direction in this matter. *Stand ye in the old ways and see which is the good and right way, and walk therein.* Antiquity deserveth that reverence, that men should make a stand thereupon and discover what is the best way ; but when the discovery is well taken, then to make progression. And to speak truly, *Antiquity in time is the youth of the world.* These times are the ancient times, when the world is ancient, and not those which we account ancient by *an inverted reckoning* by a computation backward from ourselves."[1]

To Bacon the world was like an old and experienced man who had the secret of perpetual youth and from whose informed and ever alert intelligence increasingly great things might be expected. The significance of life lies in its present and in its future, and without undervaluing the past we can only understand and solve our modern problems in the light of the best knowledge drawn from a study of facts as we know them to-day.[2] This habit of trying to settle the

---

[1] *The Advancement of Learning* (Cook's edition), p. 38. Bacon is equally explicit in his *Novum Organum.* "As we expect greater knowledge and riper judgment from an old man than a youth because of his wider experience, so it is natural to expect far greater things from our own age than from ancient times, for the world has now grown old and has been enriched with countless experiments and observations."

[2] The "pull" of the past has been well expressed by Lotze. "Modes of thought which under appropriate conditions were adopted by men of genius have withstood progress for centuries with incredible tenacity. Forms of art worked out by great minds, but not of universal validity, have continued to maintain their predominance when they had become out of harmony with the altered dispositions of mankind ; and even in science inherited errors drag on like a slow disease."—*Microcosmus*, vol. ii., p. 189. A similar thought is expressed by Prof. James Ward in his essay on *Mental Culture*, where he says that the "habit of deferring to authority, even when sound, has been one of the greatest drawbacks to the world's intellectual advance." See *Essays, Mock Essays and Character Sketches* (Rice), p. 87.

difficulties of democracy by arguing on the basis of Greek democracy is a senseless procedure : this supposition that the only true philosopher is Thomas Aquinas ; this notion that Aristotle has said the final word on the forms of logic— these, and many other quaint conceits, evince a spirit that can have no other effect than the quelling of original thought. At no time more than the present have we so much needed a protest against the dead weight of history. The socialists are among the few whose imaginations are not governed by " lessons " from political experience in bygone ages. They stand for a new regime implying almost a total reversion of civilised practice. Unfortunately they have in some respects entered the lists against human nature itself, and this, combined with a lack of reverence—to use Bacon's word—will prevent their best ideas from attaining an early measure of success. But their principle is correct : a remedy for present ills based on present facts—not past history.

Brandes in his book on *Nietzsche*—and we shall have to revise many of our opinions about the author of *Zarathustra* —says Nietzsche believed the race dragged the past about with it, like a round shot chained to a convict's leg ; historical education fetters us both in enjoyment and action (p. 16). Taking a mediate view, Brandes himself puts it this way : that history " supplies what we cannot find in one's contemporaries. This is where it may help. But it drives artists into the galleries instead of to Nature and to life— it has a monumental, an antiquarian, and a critical prejudice on our career " (pp. 17-18). That is nearer the truth as we see it. The past is not a dead weight like a round shot —or it need not be ; it should be a living thing, absorbed in a living present, just as youth is swallowed up in the vigour of mature manhood. We are always measuring ourselves by the Greeks as if they had embodied everything that was great ; but did the Greeks allow themselves to be dominated by the past ? Where did *they* get a liberal education—these men who wrote the classics ? They looked at things as they found them ; they had directness of inquiry into life ; their look was at the present and into the future. To be Greek in that sense is to have the wisdom of the wise.

III

But repressive influences are social as well as philosophical. We can understand why a degenerate with an itch for burglary is not allowed the scope that his nature asks for ; and we are glad the law is so repressive as to allow him no opportunities for the exercise of his gifts. But when a religious community asserts its right to dictate the kind of books its members shall read and not read, are we or are we not face to face with an instance of undue pressure put upon the individual by a small but controlling group ? The answer to this question is not affected by the fact that the members of such communities gladly accept and obey these restrictive rules of mental behaviour ; for resignation is not necessarily a virtue. We have to decide the issue on broader lines and the only conclusion is that individual liberty is curtailed in a matter which the great majority of self-respecting people regard as peculiarly their own province. To proscribe the works of Maeterlinck is to impose intellectual restrictions that are bound to affect freedom of thought, even though the devotee kisses the hand that thus binds his intellect. If such repressive policies became numerous the State would have to intervene and prevent the embargo on individual thought from assuming serious proportions. That this is no fanciful notion may be proved from the case of a certain large city where there is no free library because the ecclesiastical leaders claim the right to decide what books shall be included and what shall be left out. Such influences operating on a large scale would be highly derogatory to the mental welfare of the population.

The gain to the Church is no doubt appreciable ; an *Index Expurgatorius* has a salutary effect in deepening peace of mind and fidelity of disposition. Apologists claim, further, that regulations which result in moral cohesion are justified by that result alone, especially in view of the disruptive forces that spring from unregulated freedom. The *drift* can be checked only by an *anchor*. They also claim that restrictive rules are helpful mentally, because conducive to habits of concentration. It is affirmed that the power of attention in a complex civilisation is too widely distributed; the newspaper, the sevenpenny novel, the picture theatre, the music hall, games, sports—all these are pursued one after the other in order to pass the time; the result being that concentration is a lost art. Scores of men never really *think*; their lives are a mass of undigested sensations and perceptions. One remedy, so we are told, is a prescribed and proscribed reading list; only by such means can character be formed and personality developed.

It would be useless to deny that there is truth in this indictment of our common life, or that the remedy is totally devoid of sound principle. But if the indictment is only true in part, the remedy is certainly excessive. Besides, the people we are talking about are not what evangelists call "the giddy multitude," but Church members—serious, devout, chosen. Cannot these be trusted to read what critics say about them? Evidently not. The danger is too great. The super-intellects among them may get a dispensation to read any book that has been put on the *Index*, but for the many there is no such freedom.

The moving cause is fear: fear lest a writer who is outside the pale may make shipwreck of the beliefs of the faithful. Hence these beliefs must be secluded, and the holder of them preserved from danger. The principle of the action is that that which is morally beneficial cannot be intellectually injurious, an argument on the level of the old *cliché* that that which is morally wrong cannot be physically right. Fortunately, these repressive tendencies, narrowing down the life of the mind to the limits of men who lived in bygone centuries, are not on the increase; but they do exist and they are still operative.

CHAPTER II

I

AMONG the influences which affect the possible originality of a mind none is deeper or more far-reaching than that of home training; and yet none is more difficult to analyse. We remember reading somewhere that "if home training be wise, sympathetic, and individual, the best possibilities of the whole mind will be realised; but if it be narrow, restrictive and coercive—originality will be crushed." In our opinion this is a matter on which it is not possible to dogmatise, and we speak after examining a goodly number of cases, infinitely varied as to ability, education, parentage, environment and opportunity. Of the general rule—that a wise home training is better than one that is unwise—there can be no doubt whatever; but there are numerous instances where the very unwisdom of parental action has acted as a positive stimulus in a beneficent direction, and later we propose to study one or two of these cases in order that that fact may be fully disclosed.

Meanwhile, the subject itself is one that makes a direct appeal to every adult reader; for we have all passed through the home-training period, and every man and every woman can think and speak of it with the authority of personal experience. The repressive influences generally centre in religion and the conduct which is expected to arise out of it.

When a boy arrives at the age of mental discernment—and by "boy" we mean "girl" also—he sets up in business as a thinker on his own account. His capital may not be large, and his experience may be *nil*, but he has youth and vigour, and these together produce a certain type of confidence, seen

153

especially in the questioning of received opinion. He cannot understand why he should not be allowed to take a course of action that appeals to him as right and proper ; and he is still more surprised when he learns that some of his particular judgments are parentally viewed as rank heresy. Were he not already accustomed to obedience, stark rebellion would be the instant and natural result ; but from the time when his mother taught him the rudiments of living, to the present moment, when he is prepared to argue with her, he has been under tutelage ; and guidance in thought and action has become almost a second nature. How could it be otherwise ? In infancy we are helpless ; in childhood we are ignorant ; in youth, too often, we are headstrong. In almost every home there is a case which may be called Father v. Son. The father represents the ideas that are old and which have borne the test of experience ; the son represents the ideas that are personal preferences rather than logical conclusions ; the father stands for the notions that are passing away—so it seems to the son ; and the son stands for the notions that are both fleeting and dangerous—so it seems to the father. The family hearth is turned into an arena where the old and the new fight for victory ; and a family feud is the last word in bitterness.

II

Before we can say how far this kind of home discipline affects the possible originality of a youthful mind, we will investigate one or two instances where men of note have told the story of their early life.

For example, John Stuart Mill, in his *Autobiography*, and Mr Edmund Gosse in *Father and Son*, have written luminously of the effect of parental methods on the mind of a growing boy : in the first case, a boy under the guidance of a strong but sceptical intellect ; in the second case a boy slowly escaping from the influence of a father with a mind wherein faith was stronger than a love of the scientific method. The possible comparisons and contrasts of the two cases should be highly instructive. Mill was taken in hand by his father at an age when the modern boy is busy playing games and developing body and mind unconsciously. We need not outline the accomplishments of which the younger Mill could boast by the time he was seven years of age. The point that is of interest is this : What did Mill think of his home training when he became a man ? He thought it was seriously defective on the emotional side, but otherwise he seems to have been grateful for the attention his father bestowed on him. The defect on the emotional side is as obvious to readers of Mill's life and works as it was to himself. His depression in reference to the problem of musical combinations; his failure fully to appreciate poetry [1] ; the undeveloped powers due to lack of self-expression—in its turn due to repression of feeling [2] ; and his somewhat pathetic but ridiculous posturings when visiting friends in the company of Mrs Taylor—all these are the natural outcome of a one-sided devotion to what is known as pure intellect. He confesses that in one crisis of his life he had no one to whom to turn for advice ; he was afraid to consult his father, because it would bring home to that strenuous person the unwelcome fact that his educational plans had failed—in one important particular. [3]

III

The case of Mr Edmund Gosse is one with certain agreements and differences. His father, Philip Gosse, was a naturalist of some distinction, living during a period when the drift of science was almost entirely in the direction of scepticism. But he was a devout Calvinist, and in the battle that followed between faith and reason the victory was won by faith. He took his son in hand somewhat in the same way as James Mill, but a little more tenderly, devoutly, as if in the discharge of a sacred duty. There was, too, an additional factor that seems to have been absent in the Mill household. Mrs Gosse exerted a great influence on her son ; Mrs James Mill does not appear to have figured so

[1] *Autobiography*, p. 112.   [2] *Ibid.*, p. 58.   [3] *Ibid.*, p. 134.

prominently in moulding the life of the author of the *Autobiography*.

In the Gosse household both parents pulled together, but "the boy was his mother's," and, however much he imbibed of theology and science from his father, his heart was trained by his mother—to his infinite advantage. She died whilst the younger Gosse was in his early teens, and the reader of *Father and Son* knows that *that* was the moment when he began to emancipate himself from the paternal philosophy. It was a slow and, to some extent, an unpleasant task to rid himself of the tenets of a hard and brittle Calvinism, even though he had not accepted them with the conviction that characterised his father's belief. The one fact that assisted more than anything else, as it seems to us, in the work of demolishing false gods and setting up new ones, was his going to live in London, away from home. It may be a hard saying, but it is a true one, that the intellectual salvation of some young men begins when home no longer dominates them; contrariwise, it is also true that many a youth begins to deteriorate the moment he leaves the old roof for a new one in a strange city.

IV

Robert Louis Stevenson had difficulties with his father about the creeds and about attendance at church. The natural outcome was that R.L.S. took the first opportunity to escape from the unpleasantnesses of discussion, even though absence from home seems to have accentuated the trouble. The details are too well known to call for reproduction here; and as literary history is crowded with cases—George Eliot's, for instance—we may now begin the work of analysis.

We observe that (*a*) the great mistake is the parental imposition of dogma; we also note (*b*) the overplus of the masculine influence; and (*c*) the immediate advantage of new surroundings or new location.

(*a*) The early lives of Mill and Gosse—so different in type

and outcome—suggest that one of the main considerations of
parents should be the avoidance of dogma—dogma of any
kind. J. S. Mill had to *unlearn* a good deal in the sphere of
religion which had been taught him, dogmatically, by his
father; there is not much of James Mill in the *Three Essays
on Religion*, but there is a good deal of Mill the younger as
influenced by experience and a strong human affection. The
same remarks apply to Edmund Gosse; the fearsome
Calvinism, the miracles, the whole scheme of Christian values
respecting this life and the next, as taught by his father, had
to be unlearned—sorrowfully and with a strain on filial
relationship.

It is remarked by Sir Francis Galton, in his *Men of Science :
their Nature and Nurture*, that most of the men whose cases
he investigated had few dogmas to overcome; their early
education, happily, had been so conducted that even where
some form of dogmatic teaching constituted part of the
curriculum it was taught in such a manner as to render new
developments easily possible; in most cases, however, there
was no such teaching at all, and it is reasonable to suppose
that, as a consequence, the mental powers opened out more
naturally, realising their aims more easily, because no im-
pedimenta stood in the way. On the other hand, if we ask
the question: "Did the originality of Mill, Gosse and
Stevenson suffer on account of mistakes in home training ? "
we can give no certain answer. No man can say, confidently, what destiny another man has missed, and why
he missed it. We may *suspect* that Mill and Gosse, even
R. L. Stevenson, might have surprised the world with more
brilliant intellectual results, but we cannot *prove* it. That
they should have fought against accepted truths may be
taken as evidence of their individuality, and the very strife
itself must have stimulated intelligence, however painful
the domestic ordeal. Of course, we cannot argue from this
that the unwise imposition of dogma and the disputation
arising out of it, are more advantageous than otherwise;
neither can we affirm that Mill, with a better and more human
curriculum, would have become the philosophic and forceful
statesman *par excellence* ; or that Gosse would have eclipsed

ORIGINALITY

St Beuve at his best; or that R.L.S. would have written *the* novel that was absolutely unapproachable. We can only state that the imposition of dogma is an intellectual deterrent, and that in certain cases it may be highly prejudicial to originality.

V

It will be urged, here, that the profound religious convictions of parents *compel* dogmatic teaching. If a father is convinced that the Roman Catholic Church is the only source of the Truth in which there is salvation, is he to be precluded from instilling this doctrine into the minds of his children? The only possible answer is: "No." But every other "Church" must have the same liberty to teach its dogmas—the Jew, the Methodist, the Christian Scientist, and the Christadelphian. It is a liberty which an enlightened State is compelled to grant as a concession to opinion on a matter of a private nature, hoping that a native sense of humour will tend to the multiplication of charitable feelings, even if it does not undermine the egotism which says: "We are right and all the others are wrong; therefore, in order that the world may be saved, we shall impose our beliefs on the people—by force if needs be." *That* is the dangerous spirit—dangerous to the body politic and to the life intellectual.

Its presence in the parental programme has often been followed by unexpected results. There was once an ardent Protestant—we will call him Mr Robinson—who on the birth of his first-born—a son—christened him Martin Luther Robinson and dedicated him to the ministry of the Protestant Church. Martin Luther grew up; read, studied, and thought; debated doctrines with his parents, his professors and his fellow-students; and ultimately became Father Martin Luther Robinson of the ———— Street Roman Catholic Church at H——.[1] It is very pious of us to surround our children with every moral protection and to map

[1] There are several versions of this story. The real event happened in a South London family, about thirty years ago.

158

out their complete destiny from the cradle to the grave, but it is also very presumptuous, and not a little selfish. What right have we to cramp the natural developments of youthful minds, simply because they happen to belong to our children ? To cram them full of dogmas is not only asking for future trouble, at any rate where there is conspicuous intelligence, but it is hardly different, in essence, from the old Red Indian practice of producing flat heads.

Religion is not the only sphere where repressive tendencies are at work. What of politics ? There are fathers who die in unspeakable grief because their sons become Liberals, or Socialists, or Conservatives. We have little or no sympathy with such parents, unfeeling though the statement may seem to be. It is nothing short of impertinence to expect a son or a daughter to accept and act up to the political creed that we have used, however satisfactorily. True, it is human nature to desire it, especially if in war time the father feels called upon to fight on one side and the son on the other. But there are few instances where so tragic a decision must be made ; and even when it has been made, as in the American Civil War, and with Alsatians in the European War of 1914-1917, the younger man's intellectual rights are incontestable, even though at last feeling may outmanœuvre judgment.

VI

The infusion of an enlightened conscience into the mental relationships between parents and children is much needed nowadays. There are mothers who nurse a secret sorrow because their daughters hold opinions that are called "progressive"; and on the other hand there are mothers who live in utter contentment because their daughters have grown up to maintain the family religion, the family politics, the family social status, and, most important of all, the family wealth. Thus there are the dogmas of social life, some of them good, some bad, and some indifferent, which we impose upon our children with a complete disregard for their own ideas ; and, whilst all sound progress is based on holding

fast to the safeties of experience, it ought to be possible to
allow for the expansion of the individual mind. This can
be done by using the principle of adaptation instead of hard
and dry dogma, and by allowing for the natural growth of
intelligence. Mr Havelock Ellis has furnished us with some
autobiographical details that support our contention, pre-
facing his remarks by a statement of his belief that "the
harmonious satisfaction alike of the religious impulse and of
the scientific impulse may be attained to-day by an ordinarily
balanced person in whom both impulses crave for satisfaction." [1] He then goes on to show that without being in
the least conventional he, in his early years, tried to mould
his life on Christian lines. At the age of twelve he felt that
like love, religion is a private matter. Later came a period
of emotional and intellectual expansion, followed by a study
of the critical literature of the day. An inward revolution
took place, but it was " so gradual and so natural " that the
shock was hardly felt. But days of depression were to
supervene, due to the unsatisfied cravings of the religious
impulse, and it was not until he re-read and re-valued James
Hinton's *Life in Nature* that he realised how life had something to do with the heart as well as the intellect. Hinton's
soul-full pages introduced him to a new world : "I seemed
to walk in light—my feet scarcely touched the ground."
The chief significance of this development in the eyes of
Mr Ellis himself is that it was a natural and normal process,
not conversion, not intellectual suicide, but psychic adjustment. Every thoughtful man goes through these stages
although not with the same result. The value lies not in the
precise conclusions arrived at but in the educative power
of the contest.

(b) The second observation refers to the overplus of
masculine influence in the three cases investigated. To put
it bluntly, there was too much "father" and too little
"mother." We cannot find any reliable information about
Mrs James Mill, but if she had had an opportunity of off-
setting the severity of her husband's discipline, John Stuart
Mill might have been saved many heart-burnings, many

---

[1] " Science and Mysticism "—article in *The Atlantic Monthly*.

intellectual struggles, and much criticism. He is the classic example of a man with brains who was educated solely by his father, himself a man of principle but minus emotions. Gosse and Stevenson were more fortunate. The influence of the mother was patent though somewhat overshadowed during the most formative years. But it was there, working tactfully and surely, with that beneficent result which is the finest feature of maternal insight and love.

VII

James Mill, Philip Gosse and Thomas Stevenson were all strong men, but they did not always shine in their training of the youthful mind. They were all dogmatists, though very different dogmatists; and in two cases we have to thank the wives for the wisdom of sympathy, which the male mind did not possess. Are there not modern sons and daughters who can say : " The *Father* is too much with us. His views, policy, rules, regulations and prejudices are too dominating " ? [1] More feminine influence up to the age of ten at least is to' be desired in home education; from fourteen onwards masculine guidance may well take precedence on occasion. The difficulty is to persuade parents that this matter is important, and the reason for their scepticism lies in the very familiarity of the subject. But ideals are the life of youth and ideals that have personal embodiment are doubly precious. Somebody has said that the beatification of the Virgin Mary introduced a new element

---

[1] Benchara Branford says: " Now in characteristic essence, as Comte and a long line of prophets before him have urged, the rule of the Mother is spiritual; the rule of the Father is temporal. Of spiritual power and of power temporal, it is in their very distinctness and equality that lies the opportunity of healthy human emulation and noble human co-operation. The supremacy of either over the other ; the confusion of the one with the other in idea and ideal, in purpose and in practice ; above all the identification of the two and their union in one person or body ; these are the conditions precedent necessary and sufficient to despotism, tyranny, revolution and conflict whatsoever sphere of human activity we consider in which both powers obtain."—*Janus and Vesta*, p. 121.

into the conception of divinity—a Mother God as well as a Father God. To some this is no doubt true, just as to others it is superfluous, but the idea is there: a combination of feminine and masculine elements, assuring the faithful of an understanding sympathy. In human parentage these two elements should combine for the same purpose, and any disproportion is bound to bring evil results in its train.

(c) The third observation was the immediate advantage of new surroundings or a new location. Young Mill's prolonged stay in France, Gosse's escape to London from his country home, and Stevenson's journeys South—these were days of liberation indeed. And why? For the simple reason that a growing mind of considerable ability needs freedom; and where freedom is denied in the local environment it will irresistently be sought farther afield. Moreover, change in itself, as already pointed out, is a means of development. Study a group of men, from different localities, who have lived all their days in the places in which they were born. What characteristics do they show? Much depends, of course, on native qualities, but there often grows up a decided antipathy to travel, a sort of nervousness when business calls them to crowded cities, and a supreme haste to return home. This is more than a distaste for noise and traffic; it is a symptom showing loss of the power of adaptation and of growth. Such men may be acute in dealing with local affairs, but narrow to the last degree in assessing values outside their usual range. Migration of some kind would appear to be a condition of intellectual advancement.

VIII

It may be urged, and justly, that the cases we have dealt with are somewhat special in character; they concern men of notable gifts who fought their way out of the mistakes of early training into a finer liberty. What of the home training of the average boy and its effect on mental growth? Is the modern home of the ordinary type calculated to promote originality of thought, not in every case but in cases where originality is an ultimate possibility? Is parental policy favourable or unfavourable to the encouragement of individual thought ?

We may as well say at once that home is a centre of *moral* training ; at any rate, that is its first intention whether we regard the cottage of the labourer, the villa of the middle classes, or the mansion of the wealthy. In every instance *behaviour* in the all-round ethical sense is the primary concern. There are houses in every class of society where this spirit is absent—call them *laissez-faire* circles—but the presence of children usually develops a sense of responsibility that is expressed in a code more or less indicative of a desire to keep the conventions. The religious home is somewhat pronounced in this connection, and it offers certain social values that are not found in the more easy-going circles. In the first place, it has a systematic basis ; it inculcates high principles ; it fosters passion of a sort although it teaches restraint to excess ; and it has a destiny in view. On the other hand, its creed is often a handicap, and its attitude towards all material things, coupled with a love of money, is rather equivocal. But for the average man religion provides an organisation for home life, albeit it is stronger in moral impetus than in intellectual enthusiasm. To think outside the scope of the scheme is taboo. George Eliot somewhere speaks of the tragedy that is visible in the members of a family who are strikingly alike in physical features but the poles apart in religion and politics. Dogmatists in the home have much to answer for.

Then what kind of home training should be given to children if the community is to reap the full mental benefit of our corporate life ? There are three words expressing the qualities that are needed ; it should be *human, social,* and *serious.* It is not necessary to say much about the first two. A hard and brittle discipline, and a code of unrestricted individualism are alike to be avoided. To succeed life must be lived on the human plane socially construed, and there is enough organised knowledge in the world to guide youth of all ages. But gravity has not entered into the modern programme as much as it ought to have done. We are too keen on pleasures; life is not taken seriously. In other words, instead of the theory and practice of right and wrong, we should teach ethical values.

But as this section of the subject concerns intellect more than anything else, the kind of training required is almost the opposite of that which is usually given—*i.e.* children's minds should be "brought out"—educated in the etymological sense. To-day we are too much engaged in drumming knowledge into them, with the result that when in maturer years we expect originality we get indifference or conformity. A new policy of home training would do more to affect the Empire than all the schools put together; it would create energy and give it direction and this is of greater importance than knowledge in the mass.

CHAPTER III

I

It is apparently one of the easiest things in the world to criticise modern education. Why this should be so is not clear, for although we have most of us passed through an educational period we have thereby gained no special fitness to lay down the law for other people. Education is a profoundly difficult subject, as its long history and vast literature abundantly prove; and the fact that we are still debating some of its first principles ought to give pause to the most confident of critics. Education concerns the immeasurable. Two thousand years ago Aristotle propounded the question thus: "What then is education and how are we to educate? For there is as yet no agreement on this point; all men are not of the same opinion as to what the young should learn either with a view to perfection or the best life; nor is it agreed whether education is to aim at the development of the intellect or the moral character." We are still busy debating this question—but not hopelessly. Our newer professors of pedagogy are approaching solutions at any rate in part; and they realise that to limit education to the school period instead of applying it to life as a whole has been a cardinal error; they have also come to see that education concerns the whole man as well as the whole term of his existence. Such men as Vice-Chancellor Sadler, Professors Campagnac, Dyer, and Keatinge are symbolic of a better dispensation. Nothing could be better, for instance, than Dr Sadler's five things which education seeks to train and develop:—(1) character; (2) a sense of obligation to the community and to the world-wide commonwealth of good men and women; (3) the power of concentrating the mind upon the task in hand ; (4) a ready memory, including skill in using aids to memory and quickness in finding sources of accurate information ; and (5) open-mindedness to fresh truth, from whatever quarter it may come, and capacity to grasp rapidly the ground plan and bearings of a new subject.[1] Training on these lines will be directly helpful in bringing out the latent originality of all minds fortunate enough to study under such a curriculum. At present, however, the whole educational plan seems to be organised in such a way as to make it difficult to cultivate individuality of outlook. The overwhelming emphasis is still on *knowledge*. That we need the right kind of knowledge is very evident, but we need something more : we need *power*. Who has not met men with commercial degrees, possessed of great stores of information about business procedure, transport and organisation, and yet minus the ability to use it in the best way, simply because the emotional nature has been neglected ? Along with a grasp of facts there must be the spirit of the pioneer who initiates.[2] The dynamic section of consciousness, if we may so speak, calls for attention ; as much depends on that as on the other qualifications, not only for the individual but for the community. A kind of education that compels its subject to seek a living in what is called

[1] " The Future of English Education "—article in *The Times Educational Supplement* for 7th Dec. 1915. Dr Sadler's list is almost bettered by that of Prof. Keatinge, who says : " Every society needs in its adult members (1) physical strength and health ; (2) power to earn a livelihood ; (3) power to use leisure profitably ; (4) an interest in nature ; (5) in human nature ; and (6) in art ; (7) certain qualities of mind which are valuable for the individual either directly or indirectly through their social importance, *e.g.* accuracy, sympathy, and self-control ; (8) a sense of duty adequate to the necessary subordination of personal to social welfare."— *Studies in Education*, p. 17. In the same comprehensive spirit is Mr J. M. M'Tavish's *What Labour wants from Education*.

[2] " Why have so few eminently successful men been school trained ? Because the acceptance of ready-made opinions kills the original thinking power and unbiassed resourcefulness of the mind, and paramount success cannot be achieved by docile scholars and imitators but only by pioneers."—" The Disadvantages of Education" —article in *The Nineteenth Century* (1903, p. 307), by J. Ellis Barker.

an educated manner may result in a loss of equilibrium to the labour market.[1]

II

This emphasis on knowledge will continue until our examination system is changed. The examination for the Indian Civil Service and Class I. Clerkships is probably the highest form of scholastic examination in the world, but, as a test, it does no more than say that the successful candidate .has an unusual power of understanding, absorbing, and recording facts. Nevertheless the programme of the older universities is based more or less on the needs of the Civil Service Commissioners both as regards Arts and Science; the Public Schools follow suit, then the private schools, until the whole kingdom is permeated through and through. It may occasion surprise to suggest that our Public Schools lay emphasis on knowledge, but it is true despite the statement that their tradition "implants the love of health and honour but not that of knowledge and beauty."[2] The emphasis is not on *too much* knowledge, but on *too little*. The other side of the curriculum, which is broadly moral, is excellent; it is indeed the envy of other nations. It is manifest in splendid behaviour on the battle-field as well as in judicial conduct in the handling of the affairs of State at home and abroad. But the tradition for knowledge is this: that to know too much is bad form.[3] There is a story

[1] "In 1914 the University's billboard at Munich cautioned the students that there would be no use for the next ten years in taking the teachers' examination because the waiting list provided for possible vacancies for the next twenty years. What is to become of the hundreds of educated men for whom no corresponding positions can be found?"—Leo Wiener, *Interpretation of the Russian People*, pp. 145-146.

[2] *What is Education?*, p. 24.

[3] The Hon. Bertrand Russell, F.R.S., a Cambridge man, in speaking of Eton and Oxford, and "good form," says: "The evils of 'good form' arise from two sources: its perfect assurance of its own rightness, and its belief that correct manners are more to be desired than intellect, or artistic creation, or vital energy, or any of the other sources of progress in the world."—*The Principles of Social Recon-*

told about a young officer who was very "keen" on his professional advancement. He read widely and well; he practised everything he could. Of him an Eton and Oxford brother officer who was *not* keen said: " J—— is not a bad sort, really, but too quiet you know, and—and—so full of damned intellect!" Now this may be said to represent the general attitude of hundreds towards knowledge, even necessary knowledge, and so long as our Public Schools have a programme that allows this spirit to develop, so long shall we fall short in competition with other peoples, not only in sciences, but in all sorts of originalities. No doubt, changes are coming; they were spoken of long before the great war,[1] but it will take time to effect reconstructions that retain the best of the old traditions whilst implanting the new. Meanwhile new developments are at work in other directions. "Etonians must remember," says Oscar Browning, "that there is growing up every year in England, an educated democracy far superior in seriousness, in industry, in piety, in plain living and high thinking to the products of our public schools and ready to take their places. In them the real hope of England lies." Some years have passed since those words were written, and although still true in part, this deliverance is not wholly true. The centres of higher education are seeking the necessary adjustments, but if anything the new democracy is keener than ever. Its very inabilities are in its favour, for circumstances often prevent the one-sided acquisition of knowledge and turn the attention into

struction, p. 153. Speaking on the same subject, Charles Waldstein says: "'Good form,' and other causes are contributing to impoverish the English language in expressions of original emotions. We notice the avidity with which people grasp at slang, because it has such original life."—*The Balance of Emotion and Intellect*, p. 213.

[1] See "The Disabilities of an Oxford Career," by M. Wood, in *The National Review* (June, 1909); "Public School Education" (*Monthly Review*), and "An Eton Education" (*National Review*, 1905), by A. C. Benson; "The Old Culture and the New" (*The New Quarterly*, p. 257), by Oscar Browning. What could be better than this as a symptom of the new spirit? "Education . . . means training a boy's mind so that he may know how to tackle any new problem that is put before him."—*A House Master's Letters*, p. 143.

more practical channels. This leaves room for the individuality of the student, and too frequently an educative curriculum does not. Matthews, in his *Principles of Intellectual Education*—one of the best manuals we know—has put the case so forcibly that we cannot do better than repeat his words : "The aim of education is not knowledge but power —the use of our original powers in our own original way. . . . An ounce of originality, of fresh contribution to the thought of the world, is worth tons of knowledge gathered by others and simply stored away in the lumber rooms of our minds, like treasures in a chest that no one ever sees. To spend our time in cultivating thought and not in cultivating the acquisitive power manifested chiefly in memory would be . . . an infinite gain at the cost of apparent immediate loss."

III

Modern education does not give sufficient attention to individual tendencies. It is very difficult indeed to arrange any programme that will remedy this defect. Boys and girls, and older students of both sexes, have to be dealt with in large groups, and hitherto it has been found impossible to isolate individuals and detach a member of the staff to give them a special form of training. We regret we can offer no practicable scheme for relief. But the one aspect that concerns us here is this : we mercifully make special provision for the crippled and the mentally defective—we make no such provision for the youth of talent.[2] In other words, the weak get more attention than the strong. The reader will ask incredulously : "But *do* they ? What of the scholarship

---

[1] *The Principles of Intellectual Education*, p. 128. By F. H. Matthews, M.A.

[2] "The idea of the provision in all our large towns of special schools for the specially gifted as well as for the specially deficient is worthy of consideration. It seems deplorable that while money and care are lavished on those who can never do much in the world nothing more is done for those who are capable of the highest and best service than is done for the ordinary capacities which will always do hodman's work."—Welton, *Psychology of Education*, p. 123.

schemes which enable a boy like Benetsky to go from the Board School to Cambridge, and become the Senior Wrangler?" Yes; in *that* way we offer inducements to boys of unusual gifts; but if a boy has remarkable promise in any other direction than mathematics, science, or classics have we the organisation to help him?[1] We have not. We leave such boys to chance. If a master finds a boy engaged in drawing when he ought to be doing a quadratic equation, then, however good the drawing may be, the chances are that the delinquent is punished so often as to make him unsympathetic towards the use of his pencil, even in leisure hours, and especially if there is no encouragement at home. How much originality do we lose every year because we have no proper scheme for getting the best out of our scholars?

And how much do we lose because our "system" is so little adapted to the fostering of the creative attitude—that which Professor Taussig calls in business the principle of *contrivance*, and which, generally, for the fine arts and for commerce, means the advent of new ideas? Someone recently asked Mr W. W. Ellsworth, the late President of the Century Company, a well-known firm of American publishers, whether he thought there were more or better American authors as the result of the past thirty years of higher education. His answer appears to have been a direct negative. He had known a number of young people who in school had an apparent faculty for creative literature and who came out of college familiar with the writings of men like Addison and Browning, but "utterly unable to express an original thought." He adds that fifteen years ago, out of 1000 MSS. received by the Century Company 25 were accepted and 975 declined. Of the 1000 MSS. received up to 1st January

---

[1] Mr Benchara Branford, as an Educational Inspector, speaks with authority when he says: "It is, surely, one of the fundamental weaknesses of modern education that, from a false economy and other motives, we are compelled to educate our pupils in such large groups and by methods too similar. The apparently inevitable result is, in general, the stunting of valuable variations in individuality and the production of too large numbers of individuals with closely similar powers."—*Janus and Vesta*, p. 210.

1916, 41 were accepted, and not one of them was written by a new writer! In Mr Ellsworth's opinion college and university education does not develop the creative powers.[1] True; but it is an old discovery. Fourteen years ago a London morning paper published a list of authors, journalists, painters, sculptors and actors who had not been educated at a well-known Public School—like Eton or Harrow—and along with them the names of those who had. The former far outnumbered the latter, the totals being as follows :—

	Without a Public School Education	Had a Public School Education
Authors	30	3
Journalists	23	4
Painters and Sculptors	36	2
Actors	15	3
	104	12

We admit the test is somewhat different from Mr Ellsworth's, but it an English analogy to the conditions and results of education on the other side of the Atlantic. Then are we to blame education? No; blame the way in which it is administered. That is different from blaming education. Every one of the 104 men referred to above might have been even better for the stimulus of the right educational environment. But what of the hundreds whose names do not appear in the other list? Twelve men survived the ordeal and rose to positions of distinction and honour; where are their fellow-scholars whose individuality did not survive the system?

IV

Education, to be successful, must not only inform but *inspire*. If we follow out all that is contained in those two words we shall neither suffer from ignorance nor from lack of impetus. It is the personal influence, intellectual and moral, of the teacher that counts for most—even more than the best pedagogy ever conceived. Boys can be taught to think

[1] *The Literary Digest*, 5th August 1916.

things out for themselves—quite young boys too—and it is this kind of training that proves eventually to be of greater value than statical information. Mr Sidgwick, whose little book, *On Stimulus*, is so good that it ought to be enlarged into a psychological treatise, is of this opinion [1]; and there could not be a better group of models than those contained in Mr W. H. S. Jones' *Scientific Method in Schools*. Boys suitably drilled to pursue original inquiries on these lines are bound to acquire in manhood a tendency to that sort of individuality which the nation needs and on which creative activity depends. Let this question of inspiration be the test of educational schemes. The quarrel between the " utilitarians " and the " classics " is a waste of time. It forgets the personal element. The rankest " utilitarian " we ever met agreed that he did not expect his gallery of fine oil paintings to pay him dividends ; and the most prejudiced of " classics " would admit that a youth who cultivated his mind so exclusively in the acquisition of knowledge that he made himself incapable of earning bread for his body was inverting the order of Providence.

[1] " Another potent stimulus to thought and interest is supplied, by getting the pupils, whenever it is possible, in however humble a department of knowledge, to share in anything like original research."—*On Stimulus*, p. 37.

CHAPTER IV

THE LACK OF A SCIENCE OF READING

I

THE position we take up in reference to the manner in which reading affects originality may be expressed thus :

(a) That we read to excess, thereby preventing the creative powers from attaining that range of activity of which they are capable.

(b) That reading has not yet been reduced to a science.

Roughly, these complaints mean that our reading is lacking in proportion and in direction ; it is unregulated and left almost entirely to chance. Milton's saying, "Deep learned in books, but shallow in himself," brings home to us very forcibly the manner in which a plenitude of books may be hostile to individuality in thought. The question as to how far the world's leaders in thought and action were great readers is not quite an easy one to answer, partly because the sources of information are sometimes scanty, and partly because books themselves have been few in number. If we could prove that since the days of Caxton the world's total of original thought declined in proportion to the increase of published works we should stand on firm ground, and might give orders for a holocaust such as that which Hawthorne once imagined. But no such proof is either possible or probable. We can only be impressed by the fact that the finest intellectual epoch of history was marked by a comparative absence of the MSS. which were books to the Greeks,[1]

[1] Ferrero, after pointing out that the Greeks had little chance of reading, and few "books," says: "And to-day a wolfish insatiable hunger for printed paper and reading matter is the scourge of civilisation." An extreme view. Are there no other—and worse—scourges ?

and if a further analysis of the lives of men of light and leading in all ages should show that their devotion to the books of the period was slight, it will only accentuate the suspicion that even to-day we are still minus the right perspective between the printed volume and the thinking mind.

Buddha, Christ, St Paul, Mohammed—these are names of men who changed the course of history. But do they suggest vast scholarship, or a profound acquaintance with books in any sense whatever? They were great originators, even though they built on other men's foundations, but their originality was not inspired by libraries. Can we imagine Mohammed poring over ancient MSS. in order to obtain the required knowledge and impetus for his new religion? With Buddha was it not 1 per cent. papyrus roll and 99 per cent. meditation? When St Paul was struck down on the way to Damascus he did not repair to the nearest Jewish seminary to read up prophecy. He says: "I went into Arabia." The desert solitude was the only place in which to find a rationale of his new experience. And was it not in a similar life of solitude that Jesus—Essene-like—came to self-realisation. Deane's *Pseudepigrapha: Books that Influenced our Lord and His Apostles*, does not suggest that the Messiah obtained his ideas from the literature of the Rabbis, much less from Greek or other sources, indeed the New Testament suggests that in the earliest years he showed a genius for divine things.

II

It will be urged that to restrict this inquiry to great names in religion would be unfair because such leaders are confessedly independent of literature; indeed they are often the creators of it. True; but that fact alone is suggestive. If great literature can come from meditation alone, are we not compelled to ask: "Where shall wisdom be found and where is the place of understanding?" Is enlightenment to be found only in the printed wisdom of the past? We know it is not, but we also know it is useless to set one source of truth over against another as if they were enemies. The soul has its place and so has the book; but need it be said that the soul has done more wonderful things than the book ? Language is merely the symbol ; the soul is the reality.

But let us take other names with different associations —*e.g.* Plato, Charlemagne, Cæsar, Shakespeare, Napoleon, Bismarck. Can it be said of any one of these that he owed one-third of his distinction to what he learned from MSS. or books ? We do know indeed that Bismarck was a wide reader, but it was on the selective principle as a student of history and affairs. His library grew under the influence of the controlling purpose of his life—*i.e.* the unification of Germany, so that there was no vague distribution of energy. Of Shakespeare's reading we know less, but there is no evidence that he was a collector of books or that he was a student after the manner of the men of letters of his day. The best way to estimate him as a reader is to judge him by the references in his plays, and these do not show an acquaintance with literature so extensive as it is intensive. The impression he made on Ben Jonson, an all-round scholar, was not one of learning—quite otherwise. The qualities that impressed the author of *Timber, or Discoveries upon Men and Matter*, were Shakespeare's " open and free nature," his " excellent fancy, brave notions, and gentle expressions wherein he flowed with that facility that sometimes it was necessary he should be stopped." And, true to himself, Ben Jonson immediately adds : " *Sufflaminandus erat*, as Augustus said of Haterius." [1] Shakespeare, when in the company of kindred spirits, showed precisely the kind of talk we should expect—not Latin and Greek or French and Italian quotations, not a commentary on books past or present, but a stream of conversation marked by brilliant fancy, startling comparison, unique contrast and searching pathos, wherein life, not literature, was the chief subject.

III

We will now bring the inquiry down to the level of the average man, and ask how far his reading is a help or a

[1] *Timber*, by Ben Jonson (Schelling's edition), p. 23. See also the section on " Shakespeare's Books " in Prof. Lane Cooper's *Methods and Aims in the Study of Literature*, p. 164.

hindrance to originality. By the average man we do not mean the man who reads *nothing*, and takes no steps to develop his mind; we mean the man who, at least, has some intellectual curiosity—enough to induce him to read the newspapers, a magazine occasionally, and a book now and again; indeed we might even bracket him with the individual who is described as "a general reader," or "a bit of a student." The question then is this: What are the characteristics of these people, so far as the evolving of new ideas is concerned? The reply is not difficult; the great majority of what are known as reading people employ their leisure in becoming familiar with facts and ideas already revealed. They see cheap classics all around them; fiction is superabundant; travel books, books on economic and social subjects are numerous; every taste is catered for, and reading has become a sort of daily function; we have food for the mind just as we have breakfast and dinner for the body. That the average man swallows everything he sees in print is far from being true; but it is true that in nine hundred and ninety-nine cases out of a thousand there is no keen desire to arrive at new conclusions; reading is too much of a recreation for that. Life, to the average man, with domestic and civic responsibilities, does not allow much scope for sustained reflection; in his out-of-duty hours he is generally a tired man, and reads a book in order to obtain change and rest. But even where daily duties are not exhausting, and where, a little after four-thirty P.M., he finds himself free for the rest of the day, there is usually the same receptive attitude of mind; the author of the book is not met with a vigorous challenge, the arguments are not logically analysed, and there is no determined effort on the part of the reader to think out the subject for himself and form his own conclusions.

Ask him, at the year's end, to show you the list of books he has read, then to give you an account of his reflections; it will be found, most probably, that his memory will be more exercised than his judgment—it will be more in the nature of a *résumé* of what others have said than a statement of his own thoughts.

THE LACK OF A SCIENCE OF READING

Thus reading, at the present moment, is a pastime when it is not a dissipation. It is too extensive—too little intensive. Attention in many instances is distributed too widely in the effort to know a great deal ; or else it is wasted in perusing fiction that is forgotten the day afterwards. The general reader of the middle classes, who aims at being up to date, feels it a disgrace not to have read the novel of the moment, or the last volume of Bergson or Croce, or the latest whim of some paradox writer with initials. He has the reputation of being "a great reader," and he must live up to it. He is a gourmand of print. He seldom gives himself the pleasure and stimulus of a creative mood ; habit has confirmed him in a receptiveness that is now almost absolute ; and his store of knowledge grows apace.

The real working man, on the other hand, has far more individuality, mainly because he reads less and is much given to debate. A better read man may argue more scientifically, and with a greater fulness of knowledge, but the "worker" has a directness all his own. He is often mistaken, but even in his mistakes he carries that atmosphere of individual conviction which is frequently lacking in the more academical methods of the other man. It was St Beuve who said: "All peasants have style." One can predicate almost as much of the working man. In the etymological sense there is more *wit* in his contentions, as well as in his manner of expressing them ; the habit of consulting and using authorities has not robbed his mind of the "native hue of resolution." We must admit, however, that his uninstructed and untrained mind is not a model to be imitated ; indeed its value, from a psychological standpoint, is mainly negative ; it shows us how we suffer from the pressure of print in carrying out our educational policies ; how books become an end in themselves, instead of a means to an end ; and how individuality is crushed beneath the burden of mastering other men's opinions.

IV

To the objection that we do not expect originality from the average man we cannot but demur. In the broad sense we are justified in expecting every man to express his individuality instead of sacrificing it; at any rate he ought to be encouraged in this endeavour so long as he does not transgress the social laws that protect the rights of the majority. It may be true, as a theory, that the average mind is essentially incapable of striking out in a new line of inquiry, but, as a matter of fact, original thinkers have often sprung suddenly from the ranks of the average man; indeed we never know the moment when genius may rise from the lives of ordinary intelligence to dazzle us with the light of some great conception or amaze us with an unexampled deed. No hindrance, therefore, should be put in the way of developing the personality of the man from whom we have been taught, erroneously, to expect little; for with a superior system of using books—and we need such a system—the native qualities of the mind are retained, not destroyed, by being moulded in the fashion of another. To look for original minds among the great devotees of books is a mistake, if we do so under the impression that learning is productive of individual views; and a census of genius in its relation to printed matter would reveal the fact that the larger the library of books read the smaller is the output of originality.

V

This brings us to a very important discussion, one that has often been the subject of addresses by professors of all kinds—*the right use of books*. We have ploughed through—there is no other expression for it—a score of volumes on how books should be chosen and studied, but we cannot say we are much the wiser. Each writer speaks to a particular kind of reader; not one of the authors consulted seems to apprehend that the problem is both serious and difficult, dealing not merely with a type of book-man, or general methods of study, but with the relation of published ideas to the nature and requirements of a growing mind. In a large measure the issue is strictly educational, and comes within the province of pedagogics [1];

[1] In this sense it is discussed by Prof. Dewey in his *How We Think*, p. *197 ff.*

but it is also one that concerns the private person, especially in those formative years that come when the school period is over—years when, as likely as not, a youth has little intelligent guidance on so important a matter. He may follow his own instincts and use books in a special way for some end which he pursues ardently, in which case he is rather fortunate ; or later on he may fall a victim to some mania, such as the desire to read all that has been written on Alchemy, Poor Law, or the Eleusinian Mysteries, becoming an authority on these subjects. We have no objection to urge against the acquiring of knowledge ; it is necessary that somebody should organise useful information on a sound basis ; but when this accumulating of facts is made into an ideal, as if it represented the highest use to which books could be put, it is time to call a halt.

With a touch of impatience the reader may say : What, then, is the true relation of the book to the mind ? In theory, and this applies to all external stimuli, there should be no excess of impression over expression. It is an old and healthy law of the life psychological ; and yet the manner in which thousands of people live, mentally, is that followed by the fattener of cattle for an agricultural show—it is "stuff—stuff—and stuff again." Input and output have no scientifically regulated action ; even in educational treatises there is no rationally established system of adjusting external stimuli to internal needs. We are certainly improving in this respect—at least in some quarters—but we have a long way to travel before we can say we have found the true criterion. Probably there is no criterion that can be applied to every mind, except in fundamentals ; for although all minds work according to fixed laws of thoughts, the bases are individual in quality and call for individual treatment. The Jesuits had the right method but the wrong purpose.

Now, as between impression and expression there is a hiatus that can only be filled by reflection. To gather together a vast store of things seen and heard, and to give them some sort of expression in speech, in writing, in art, is to obey the law ; but the quality of the obedience is determined by the thinking that has preceded it. The reader who goes through a volume of economics, leaving it for a book on eugenics, passing thence to a problem novel, and closing with a volume on futurism, has brought together a great store of ideas, suggestions, policies, and arguments; and if he be possessed of a glib tongue, and a good memory, he may have much to say that sounds entertaining; but in most instances he has merely filled his mind with information about which he has not reflected in a manner worthy of the name; his impressions are numerous and extremely varied, his expressions are voluble and confident, but his thinking is practically *nil*. As for originality—well, he is only a vociferous echo.

In varying degrees this devourer of books has his imitators in all classes of the community, and the only remedy is (*a*) to reduce the number of impressions from books, so that the mind may not be overtaxed, or its reflective work made otherwise impossible; and (*b*) to take steps to secure adequate means of expression.

Now who is to determine these relationships between stimuli from books and creative thinking? No one, apparently, except the man himself. We cannot find an author who has attempted to solve the problem with even a degree of approximate success.[1] Then is it insoluble? It ought not to be; for whilst there is a specific individual factor that cannot be measured, the other factors are certainly not incalculable. Let us first try to simplify the problem.

VI

The first defect in our modern reading is lack of discrimination. We do not know what we *ought* to read, nor do we understand ourselves, individually, with sufficient fulness to know what books are best adapted to our intellectual requirements. We have not decided the relationship between humility and self-confidence when we stand face to

---

[1] "The true use of books has yet to be found and admitted; we do not sufficiently recognise their value as stores of information and savers of brain waste."—Prof. Armstrong, in an address before the British Association in 1902.

face with the great authors of all time. When we learn that Nietzsche often regarded a book as an impertinence, saying: "It would never occur to me to allow anyone to speak or even to think in my presence—for that is what reading would mean,"[1] we probably take a step in the other direction where more modest conceptions prevail; and if we stay there long enough we may end in mere receptivity and hero-worship. But is not intellectual modesty compatible with a sincerity that respects the opinions of great men without a blind acceptance of them? Do we not owe it to our self-respect to make a wider margin for our own ideas—not for the sake of the ideas themselves, for they may not amount to much, but for the sake of dignity, the dignity of being a conscious soul in the presence of infinite things? That the quality of our ideas would improve there can be no doubt, but there is a factor in the situation that is more than utilitarian. It is not "How much do you know?" but "*What* do you know?" Have you read literature by a process of selection that has put you into possession of the best which has been thought and written? Have you had the courage to be ignorant of the thousand and one things, a knowledge of which other people call culture? And have you accomplished this because you have respected your own individuality, forsaking books altogether for a period and, in solitude as well as in society, reconstructing the fabric of your thought?

In Mr S. M. Crothers' essay on "The Honourable Points of Ignorance,"[2] there is recorded an incident in which the writer sees a parable with deep meaning. "What is behind the secret panel?" he asked, addressing his host, the owner of an Elizabethan mansion. "I do not know," was the reply, "and while I live it shall never be opened, for then I shall have no secret chamber." Some readers will say: "How stupid!" others will say—nothing. They *see*: for as Mr

[1] *Ecce Homo*, p. 36. Thus also Schopenhauer: "Reading forces alien thoughts on the mind. The safest way of having no thoughts of one's own is to take up a book every moment one has nothing else to do."—*The Art of Literature*, p. 60.

[2] *The Gentle Reader*. By S. M. Crothers. Boston, 1903.

Crothers remarks, his host "was wise enough to resist the temptation to sell his birthright of mystery for a mess of knowledge." With what shame do we utter the phrase: "I don't know." A keen sense of disgrace, as if caught in a flagrant sin, overpowers us; and we are conscious of a sad fall in the estimation of our fellows. Ignorance is made into a crime; not merely my ignorance of the subject in which you have specialised, or your ignorance of my speciality, but ignorance of the exact science of the moon, of dates in history, and of the authorship (chapter, verse and page number) of notable quotations from poets and prose writers. So long as the knowledge-in-the-mass ideal prevails, so long will it exact punishment for disobedience to its laws. He that knoweth shall be saved, and he that knoweth not shall be damned; such is the law. Is it far better, then, to know the history of Westminster Abbey from the remotest crevice to the topmost stone, and to rest in that knowledge, than to be comparatively ignorant of these details and yet to be deeply moved by the spectacle of the stately building in which the past is so potently present as to be almost disturbing? We think not. Knowledge gained *after* an impressive experience assumes its rightful position; it becomes memory charged with emotion, and in that way is changed from a record of facts into living consciousness. Such a procedure is not possible in every sphere, but it is the ideal to be aimed at; and the student who, after studying nature with his own senses, thereby creating interest, goes to the text-book on Physiography will master it more quickly, remember it more unfailingly, and appreciate it more fully than the mere "reader."

VII

The secret is to maintain the needed balance between subjective impressions and objective realities. If we study the stars for long periods we are glad to get back to earth again for a rubber of whist or a round of golf; but when earthly troubles oppress us there is nothing like astronomy for belittling mountains to their original molehills. The emphasis here is not on the range of our knowledge but on the effect it has on our imagination—the extent to which it inspires us. Hence the literature of *inspiration*, what De Quincey calls the literature of power, must have a first place in the reading curriculum. And because more than one kind of originality springs from imitation there should be an effort to individualise one's own experience, not with a view to enlarging the wisdom of the world, but as a duty carried out in the spirit of self-respect. Books will then begin to assume their true perspective, and knowledge will only be knowledge when it can be assimilated into the great unity of consciousness. Physiologists tell us that stored material and superfluous fat are almost synonymous terms. And are there not many corpulent minds, unwieldy with bulky masses of unused information ? These flabby and monstrous products are the outcome of wrong methods of reading, whereby the life of the intellect becomes a perpetual gourmandising ; indeed, to carry the figure still further, such men live in the dining-room and never have the table napkins out of their hands. And the dish is always the same—*Information Pie.*

There should be a greater effort towards synthesis than analysis ; that is another aspect of the relation between the subjective and the objective. Nowadays we are mostly analysts ; we use the microscope freely ; we take things to pieces ; we love to be scientific. But synthesis is just as scientific as analysis, and although some of our present-day syntheses are often hasty, showing scamped analysis, that is no reason why we should discourage the thirst for unities. All the great ages have been synthetic, and all the best minds have been positive and constructive,[1] even Schopenhauer's. Reading carried out in this spirit will introduce almost unconsciously an art of selection, a principle of guidance,

---

[1] " If one were to endeavour to express in a single word the fundamental difference between ancient and modern ways of thinking one might say that the keynote of the former is synthesis, that of the latter analysis. The ancient delighted in wholes ; the moderns delight in resolving a whole into its component parts."—*The Vitality of Platonism*, by James Adam, p. 222. A little too sweeping, but with an underlying|truth.

a method with creative possibilities in it; and it will therefore destroy, automatically, the tendency to read for reading's sake; all mental processes will have a right direction because a purpose has been found.

These general principles—*i.e.* (*a*) the balance between a knowledge of external facts, and an appreciation of their inward meanings; and (*b*) the proper relation of synthesis to analysis have to be made personal in order to be successful, and in that respect every reader must be his own judge and guide. But since it has been possible to produce evidence that the modern reading of books in the mass is to some extent repressive of individual qualities, and therefore of originality, it ought not to be difficult for an intelligent man to edit his book list in such a way as to prevent the inefficiencies of the past. The one safe rule for everybody is: Follow your interests *intelligently*. The adverb is important. To follow one's interests exclusively, riotously, and aggressively is to ally oneself with the devotee who never thinks outside his rigid little circle: but to follow one's interests wisely is to see a sphere of knowledge in its intimate relationships with all other spheres of knowledge, thus avoiding a fatal narrowness of outlook. But there are other factors at work; interest means sympathy, joy, admiration, and, as will be evident later, these are among the qualities that lead to discovery and originality.

CHAPTER V

I

IT would be possible to occupy a good deal of space, quite interestingly, in discussing the origin and operation of *standards* in human affairs, but this is outside our purpose. We shall be content to draw attention to one aspect of the subject—namely, the influence which defective standards exercise on creative thinking. It must be evident, even to the bitterest opponent of Nietzsche, that our standards of merit need overhauling periodically. The best of literary critics has a far-away, half-hopeless look in his eyes when you ask him : " What is the difference between a good book and a bad one ? " He knows, of course, but it is so difficult to put it into words ! Besides, there are so many kinds of books, and each kind has its own standard of value. *Value !* Ah ! that is the keyword. If we can define it we shall get near the truth, for all standards depend on the sense of value. He who has written the most scientific treatise on brick-laying—one that is sound in every instruction, and tested by much experience—has produced a standard work for builders because, of all such works, it contains the most value. Value, then, is some special form of service in the interests of man ; for the writer who, on a higher plane than bricklaying, creates an ideal value, is also serving the interests of man, albeit in a different way—in poetry, in music, in art. This view does not compel us to look for our standards solely in the past : they are being recreated and renewed all the time. Once we used to look exclusively at Greek models,[1] and whilst we shall never cease to reverence

[1] Mr R. W. Livingstone, in his illuminating book on *The Greek Genius*, says: " Greece never learnt, like the symbolists, to indicate

their achievements we shall no longer bind ourselves by their standards. Values have changed. We think we have a more comprehensive view of life than they had—one with more sympathy and justice in it—consequently the measures they applied to literature and civilisation are too free in some instances and too narrow in others. We might study the evolution of values and standards throughout the ages, but all that is needful here and now is to remember they are always changing even though there are elements that are permanent.

Unfortunately they sometimes change for the worse. The permanent elements become obscured; the newer additions are perhaps tawdry and evanescent. One main reason for this deterioration is the raising of the average standard of merit at a time when there is at work no original mind of the first order. A period of creative activity is usually followed by a tamer period, in which we say what a wonderful age the age was that went just before our own; and we write critical valuations and issue cheap editions of the classics. The few creative minds that remain use the principles of imitation, and, in the absence of the superman, these imitators are hailed as men of genius. That is how standards fall because the sense of value has been lost.

II

If we take up a modern literary journal—one that appeals to the general reader as well as the private student—we are surprised to find, from the reviews, what a number of geniuses there are in the world whose names are absolutely

the vague emotions which hover on the verge of consciousness: it ignores the infinite mystery of things or reduces it to a minimum. Its clarity falls on us like the transparent atmosphere and vivid colours of Switzerland, till we long for mistier outlines and bluer distances. And more. It is hostile, a critic might argue, to sentiment as well as sentimentality. A whole range of thought and feeling is wanting in Hellenism. There is hardly a trace in it of that poetry of failure in which, writing of weakness and disaster, a poet so treats his subject that we almost feel the weakness to be a virtue and the disaster a success " (p. 97).

new to us.[1] The discovery is chastening to our belief that we keep in touch with the times. Evidently we are quite out of date, for here is a novel by Gerald Herriter "full of the same fire of genius as was his first . . . the perfect portrayal of character . . . the cohesive movement of the plot, sure as Nemesis. . . ": all this is bewildering to a reader who, if he would not miss the best of new things, feels compelled to go through two new novels in order that he may not be conversationally impotent among his friends. If Herriter had been a second-rater we could have ignored him; genius we are obliged to know.

But the matter does not end here. There is Aloway, the new poet, who after philandering with the Cubists and Futurists joined the Imagistes, feeling his real call was poetry, then broke away, and published his *Voices from Italy*. We have to read him also, together with a new philosopher who is said to out-Bergson Bergson. Feverishly we begin to study these expressions of the modern spirit; and if, in the interim, we are asked for our opinion of Herriter, we reply, loftily, that, like Emerson, we never read books until they are a year old. . . .

Then the truth dawns upon us. Herriter turns out to be a second-rater after all; he has exploited a sex problem with a rather new plot—nothing more. Aloway is merely a designer in the use of colour words, and the thinker who has put Bergson into the shade is proved to have climbed on Bergson's shoulders in order to obtain his own elevation. These discoveries bring us back to the notices in the journal, and we have a natural desire to cross-examine the reviewing staff about the origin of their standards of criticism. We ask: "Why have you described second-rate work as if it were the offspring of genius? What do you mean by telling Herriter that in some ways his book is superior to Hardy's *Jude the Obscure*, in its insight into human nature? and that even Stevenson gave no better example of wizardry in the

---

[1] We have before us a literary journal with a review of three novels—certainly good—but not meriting the heading "Novels of Genius."'

use of words ? " Perhaps the reviewers honestly believe these judgments. If so, then since Herriter is only a facile scribe, handling a problem that has all its attractiveness in itself, the need of higher standards is as clear as the day ; if they do *not* believe in these judgments, well, then we require more conscience as well as a better criticism.

III

Mr Edmund Gosse, writing of his friend the late Maarten Maartens, offers an apposite criticism. "Maartens was a great lover and buyer of books, but he lived in the depths of Holland, and had no means of seeing his purchases before-hand. He was in the habit of appealing to acquaintances in London to assure him what was, and what was not, worth buying, because he found it impossible to discover by merely following the lead of the English reviews.

"So much trade interest, so much laxity of judgment, so great a fear of giving offence, entered into the writing of these articles, that—so Maarten Maartens avowed—it was hopeless for a foreigner at a distance to be guided by them. The reviewer follows the line of least resistance, which is the idle line of indiscriminate praise." [1]

Consider the effect of undeserved praise on the future work of Herriter. He is now a satisfied man, and therein lies his danger. He feels he has *attained*. Further effort is unnecessary. He need do no more than try to preserve the standard he has already achieved. Worst of all, it is a low standard ; and the chances are that his next book, the offspring of smug self-satisfaction, will not be even as good as the other two. Not only so, but contemporary and perhaps younger writers, knowing Herriter's reputation as a genius, and believing they can achieve greater results, enter the literary tournament ; and eventually we have a group of men and women who form "the Younger School" of this, that and the other art. Can we wonder that literary and artistic values get into a tangle, that attainment becomes

[1] *The Athenæum* (No. 1, Monthly Edition).

cheap and easy, and that a reputation for originality is obtained by following the prevailing fashion ?

Primarily the critic is to blame, especially the critic as reviewer. There are three types of reviewer. He is competent but too kind ; or he is incompetent ; or he is not his own master. In the journals that count for anything the critic generally belongs to the first class : the other two classes have the remainder of the literary world in their care and keeping, and book values often depend on the amount of advertising given out by the publisher. All the more credit, therefore, is due to those publications which aim at the preservation of high standards, and are prepared to sacrifice a page of publicity rather than promise a favourable review in advance. True, there are journals that carry the spirit of independence to an extreme degree ; the only true standard of criticism, in anything, is a foot rule that appears to be kept in the editor's desk ; and, seemingly, a book is never written that is equal to this standard. An impossible standard is not quite as mischievous as a low standard, but it is essentially uncritical : it seeks not to appraise but to destroy. Nevertheless, the existence of this type of publication is a necessity ; for one set of critics discovers so many geniuses that we require a strong band of " slashers " to kill them off. The " slasher " can be wickedly " exaggerated " and unfair, at times, but without him we should lose the needful balance, and our values would sink to nothing.

We have heard a man state, with utter complacency (during a railway train conversation), that he considered himself a first-class musician : " 'E'd given five years to it, and there was not one thing among the hundreds of Sankey's he could not play—'e'd even composed two 'ymns of 'is own —said to be better than *Will you meet me at the Fountain ?* " This man clearly had a standard ; he also had originality of a kind, but the low value of it decided the status of his creative work. He was asked what he thought of Wagner, Strauss, Debussy. He " 'ad 'eard of 'em, but 'ad no use for 'em—not in ma line ! " He said it quite sympathetically— as though he was rather sorry for them. Now, to-day, in art work of all kinds, there is too much "Sankey." The Sankey standard in fiction, in poetry and drama, perhaps in painting, too, will have to be destroyed if we are to increase the kind of originality that is worth while. What passes as meritorious is quite frequently either mediocre or merely mechanical brilliance of the paradoxical order.

IV

There is, for instance, the method of being original by turning a truth over on its back. Oscar Wilde, in his earlier days, was one of its shining lights. To say: "Discretion is the better part of valour" was too tasteless, too obvious, too plebeian; so he said: "Indiscretion is the better part of valour." How subtle it sounded to his contemporaries—and how clever! Indeed the critics said it *was* clever, and when they further read such a luminosity as this:

> "The amount of women who flirt in public with their own husbands is scandalous. It is simply washing one's clean linen in public,"

they talked of brilliance—even of genius. Having found his market, Wilde supplied it with the necessary "sparkles":

> "Divorces are made in Heaven,"

and

> "I can believe anything provided it is incredible,"

but if the critics had told him the truth—that he was only acting the part of a literary trapeze artist—they would have saved him from the years that were spent in posturing before the public, or in polishing the pebbles of speech and coining literary couplets; they would have hastened the advent of the higher work of which he was capable. Less flattery, strenuous criticism, and loftier standards generally might have saved Oscar Wilde from a good many misfortunes.[1] His possible originality never reached its maximum, not even in the remarkable qualities of *De Profundis* ; and the possible maximum was very high indeed.

V

For some years, on occasion, Mr G. K. Chesterton followed the method of inverting facts ; indeed we are not quite sure that he has, even now, altogether renounced it. A specimen of his process is seen in his handling of the question : "What is tyranny ? " He replied : "Broadly speaking, the common theory of tyranny is this : that men have groaned under some system for centuries and have at last rebelled against it ; but I think that men have actively done quite otherwise ; they have rebelled against the system under which they have not groaned." He then proceeds to show how the world has been mistaken for some hundreds of years, until his article in *The Daily News* (from which we quote) discovered the real truth to a grateful public. Was he fooling ? Most likely ; but anyone with nimble intelligence can make out a case for the flat contradiction of accepted opinion by postulating the opposite, thereby "proving " that optimism is really rank pessimism, and that appearances are more substantial than realities.[2] This is the sort of work that falls to the man who takes the negative in the Mutual

[1] It is only fair to say that Jeyes, of the *St James's*, warned him about *Dorian Gray*. "What is the use," he said, "of writing of and hinting at things you do not mean ? " "I assure you," replied Oscar, earnestly, "I mean every word I have said, and everything at which I have hinted in *Dorian Gray*." "Then all I can say," answered Jeyes grimly, "is that if you do mean them you are very likely to find yourself in Bow Street one of these days." A few criticisms of that kind might have had a cumulative effect, even on a vanity as great as that of Wilde.

[2] Max Stirner, in *The Ego and his Own* (p. 60), quotes from Feuerbach: "If one only *inverts* speculative philosophy, *i.e.* always makes the predicate the subject, and so makes the subject the object and principle, one has the undraped truth, pure and clean." Yes; Germany often put the cart before the horse.

Improvement Society debate; and it is to be regretted that a writer of Mr Chesterton's powers ever wasted his time playing with these fireworks. But here, again, the critics are the real sinners. They appraised the display as "brilliant," [1] and the author pursued his efforts accordingly until ripening experience rendered him a service that ought to have come from other quarters—and much earlier.

VI

There is one other method of obtaining a reputation for originality, and that is to challenge accepted truths—and deny them. This is pre-eminently the method of Mr Shaw. In the new preface to *The Irrational Knot*, he says: " I define the first order of literature as consisting of those works in which the author, instead of accepting the current morality and ready-made religion, without question as to their validity, writes from an original moral standpoint of his own, thereby making his book an original contribution as to morals, religion, and sociology as well as *belles-lettres*." No more inept utterance on a vital issue was ever delivered. The first order in literature is surely that of genius, and the works of genius have not, in the main, been concerned with the truths of either religion or morality, not even in the widest sense; they have dealt with the human mind and heart in every phase, not merely in relation to the universe and personal destiny. And their first principle has not been that of challenge—an antagonism to the truths accepted at the time—but the insight of sympathy. A genius is not pre-eminently an Ishmaelite whose hand is against every man; he is rather a man with a superlative gift of seeing *into* and *behind* phenomena, and of feeling *with* his fellows.[2]

[1] For instance Mr James Douglas, in reviewing Mr Julius West's *Chesterton: a Critical Study*, says: " The central truth to be uttered about Mr Chesterton is that he is the greatest prophet of our generation. He is as great as Tolstoy or Ibsen."—*The Observer*, 20th February 1916. Mr Chesterton is probably not comfortable when his friends take up their pens.

[2] Speaking of Shakespeare's comprehensive sympathy with life as he knew it, Bagehot says: " To him more than to anyone else has

The secret does not lie in antagonism but in vision. Hence Nietzsche has it that originality is seeing "the old, well-known thing, which is seen and overlooked by everyone, as something new."

Mr Shaw affirms that a genius—a member of the first order—is pre-eminently a challenger of the prevailing religion and morality. If that were true, in the sense described, the literature of the Ethical Society, representing specific attacks on accepted religions and moral truth, would take as high a place in *belles-lettres* as it does in the record of progressive philosophy. We know it does not ; its aim is to teach people to think on what it believes to be better lines ; and although some of its publications are written in excellent English they cannot claim to be classics. And yet they fulfil Mr Shaw's conditions : they challenge the validity of current beliefs about religion and conduct ; the writers write from "an original standpoint" of their own ; they offer in consequence an original contribution to theological truth and to sociology, but they are not included in *belles-lettres* and the authors are not geniuses : they are moral reformers.

It is not surprising that with this notion of originality, as a motive, Mr Shaw's own works are essentially lacking in that quality ; we can never think of them in association with *belles-lettres*. That some of them have piquancy we may admit ; indeed it is this which has given them their popularity. The man with nimble wit and glib tongue who makes it his business to shout : "You're a liar," to everything and everybody, is certain to get attention. In all fairness to Mr Shaw it must be admitted that he has done his shouting with a good deal of skill ; and, having a sense of humour, he must have laughed quietly to himself when an American professor wrote a book on Shavian history and philosophy, and associated the

it been given to see that they (*i.e.* life's varied aspects) were a great unity, a great religious object ; that if you could only descend to the inner life, to the deep things, to the secret principles of its noble vigour, to the essence of character, to what we know of Hamlet, and seem to fancy of Ophelia, we might, so far as we are capable of so doing, understand the Nature God has made."—*Life of Walter Bagehot*, p. 217.

name of Shaw with that of Ibsen. We should not wonder if, in a momentary fit of anguish, the words: "Poor Ibsen!" escaped the Shavian lips. For Shaw knows himself as few men do ; and he knows that whilst skilful advertising and the method of challenge have made him *different* from others, giving him an eccentric individuality, there is nothing in his work that is distinctively original.

VII

We claim that a dispassionate analysis of the type of brilliance associated with much of the work of Oscar Wilde, G. K. Chesterton, and G. B. Shaw—taking them as specimens of some modern literary fashions—proves it to be the result of artificial methods ; it does not spring from greatness of mind so much as skill in dialectics ; in short, it is merely the outcome of a trick. The popularity of this kind of writing is, in part, due to the low standard of merit by which our literary output is judged. The critic is content to regard a book as a great achievement when it is nothing of the kind. He lives too much in the atmosphere of the mediocre, and does not ask himself as often as did St Beuve : "What is a classic?" If he did, the word-pyrotechnics and the self-conscious art of to-day would not receive the gratulations bestowed upon them, and the rising generation of writers would have what they need most of all : a higher ideal.

That our attitude towards the three men is not hard, unjust, ill-informed, or incompetent will be evident if the thinking reader cares to make a few inquiries into the artistic quality and possible immortality of such work as they have produced. Wilde is greatly superior to the other two, and his *De Profundis* will take its place among the great Confessions. But the critics did not help him to write it ; he is indebted to suffering for that service. Had disaster not overtaken him, the possibilities are that he would never have produced anything higher than a little group of bright plays, and a few polished essays. Chesterton and Shaw remain where the critics have placed them, and one cannot think of any work of theirs that will last. Mr Shaw is steadily advancing in years and will probably only repeat himself. Mr Chesterton is younger and possesses an emotional quality that may yet result in something truly distinctive. But he has not yet reached that level.

VIII

The questions opened out in Mordell's *The Shifting of Literary Values* (1912) and his later book, *Dante, and other Waning Classics* (1915),[1] are not so much concerned with low standards as with false standards; but both books may conveniently be considered in this place. The standpoint of the first is thus stated in the author's preface. He undertakes to establish the fact "that changes in morality must affect literary values; that some of the classics idealise views of life now obsolete; that these books are therefore responsible for the existence of some of our moral and intellectual stagnancy; and that a new critical outlook upon them is called for." The keynote is struck in the first contention; for if changes in morality mean changes in literary values, the other contentions necessarily follow in logical sequence. But what proof have we that moral values change in such a way as to affect the principles of literary art? The morality of Greece in the time of Sophocles is separated, in point of time, by over one thousand years from the morality of England in the days of Shakespeare. In what sense, therefore, has the process of centuries, considered morally, affected the principles of the drama? Religion and ethics passed through a whole series of revolutions during those ten or more centuries, but our valuation of drama, as a form of literary expression, is still largely influenced by Greek models and by the teaching of Aristotle on that subject. Indeed we have scanned Mr Mordell's pages closely for the kind of evidence required to support his main contention, but we have not found it. On the other hand we have discovered many statements that are decidedly curious. For instance: "One cannot really admire the book without accepting the leading ideas of the

---

[1] The Acropolis Publishing Co., Philadelphia.

book." [1]   This suggests an inability to distinguish *form* from *contents*; but let us take an illustration.   Referring to Bunyan's *Pilgrim's Progress*, Mr Mordell says: "It reeks with error and falsehood, couched in alluring images, . . . there is little wonder it appeals to aborigines who are deficient in intelligence and morals." [2]   Mr Mordell is not a Christian, therefore any book containing Christian ideas is nauseous to him, and cannot be good literature.   But it is not necessary to be a Christian in order to see truth and beauty in Bunyan's ideas and literary power.   The fact is, Mr Mordell has little sympathy—in the Greek sense of feeling *with*, not *for*—and practically no sense of humour.   He says: "Let us first examine the dangerous places through which Christian passed.   We come to the Slough of Despond, but *we* do not fall into it, for it is made up of the doubts and fears afflicting repentant sinners.   Only those who have upon their backs the burdens of sins against religion stumble here."   Clearly our critic has never thought that there may be other Sloughs of Despond; Bunyan's parable of human progress through effort has been lost upon him.   But when, with seeming annoyance, he watches the fight between Christian and Apollyon, and passes comments on the contest, we are inclined to laugh.   "We observe with indifference and incredulity," he says, "that though Christian's strength is spent he picks up his sword and drives Apollyon away." Mr Mordell is entitled to his indifference; its penalties are manifest everywhere in his pages.

IX

In this spirit he castigates Dante, Milton, à Kempis, St Augustine, and Pascal, claiming that they have been overpraised and ought not to be regarded any longer as classic authors.   Evidently they have lost their reputations because their ideas are now out of date; and however marvellously they wrote the language of spiritual things the marvel has departed, for the change in moral values decides the change in literary values.   "The bringing in of God has spoiled

[1] *Literary Values*, pp. 14-15.   [2] *Dante*, etc., p. 83.

St Augustine's *Confessions* as a piece of literature," says Mr Mordell plaintively. Really our critic is almost hopeless ; and, as often happens, he defeats his own aims eventually. For on page 66 of his *Literary Values* he says that : "All literary criticism is really subjective. Our critical estimate of a book depends upon our prejudices and beliefs, upon our past experience, upon our physical and psychological constitution." This deliverance comes as a surprise, for Mr Mordell's methods are not Impressionist in any sense ; they aim at measurement and valuation by a scientific analysis which can be used by almost anyone. A beautifully written book about the life of Moses, setting forth the ideas and customs of the Egypt of the Pharaohs, would be an impossibility, for the ideas of such a book would be untrue, and no fine literature can be written that does not tell the dry truth. Poetry, we suppose, is mere imagination. But the point is this : that the despised Christian has as much right to affirm his valuations as Mr Mordell has to affirm his : and apparently one opinion may be as good as another. That uncertainty, however, is the weakness of Impressionist criticism. Jules Lemaître may describe his adventures among books and deny the old rules of valuation, but all the time he is obeying them, in spirit if not in the letter. And, on Mr Mordell's individualistic view, the people who still believe in Dante and Milton as classics are just as sound in their criticism as he is. The only difference is that they have a standard and keep to it ; he has one and departs from it, for he starts out with the intention of using the objective method—*i.e.* exact truth and beauty—and he closes by admitting that after all the literary judgment is subjective. If truth, in the exact sense made clear in these two books, is the true criterion, then Euclid's *Elements of Geometry* must be the greatest book in the world. The demonstrations are beautiful.

X

Now we are disappointed that Mr Mordell has not made a better showing. We read his pages avidly, hoping that he would prove his case by introducing us to some new, startling,

and beneficent principles of literary criticism. Nothing
better could be desired. We are of his opinion that there
should be a periodical overhauling of our classics, and with
some of his criticisms of à Kempis we find ourselves in full
sympathy; but there is a right and a wrong way of taking
down a classic from its pedestal. We ought to be glad if,
after a close inspection, we have to put it back again : sorry,
if we must look round for another to take its place. Mr
Mordell's way is to knock down both pedestal and classic,
and then to rejoice as he surveys the débris. His temper is
militant, not judicial. He is an evangelist who preaches
against the other preachers, and he has some of the other
preachers' vices. He is a hot gospeller who will show no
mercy to an author with Christian ideas. Mordell, among
his broken idols, is like a Crusader surrounded by the bodies
of the unholy pagans he has slain.

XI

To talk of British low standards in business is almost to
talk sacrilege. The British people have won for themselves
a reputation for good goods, and for a trustworthiness of
dealing that is second to no other. In what sense, therefore,
can we, without impropriety, talk of a possible loss of originality due to a lack of proper ideals ? The answer is this :
because in these islands there are too many business men
who have to be *forced* into a progressive policy. We do not
say it is conduct that is typically British : how could we have
held our own as we have done if the Britisher had been as
inefficient as rumour has painted him ? But there are still
a good many who are too cautious, and lacking in initiative ;
and this is due to their low standards of merit. One of
the watchword phrases is : "What was good enough for
my father is good enough for me." Another and more
dangerous phrase is : "It will do." They cast a brilliant
light on the psychology of the manufacturer and the
trader. Reverence for the past, personal or otherwise, is
in itself a commendable quality, but the world of trade
never stands still, and it is safer to say that "what was

good enough for my father will most likely not be good enough for me."

Fifty years constitute a period in which a hundred vital changes may take place, and he who would be saved commercially must enter through the strait gate of adaptation —often with effort and after much expenditure of time. But the phrase: "It will do," is a fatality. The advertisement copy that is not *quite* satisfactory, and calls for another hour's revision, is thrust into the envelope and sent off to the printers. "It will do"—besides, you have the golf train to catch. Those accounts that have been waiting for a week already—after half-an-hour's cursory study—are filed for a future opportunity: it is Saturday, and the matinee can't be missed. The philosophy of "It will do" follows us everywhere, and it becomes a habit. Our business ideals are not crisp enough; our standard of work is—or was —becoming too low; the ca' canny of the worker, and the Friday evening to Monday morning week-end of the wealthier man, offset each other.

Who sets up the standard then? His name is *Competition.* To work and to have a reasonable margin for recreation seems to us to be the true ideal. But if other nations are prepared to work harder than we do, for lower wages, and with a smaller recreational margin, how are we to keep pace with them? Only by falling into line. We should prefer to follow our more peaceful methods of doing things—sans excitement, sans struggle, sans cut-throat prices, and sans everything that does not suit our comfort; but if the others are capturing our foreign markets and getting our home business as well, the only policy to pursue is to fight. America and Germany set the pace and we objected to it; we were doing a large business and did not want to be disturbed. But they insisted, and grumblingly we agreed to contest them for the world's markets. Now the point is this: that whatever value the conservative instinct has— and it has some real value—we are losing a great deal intellectually and economically because we are not sufficiently alive to the needs of the moment. More than that—we are not as good as our forefathers, the Merchant Adventurers, for instance. They were men of imagination in those days. They were the real founders of England's commercial greatness. They created the tradition, and although we have not lost it, we have developed a keen love of sport, of games and of the pleasantnesses of life generally. It is a thousand pities we cannot continue this spirit, in a modified degree; for the present hunger after mere money, and business expansion, has a deadening influence on the soul. But if other nations press us closely and threaten by competitive methods to take what we have won, then the only sensible action is to cut down the margin of recreation, to make the business ideal more tense in its appeal, and to introduce conscience into the efforts to realise it. And it can be done without losing our sense of proportion. Business pursued with the interest and zest of a game acquires a dignity and attraction all its own. The radical weakness is that too many people regard work as a necessary nuisance, a thing that is contemptible in itself, and one to be dispensed with as soon as possible. There is no need to preach a homily on the sacredness of labour; those who preach it most lustily are as ready to retire from it, at any time, as those who look upon it as a curse; but is a community of men with such views of its various occupations likely to be guilty of original ideas in relation thereto? Certainly not. And it is the lop-sided man who has been our greatest business benefactor; the man who lived like a hermit that he might make a valuable discovery; the man who neglected himself and his family that he might bring out an invention; the man who starved both mind and soul to spread his business all over the world. This, more often than not, was the type of man whose work led to national prosperity, provided work for immense populations, and helped to promote our foreign trade. Nowadays we aim at a better perspective. We believe in work and we believe in play; indeed we believe too much in play. We are in danger of becoming lop-sided in a new manner quite distinct from that of the men just referred to, who were content to remain in ignorance of a thousand fine thoughts, and to lose all the benefits of a great culture, so

Hawker's Flight (may 1915).

long as they could compass a worldly ambition. We are raising sport to the dignity of a small deity ; and we never tire of saying that the battle of Waterloo was won on the playing fields of Eton. Professor Taussig remarks that "the experiences of the American Civil War and of the Franco-German War of 1870 throw doubt on the validity of this pronouncement, even in the military sphere. Still more does modern industrial development in the United States and in Germany throw doubt on its applicability to that of economics. The truth would seem to be that much play, elaborate play, is a result of industrial prosperity, rather than a cause of industrial efficiency. It is a concomitant of the ample income and the leisure which follow success in economic activity, but negligible among the causes of success."[1] There can be no doubt that thousands do not take their work half so seriously as they take their recreations ; then, when the foreigner steals a march by working longer hours and sometimes more intelligently, there is a mighty grumble. The fact is, the British business brain is not giving us even fifty per cent. of what it is capable of, and it never will improve its output until it has reconstituted its ideals. The reconstruction is going on slowly—too slowly. *Laissez-faire* principles have gripped us until we can hardly shake ourselves free. We believe in the self-movement of things with a pathetic assurance, and we act as if our business had individual rights which ought to be "respected." Freedom is our national idol, and we insist on it everywhere— even in trade. Free trade is popular, or it has been, because it suits our temperament ; but in the next few years we may have to pipe another tune. The men who do our trading will not be labelled with this or that : they will be men of science acting according to needs and not according to political shibboleths of any kind.

A better and a higher standard of commercial life is needed, otherwise our long history of original enterprises will cease.

[1] *Inventors and Money-Makers*, p. 10. By F. W. Taussig, Ph.D., Professor of Economics, Harvard University. 1915.

CHAPTER VI

I

To discuss the hindrance to original work that lies in incompleteness of effort may seem to be churlish in spirit when our examples have been studied, inasmuch as the works we shall notice have, in some cases, more than a touch of originality in them. Our complaint is that the authors have gone far but not far enough, and that this hesitation, with a possible lack of high method, has probably prevented them from producing volumes of universal value. We shall confine ourselves to a series of volumes dealing with the creative spirit of analogy, and the first is *The Romance of Mathematics, being the Original Researches of a Lady Professor of Girtham College*, by P. Hampson, M.A., Oriel College, Oxford.[1] The playful element leads us to expect a merely humorous treatment, but Mr Hampson, whoever he (or she) may be, is intent on suggesting serious analogies which he has not the courage to put before us with gravity. His theme is stated thus: "We have one great problem to solve: and all questions, social, political, scientific, or otherwise, are only fragments of that great problem. All truths are but different aspects of different applications of one and the same truth; and although they may appear opposed they are really not so; and resemble lines which run in various directions but lovingly meet in one centre." The first study is "The Theory of the Brain Wave," and he finds the exact analogy in rays of light which travel in waves. The equation is:

$$y - \frac{a}{r} \sin \frac{2\pi}{\lambda}(vt - r)$$

[1] Elliot Stock, 1886.

y is the initial disturbance of the ether, *a* the initial amplitude, *r* the distance from the starting-point, λ the wave length and *v* the velocity of light. Mr Hampson argues that "the waves of thought are governed by the same laws and can be determined by an equation of the same form." But the exposition is finished at the end of the fourth page (after this introductory matter) and just when the reader's appetite has been whetted by the finding of λ in *mesmerism*, the author concludes with some playful verses. "Precisely," says the cynic; "he is fooling."[1] We are not of that opinion, and after reading the later chapters on "The Social Properties of a Conic Section," "Polemical Kinematics," and "The Laws of Political Motion," we are convinced that Mr Hampson, believing in the reign of law everywhere, tried to suggest the interaction of physics and politics, not in the manner of Bagehot, but as a traceable connection. He trembles occasionally on the very border-line of a new and striking analogy, and it is our criticism of his work, from the standpoint of originality, that if he had persisted on such lines as are laid down in the preceding pages he would have produced a volume as new as it was instructive and entertaining.

II

The next book on our list is Gratry and Boole's *Mathematical Psychology*.[2] Its avowed aim is the investigation, mathematically, of questions of general psychology. A more direct statement is this, that "if we wish to think out for ourselves the meaning of phenomena, *i.e.* to receive without human instruction new light about facts we already know, then we must keep mathematical order in our sequence of mental operations, or a delusion may come upon us and we shall be likely to believe a lie, and perhaps fix it on the texture of our thinking machinery." Gratry, who in 1868

[1] The extension of mathematical ideas into spheres apparently alien to them is by no means on the decline—Haret's *Mécanique Sociale* (referred to in Lynch's *Psychology*, vol. i., p. 191) is a case in point.

[2] Swan Sonnenschein, 1897. (Based on the works of Gratry and Prof. Boole, by Mary E. Boole.)

was Professor of Moral Philosophy at the Sorbonne, followed this method, which is claimed to be that of the calculus, and designed to develop brain action in normal sequence. "He studied several sciences . . . and formed the habit of sitting alone, once a day, and so far as possible at the same hour, pen in hand; he suspended thought, making silence within the soul, and then wrote down whatever thoughts came to him about the unity of Nature. What is so written is found fruitful of suggestions of syntheses which prove useful for future study. When the habit is fully formed the brain will do synthetic work even during sound and refreshing sleep." Very well. Now let us turn to the exposition. They deal with "Geometric Co-ordinates," "The Doctrine of Limits," "Newton," "The Law of Sacrifice," and "Practical Examples." Here there is no playfulness: the whole treatment is grave. But it is by no means a clear treatment, and some points that are worthy of extended notice receive the briefest mention.[1] Let us, however, take an illustration from the chapter on "The Law of Sacrifice." James Hinton had been talking about fluxions, and he talked so well that even a little girl of ten became interested and she said: "Do tell me about the fluxion." So he began. "Multiply 17 by 8. . . . We get 8 times 7 =21—*i.e.* 1 and carry 2; 8 times 1 =8, and 2 =5—*i.e.* 51. Now do you see what you have done with the 2? You have put it down and then rubbed it out; it was necessary to have it, but not to keep it. Now a fluxion is this: it is a thing we used to have, but are not intended to hold; a thing we rightly make, but in order to unmake." The explanation might not satisfy a professor, but at any rate it makes the fundamental notion quite clear; it is change or progress by a form of sacrifice. Now what trace have we of this in psychology? Mrs Boole has attempted to answer that question by the study of a diagram of a dust-whirl as representing the thought currents of the time. "A man . . . cannot let himself be blown about by

---

[1] For instance, the reference to Boulanger's *Origine du Despotisme Oriental*, where he says that no tyranny could keep itself in existence were not the minds of the peoples weakened by some form or other of the practice of putting a concrete ideal in the place of God.

every wind ; he must organise, formulate, translate momentary direction—impulse—into definite tangential direction." How ? When he " sees that another has been blown in the direction exactly opposite to the one in which he himself is drifting, he has the clue he requires for finding out where lies the still centre of calm and orderly progress " ; and he will reach this by " steering towards his absolute opponent—not in the direction towards which the opponent is drifting, but towards himself." The rank capitalist and the rank syndicalist now know what to do. Mrs Boole affirms : " The sacrifice appropriate to any given situation of difficulty or doubt is that which converts the force which is taking the individual along his habitual path into energy of union with opponents." It is all very interesting, but what of the men who conscientiously pursue a straight-line policy and ignore their opponents entirely ? We fear Mrs Boole has not been fortunate in her choice of illustration ; for in spite of everything the idea of the fluxion, as an element of progress everywhere, strikes us as one that is worth working out. Hence our complaint ; the enthusiastic authoress has not gone far enough. If she had she might have produced a book of rare interest.

III

The Curves of Life, by Mr T. A. Cook, is perhaps one of the most distinctive illustrations of incomplete originality. The comprehensiveness of his aim is seen in the sub-title, which reads: " An account of spiral formations and their application to growth in nature, to science, and to art." A perusal of the four hundred odd pages is a pleasure in itself, and when we close the book we feel that another aspect of the vast unity of life has been unfolded to us by a competent revealer. But there is also a feeling of disappointment. The curve in nature, in science, and in art has proved so deeply interesting that we are curious to know whether Mr Cook can tell us how far all progress moves in the spiral formation. That we are not expecting too much is evident from the author's Preface, for " spirality (if the word may be allowed) is a generalisation of far-reaching importance." Is the ascending arc of life a mere figure of speech or a real process ? Can we speak of advance as a forward movement in a straight line, or is it better to include it under spirality ? And as to *Music*—does sound spiralise itself ? The rainbow's curve is one of the most beautiful things in nature, but is there a real *colour* curve ? and have any artists followed it as a principle ? Then there is *Thought*. Can we imagine that the syllogism takes on the form of an arc ? An absurd question ? By no means. Lafcadio Hearn, in his *Out of the East*, says : "The Occidental mind appears to work in straight lines ; the Oriental in wonderful curves and circles." What a field for the experimental psychologist ! These and many other notions come to us as we reflect on Mr Cook's pages ; we feel as if the writer might have discovered some new unity had he given himself further time and patience. As it is, he has gathered together the phenomena and we must wait for the full rationale. Perhaps in another book he will tell us why the curve is superior to the straight line. It sounds very much like the question : Why is a square morally better than a circle ? but there does appear to be in nature a progression that uses the curve and not the prism.

CHAPTER VII

I

IN the professions of the Army, the Navy, the Church, the Law, and the rest of them, we meet with a type of mind which has a tendency to think according to accepted principles, precedents, fashions, or usages rather than according to freedom ; indeed the professional man is a member of an intellectual caste who has, so to speak, " signed on " to think and act in a particular way, at any rate about certain things. There are many and just reasons why he should do so, but he must not be surprised if the habit of thinking and acting according to rule unfits him, to some extent, for free thought on his own as well as on other planes. Such an outcome is not inevitable, but it has happened often enough to justify a warning ; indeed, the jealousies of professional men shown towards a progressive brother form a very unpleasing chapter in the history of the progress of knowledge. It is usually supposed that the priest has excelled all others in the art of preventing advances in science and civilisation, but, although this may be true in some respects, we have to remember that lawyers, men of science, doctors and politicians have looked askance at original thinkers, being blinded by the prejudice which the trained acceptance of received truth seldom seems able to evade. The radical evil has two facets : (1) a belief that in specified matters the best is already known ; and (2) a belief that new truth can be arrived at only by a study of the past, or by the use of the scientific method. On the face of it there is nothing much to complain of in these simple contentions, and it may be puzzling to know in what sense they are an evil. But when we come to study the professional mind in *action*, we shall see how a

207

healthy conservatism becomes reactionism, and how even the scientific method may be nullified by brittle prejudice.

For instance, if a medical man sees a non-medical man evidencing a knowledge and skill in particular diseases which he himself does not possess—a few such instances have occurred—he will refuse the new knowledge because the discoverer of it is not a qualified man and cannot toe the professional line. There is no case on record that is more striking than that of Mr H. A. Barker, the manipulator of bones and muscles, or whatever he calls himself; for despite the support of doctors whom he has cured, of aristocrats and democrats, of newspaper editors and other champions, he has been steadily refused any recognition from medical men as a whole. One cannot but admire the vigour with which the doctors have defended their rules and regulations, but really their attitude in this instance is too much like that of a Church Council in the Middle Ages. Men of the world respect the concern of a profession to keep its members up to the required standard, and to preserve the public from quacks and impostors, but this Barker case is quite different. Here is a man who wants credit for a valuable discovery, the principles of which he is willing to place at the disposal of the profession free of all charges. But no; to learn from a layman, even a smart layman, who has mastered a section of disease as few have done, is impossible. The teacher is not a scientific man; he is not a physician; he is a stranger to surgery; he has never walked a hospital, or passed an examination; and if any qualified man is found consorting with him—well, the sentence that will be passed is everlasting destruction from the Presence of the G.M.C. It is just as if a Salvation Army captain had discovered in Palestine a new Sinai Codex that completely changed the interpretation of a part of the Greek Testament, but which an Anglican parson refused to recognise because the Salvation Army captain had not been episcopally ordained !

II

Is this the type of medical mind that is likely to be fruitful in research, in adapting itself to new methods, and, generally, in furthering the health of the community ? No; at any rate not so far as it affects the men whose business it is to foster progressive principles. There was a libel case before the courts some years ago where a distinguished M.D. of London University very properly complained that he had been called a quack by one of his *confrères*—and all because his ideas were not considered orthodox. These ebullitions do more than prove that doctors are human; they prove that doctors and priests have often a good deal in common because of their professional training. At a congress of alienists held in Baden-Baden, a year or two ago, the Professor of Psychiatry at Freiburg described the Freud movement as an outbreak of insanity *among doctors* l Similarly a French neurologist said : " It is true I have not read Freud's works but as for his theories they are nothing but a *mauvaise plaisanterie* l " [1] How like the priest who has never read the works of Voltaire but who knows Voltaire is " quite wrong " from centre to circumference. Truth from a source banned as heretical, even science from a Galileo, must be suppressed; truth for medical men, from an unofficial and unrecognised quarter, must be ignored.

It is by the purest chance that we have thus begun to illustrate the working of the professional mind on its defective side ; any of the spheres, except perhaps one, would have supplied data similar to that of medicine. We will begin with the priest.

III

The priest—who must here stand for every leader of Christianity in every age—is a member of a profession which is the reactionary profession *par excellence*. From the days of the early Church up to modern times his lack of intellectual sympathy, both within his own borders, and outside of them, has originated controversies of a peculiarly embittered

[1] Jung, *Analytical Psychology*, p. 355. A similar outbreak of angry comment is recorded by Dr E. F. Bowers (U.S.A.) in reference to Dr W. H. Fitzgerald's zonetherapy and relieving pain by pressure.

character, often ending in wars that have devastated entire populations. The cynic has full scope for the exercise of his gifts when he deals with war and Christianity, for if there is one thing to which the Messianic Jesus was opposed it was the use of force against force. But the story of those warring centuries has been written many times already and we need not dwell upon it here except so far as it is an expression of the clerical mind. There will always be trouble in the world where we have to do with men who believe that they alone have the Truth, and that it is their duty to compel others to accept it, the compelling force being moral suasion or the secular arm. We see this type of mind at work to-day, both materially and spiritually. Take *Kultur*. This was a gospel of civilisation invented by the Prussians, and they became so infatuated with it that they believed their old German god had commissioned them to impose Kultur on the whole world, otherwise the world would sink into decay. So the fiat went forth that all the world was to be kultured. Rational people in Europe said they would much rather be damned altogether, and they resisted the threatened imposition successfully. Now when we turn to the religions which have acted in the same way—*i.e.* by fire, sword and persecution have forced whole populations to accept a new creed for their good, whether they wanted it or not—the story, bloody as it is, has not the same reeking conceit as that which marks the Prussian infamy. Otherwise the analogies are fairly close. The Roman Catholic put the heretic on the rack ; the Prussians gathered the girls from the houses in a square in Liège and raped them in public. The Protestant has burned the Roman Catholic at the stake, and the Roman Catholic has returned the compliment with interest ; but the Prussian puts men, women and children together and turns a machine gun on them. These and a thousand other abominations have been committed throughout the ages : but to-day the Churches are wiser than they were, and charity for all worshippers of God, known by whatever name, is growing, even though dogmatic theology in the older Churches shows few signs of adaptation.

THE PROFESSIONAL MIND

IV

Where is the root error ? It lies in the *ignorance* that poses as *final knowledge*, plus the spirit that riots in forced conversions. The ignorance manifested in the notion that Germany has been called of God to dominate the world for the world's good is abysmal to the point of insanity ; it is a delusion unspeakable, for a Teuton world is the last thing conceivable in tyranny. And yet Churches and priests have claimed and still claim to possess final knowledge, perhaps not in detail but in bold outline. In science, Prof. Ernst Haeckel assumes the same position : and if we were to put him and a hustling bishop side by side we should find that both men were apostolic in their ardour, and in their desire to proclaim Truth as they understood it. Haeckel preaches monism so earnestly that he ventured to attack the theologians who opposed him, evincing the slipshod methods which the clergy sometimes display when they attack science. Loofs showed the Jena professor to be a very, very amateur theologian, and hardly honest or sincere at that. But the theologians are not always in better shape. How can they be ? If all truth on important issues has been revealed already, every new attempt to "discover" it is an impiety to be rebuked, perhaps to be dealt with more severely still. Any man, scientist or ecclesiastic, who says : "I, alone, have the truth," closes the door to new ideas : originality is out of the range altogether.

But better days are dawning. When on the battle-field a Jewish Rabbi holds up a crucifix before the eyes of a dying soldier of Christian faith—and this actually happened in the Great War—we see how a religion becomes human without losing its historic identity ; and we see also the approach of a time when the emotions of the infinite will help, not hinder, the production of original thought.

V

Who makes our laws—the laws that control our commercial prosperity, our relations with other countries, and our domestic affairs ? The natural answer is that laws are made by the Houses of Parliament, and that if we wish to insinuate that laws are made by lawyers there is a sufficient refutation in the fact that laymen preponderate in both Houses. Yes; but what of *leadership* ? A majority of lawyers in a Cabinet, and in its closely associated group of officials, cannot be regarded with complacency by those who have studied the legal mind in action. There is something about a training in law which, unless a man is blessed with high ideals and great talent, unfits him for large views ; the prevailing motive in his mind is *administration*, not *creation*. To be a good leader of the people he needs both qualities, but if he should have the first only—as is the case with most lawyers—a comparatively fruitless period of office is the certain result. whether that period be Conservative, Liberal, or something else. Consider, for a moment, the vast responsibility of a Cabinet in relation to the past, the present, and the future. It must conserve the good and dispense with the bad—we use common terms advisedly—and create new political unities that will anticipate the needs of the years ahead. The "legal" Cabinet, however, is more concerned with policy, law, agreements, treaties and history in general : it does not come down to the level of the people for whom it is legislating, nor does it enter into the details of trade before announcing laws for its governance. These are serious statements to make, but they are unfortunately true. Great Britain owes its position not to skilful management but to good luck more than anything else, unless it be a keen respect for honour. And the bad management is due to the overplus of lawyers who have controlled our affairs. They did their best, and a few of them succeeded, but a good many have failed. It might be too much to include Mr Lloyd George among them, but we fear we shall have to do so, at any rate up to August, 1914. He showed a keen interest in the welfare of the common people, and in this he did well, for the Tories were seldom or never constructive in their policy : their actions always had the appearance of modifying Radical Bills and passing them as their own. But Mr George's plea for the people, as seen in his Land and Insurance policies, had "lawyer" stamped all over them. He seems to have said: "My client is the British people; my opponent's client is Vested Interest in land and property and capital. I will defeat my opponent." And he *did*. But events have shown that the judgment he obtained was not a sound one; it was not *creative* in the sense of dealing with the needs of the country as a whole; it was *penal*, causing loss, injustice, and even real suffering where his generous disposition never intended such things to happen. Mr George, indeed, is *essentially* not a lawyer. His disregard for precedent was always a source of concern to his friends in the Cabinet.

Now the scope for genuine originality, for great and moving conceptions respecting the government of a vast community, is as wide in matters of State as it is in literature, science, and art; but the last man in the world who ought to be allowed to attempt it is the lawyer, be he distinguished or not. The reasons are two: (*a*) that the legal mind has too strong a tendency towards guidance by precedent; and (*b*) that it is accustomed to a form of mental procedure which is ethically injurious. No professional men are so lacking in originality as the men of the Law.

VI

(*a*) The search for a precedent is fatal to originality. If some new shipping laws are needed the lawyer has no tendency to study modern shipping itself: he looks back into the past, revises his knowledge of the Hanseatic League, consults the first shipping Acts, compares and contrasts them with the present Acts, with foreign Acts—indeed he does a lot of hard work, but most of it in the wrong direction. Schemes that have worked well in years gone by certainly deserve respect: the men who formed them were no doubt ahead of their time. But is not that a strong reason why modern legislators should formulate laws that spring out of the needs expressed rather than out of a study of the past? Our present law-making is hide-bound by history, and it always will be until a new spirit and a new and unfettered type of intellect is brought into action. Probably that is too much to hope for.

The parliamentary pushfulness of the modern lawyer and barrister is due to several factors : like other men of ambition, they love the limelight, and they take pride in all forms of power ; but the main factor, behind every other, is this—that politics is the best method of advertising. Ordinary trade publicity is odious and could not be tolerated ; and yet publicity is needed. The House gives it, plus a useful salary. Consequently we have a plenitude of the wrong kind of minds at the headquarters of Government : men whose training is in most cases the reverse of the kind we want. The originalities of the Commons have nearly always come from laymen. If such men had had to deal with the initiative and control of parliamentary business, would they have taken nearly a quarter of a century to settle Home Rule ?

VII

(b) The second point may be illustrated by quoting a portion of Lord Brougham's speech at the trial of Queen Caroline. He said :

"An advocate, by the sacred duty which he owes his client, knows in the discharge of that offer but one person in the world—that client—and none other. To save the client by all expedient means, to protect that client at all hazards and cost to all others, and among others to himself, is the highest and most unquestioned of his duties : and he must not regard the alarm, the suffering, the torment, the destruction which he may bring upon any other. Nay, separating even the duties of a patriot from those of an advocate, and casting them if need be to the winds, he must go on reckless of the consequences if his fate should unhappily be to involve his country in confusion for his client's protection."

This is a point of view that has strong analogies with Treitschke's theory of what the individual owes to the

State, or of Bethmann-Hollweg's "necessity knows no law."

The truth is, a lawyer's honesty may be merely professional. In cases where he is absolutely convinced that his client has a just case, the honesty is as real as any other man's honesty; but in other circumstances a lawyer may become so easily sincere—no one has raised self-suggestion in business to so fine an art as he has raised it, and in politics he can persuade himself that any policy he espouses is right: his mind has been made that way by the training he has had. He is the modern sophist, and quite unsuited to dealing with the practical needs of a vast population, with the mysteries of foreign trade, or with the construction of a battle fleet. These matters call for expert knowledge and sympathetic insight. We who have seen the lawyer-politician cross-examine an innocent and truthful but nervous witness, flaying him alive, and then holding him up to ridicule, have left the court with a feeling of disgust for the iniquities of an out-of-date court procedure, and with a feeling of contempt for the barrister who can draw fat fees for prostituting his conscience in the service of his client.

VIII

Readers of Lord Alverstone's *Recollections* will recall an instance less brutal but typical of what we mean. Anthony Trollope, the novelist, had to give evidence in a Post Office prosecution—he was a Post Office official himself. Counsel for the Defence rose to cross-examine him. Asked for the title of his last book, Trollope gave it, and Counsel then inquired: "Is there a word of truth in it from beginning to end?" Trollope's answer, of course, was that the book was a work of fiction. "Fiction or no fiction, is there a word of truth in it?" demanded Counsel. "Well, if you put it that way, there is not," replied Trollope. Will it be believed that Counsel, in addressing the jury, asked them to acquit the prisoners on the ground that Mr Anthony Trollope, the principal witness against them, had admitted writing a book in which there was not a word of truth from the beginning to the end? No educated man, not a lawyer or barrister, would ever stoop, in a public address, to such low sophistry as that. The Bar has often aired its moral indignation in court when some over-ambitious man of business has brought himself within the law, but what of the morality of the Bar itself? When Counsel inveighs against "this wicked person who, with a lack of scruple that is as cynical in its spirit as it is criminal in its results, robbed his employers of a five-pound note "—is the prisoner so sinful and the barrister so sinless? Is the Bar never cynical and never unscrupulous? That it is better than the Bar of other countries we cheerfully admit, but it ought to be ashamed of its legal dodges, its trumperies, its half truths, its dissimulations and its professional insincerities.

In America the conditions of business and government give the lawyer-politician a strong position, for Americans have not the same faith in government on business lines as we have; the phrase means something different to them. A Cabinet of business men would be regarded as "out for business": whereas a lawyer would be more likely to uphold the interests of the people—the lawyer class has "the wider vision and the smallest equation of personal interest obtainable anywhere." [1] Hence an ambitious American uses law as a means to an end; it is in itself a secondary matter, and he is never subdued by it, never allows it to dominate personality or to become a habit of thought.

IX

The intellectual idiosyncrasies of the Civil Service call for some remark in this connection. In most democratic countries the work of government, partly in regard to its policy and almost wholly as to its administration, is performed by the permanent staff. Speaking broadly, this work is well done, although it costs a great deal more than the same amount of work carried out in business concerns, where discipline is known and where errors of a serious nature mean

[1] Article in *Westminster Gazette* on "Lawyer Politicians," by J. D. Whelpley.

instant dismissal. The call for originality is met by the permanent heads of Government Departments, and as they have been trained in Service traditions, they are not likely to meet that call with anything like freedom. Too often they, like other professional men, lean on precedent, and this is one argument for the bringing in of a Secretary of State who is not hide-bound by tradition, but looks at the matter of legislation from a wider and national standpoint. Cabinet changes are our only hope of originality in politics both as to its projects and its methods of materialising them. If we were left to the office men we should be in a poor plight. The office mind dealing with native questions in distant colonies has often been woefully inept ; dealing with such important items as the delimitation of the Canada-Alaska frontier it has been a tragedy. And nothing could have been more humiliating than some of the weaknesses and illiteracies of the London War Censorship, 1914–1916, especially in its earlier days, and in some of its later developments. Things were done which were absurd to the very limit. The wrong men were used—the " system " again—but even if the right men had been put in command, they would have been right only in the sense that they had a good Service record. What was wanted was a mind that could face a new situation with confidence and grip, and very few Service men have had a training that would enable them to perform such a task. Consequently fixedness of thought and action is the staple element of the Civil Service mind.

But, it will be asked, in what sense can you have originality in a Government Department ? You cannot change Whitehall from a democratic to an autocratic *régime*. What possible room is there for newness in taxation when the only difference in, say, the income tax is made by addition or subtraction ? Yes ; the old questions and the old spirit. A clean sweep of the chief Service men, replaced by men of commercial efficiency who would " fire " subordinates for serious errors, would save the country millions a year. Is not that an originality worth thinking about ? Even in offices where professional men are engaged—lawyers, engineers, and so on—there is the same room for speeding up and for profitable change. The Service is regarded as a safe port, a haven of refuge, a place for the dull daily round that brings security and a pension. We need a new era for the servants of the State, and only the living voice of a people called upon to make great sacrifices for the community is strong enough to inaugurate this era, with a new ideal of competence, a better notion of speed and courtesy, a truer conception of straight-line methods, and finally a sane understanding of the What-Am-I-Here-For ? text.

X

Those who have, observingly, mingled with Army and Navy officers know that psychologically there is a perceptible difference between them, but it is a difference that is not easy to put into words. The brainy man who wears a naval uniform seems somehow to have a freer mind than the brainy man of the Army ; he is not so hide-bound by precedent ; he is more open to consider a new idea or a new method ; there is with him a greater expectancy of development. Both men will probably have mastered the same number of text-books, and both may be good technical scholars— possibly the naval man in this respect has the advantage, his training being longer and his subjects rather more abstruse. But the army officer's studies, his discipline and his dependence on military history, appear to make his intellect less supple. We here refer, of course, to the generality, not to unusual individuals who have risen above the ordinary limitations of the system. The Great War was a year old before British officers allowed that the German use of heavy artillery on the battle-field had justified itself.

In another and previous warfare we had a similar illustration of devotion to theory. General Buller, held up by the Boers, suggested in a dispatch that he would try to engage the enemy on a terrain "more suited to our tactics." The ungallant foe had actually chosen ground for defence that did not suit the instructions of the British text-book ; indeed it was ground that made the tactical theories very confusing. The remedy, clearly, was not to adapt the theory to the ground but to change the ground on behalf of the theory. Buller was a man of fine characteristics, and popular with his men, but his very considerable military knowledge of warfare was not equal to the practical wisdom of the farmer general who opposed him. And our criticisms are offered in no carping spirit ; they do not touch the *soul*, for there is none better than that of the British soldier. We confine our strictures to the effect of professional training on the mental powers ; and we say it is narrowing. The very exactitude of military science, and the need for decision of mind and instant action, provoke a kind of impatience with anything that is inexact, uncertain, mysterious, elusive, indistinct and inactive. We remember taking shelter (from a storm) in a hall where a colonel of high repute was giving an address on the Bible. The Higher Critics never had such a dressing down in their lives. If the colonel could have got them together he would have court-martialled the lot. "These traitors," he exclaimed, "ought to be dealt with according to their deserts. Drum them out of the Church to whose faith they have been utterly disloyal." He was equally severe on those teachers of religion who cast doubts on the eternity of future punishment. "I believe in a Heaven for the good and a Hell for the wicked. These fancy theologies about future probation, universalism, and the larger hope are all wrong and mischievous. Death and life are the Scripture terms. Don't monkey with them. Accept them as the inspired word and avoid the plausible teacher who would have you believe that there are plenty of chances for salvation after death. After death—the judgment." Yes ; he had an exact mind, and on the battle-field would have been a brilliant commander. He could see things clearly, generally one at a time ; he acted promptly ; but, when a subject with remote boundaries had to be surveyed and appraised, his mental limitations were immediately revealed. There were no shadings : white and black, or good and evil, were the chief realities ; the half good or the half evil were outside his radius.

ORIGINALITY

XI

It would be unfair to take this instance as an illustration of the general type. It is not ; for army officers are various, just as other professional men are. But the case does illustrate the necessarily narrowing tendency of certain forms of mental training, not so much for military subjects but for other and different subjects. And it must be so—always. To obtain a good soldier a specified mental disposition is a pre-requisite—*i.e.* the fighting spirit ; and this is intensified by scientific instruction. Action is pre-eminent. If the army officer's training were of a kind to give him a liking for comparing and contrasting *ideas*, and if, when decisive action was an immediate necessity, he saw six possible ways of attack or defence, alternating between the first and the fourth, and the third and the sixth, with affectionate glances at the others, we should condemn the system *in toto*. A soldier must not see too many sides of a campaign ; he has his own and the enemy's, and these are quite sufficient. The less of the philosopher there is in him the better, at any rate so long as he is on active service. After retirement he can give himself more latitude, and he has often done it with good results, although it must be confessed that the number of inventions for war, emanating from military men, is not so large as one might expect. Retired officers, as a whole, show disinclination to mental effort, and if they do take up a subject enthusiastically it is often of a "cranky" nature, or else it is a practical business in which they achieve not a little success.

In Government the military mind does not show to advantage. A barrack training is good for order and efficiency but not for dealing with civilian difficulties and the thousand and one little problems of a vast population. The soldier's mind is one that aims at a quick solution, and rather favours a drastic remedy. Those qualities are unsuitable in statecraft, and however great the Duke of Wellington was on the battle-field, and he *was* great, he was never guilty of originality in his functions as a political leader.

THE PROFESSIONAL MIND

XII

The naval officer belongs to another grouping. His training is long in point of duration and intricate as to its details ; and yet he never seems to be "narrowed" in quite the same way as the army officer. He shows a greater readiness to welcome and adopt new ideas, even when they concern guns, torpedoes, submarines, or armour plates. Of course, he will have his preliminary grumble, and a new Dreadnought is sure to have a crowd of deficiencies at first, just as every new hoist never works like the old one until it has been in use for a week. But this is because he is an Englishman. It is surface irritation until the new thing has been mastered. Deep down in his inmost self he is more of a progressive than a conservative, and the question arises as to whether there is anything in his training that brings about this result. Yes. First there is the vastness of the *sea* and a great sense of *space*. His school is the ocean ; the broad expanse of the heavens is never without a meaning, and he is on intimate terms with its friendly aspects as well as with its ugly moods ; the planet is not an undiscovered country ; he often visits foreign ports, sees other forms of human life, learns in a fundamental sense what it means to live and let live : in a word, his education is that of an open-air academy, plus travel, plus discipline, plus a perpetual spice of danger.

And that brings us to another point : his training has a responsibility in it that is probably not found in any other form of national defence, the air service excepted. The naval manœuvres constitute a more wonderful performance than the army manœuvres. The commander of a Dreadnought, a destroyer, or a submarine must not make a mistake or he endangers the safety of his vessel and crew. Is there any army operation analogous to the possible loss of a £2,500,000 ironclad with hundreds of valuable lives ?

A sense of responsibility—and it is everywhere the chief agency for developing mental ability—added to the education of sea and space, is responsible for creating the psychology of the sailor. He lives a more comprehensive life than the soldier because he has no other option ; his mind has a constant change of environment ; a rigid system of instruction has its offset in ocean travel, and the influence of past tradition is counterbalanced by an ever-progressive present. The effect is visible in the mental deportment of the naval officer, taking him in the mass. The physical *handiness* of Jack has its complement in the mental readiness of his officers. A new situation, such as the unscrupulous methods of German U boats during 1915-1917, was not met by consulting the text-books, or falling back on tradition ; instant adaptation to circumstances was the need, and in a few weeks the Navy was doing something on a scale it had never before thought of doing. The U boats were sent to the bottom in unorthodox ways. To be original is not the aim of the naval officer, but he takes to it easily and effectively, because exact training has not grooved his intelligence.

XIII

A survey of the preceding sections might leave the impression that there is not much hope for originality in the ranks of professional men as a whole. That impression is right, and yet it is wrong. It is right so far as the *tendency* to uniformity is concerned ; professional prestige is more often won by excellence in things as they are than by new conceptions of things as they might be, or ought to be. A careful training, extending over years when impressions are deep and abiding, cannot but result in a fixity of mental habit, a fixity which, as we have seen, has undoubted merits. But the training is too dogmatic ; it does not make sufficient allowance for future developments, except in science, and even there we find room for a teaching with less confident affirmation and more encouragement to research. We must not expect a great deal of original thought from the ranks of professional men, but we may expect most from those who can hold fast to ascertained truth without limiting their expectation of greater discoveries to come.

Isaac Taylor made out a good case for the originality of the lay mind as against the professional mind, at any rate in the realm of invention. "Almost every one of the original modern inventions," he says, "and a large proportion also of those supplemental improvements which have followed in the track of the principal, have been the offspring of minds which were untrained in the professions—undisciplined—untaught; or to say all in a word . . . it is *laymen* who have placed the nineteenth century so far in advance of its predecessors." [1] Then follows a rather surprising list of achievements due to lay originality: and Taylor devoted a special chapter to lay theologians, so many and so distinctive were they. It is like the old division between the classic and the romantic: the mind of the professional man is held down by rule, and precedent, and ideal; the mind of the layman, on the other hand, has a freedom which, even if it sometimes results in ridiculous mistakes, is nevertheless a type of intellect we cannot afford to do without; indeed we owe more to it than we can possibly state. Without undervaluing the professional mind or over-estimating the lay mind, we may embody the truth in such a phrase as this: that both types of mind are necessary, but no element of exactitude, of conservatism, or of experience, no rule or regulation, is so important as the freedom which allows the intellect sufficient impulse to discover new principles.

[1] Chapter on "Modern Advancements," in his *Ultimate Civilisation*, p. 193. 1860.

SECTION V

LOOKING AHEAD

CHAPTER I

IS ORIGINALITY NOW IMPOSSIBLE ?

I

THE possibility of further originalities of every kind is bound up with the larger question of progress ; consequently it is difficult to discuss the one apart from the other. If there be no such thing as progress there can be no originality worthy of the name. Assuming that progress is any kind of change that brings advantage, external or internal, it would be difficult to deny the existence of such changes, just as it would be futile to deny that there have been changes leading to deterioration and disaster. Unless we are to abolish all the distinctions which thought and experience have set up, it is impossible to read the record of history without acknow-ledging the existence of a plan of operation governed by laws as certain as those of inanimate nature ; nor can we intelli-gently deny that the changes which have taken place are such as to justify the use of the word advance.

By the practical man the question is looked upon as absurd. To him every new development is an originality, and there-fore a part of the great scheme of progress. He is very certain about most things, and this is no exception. He knows what he has read and what he has seen. Some years ago he went to a motor exhibition and saw one of the first motor cars ever made. He got somebody to set the machinery working, and as the old car shuddered and shook in the early manner he laughed long and loud : the thing was so foolish, so pitiable, so pathetic. Progress ? Well—he is angry with

P 225

scholars who deny it ; indeed he will confute them out of the pages of a notebook he keeps in his office.   Here is the first extract :

Sir Henry Savile, one of the most eminent mathematicians of his day (who died in the same year as Shakespeare), closed his career as a Professor at Oxford with the words : " By the grace of God, gentlemen hearers, I have performed my promise.   I have redeemed my pledge.   I have explained, according to my ability, the definitions, postulates, axioms, and the first eight propositions of the *Elements* of Euclid. Here, sinking under the weight of years, I lay down my art and my instruments."

"Have we made no progress since then?" he asks gleefully. " Or since this ? " and he reads another quotation :

Pope Alexander VI. once divided the unexplored portions of the globe between the Spaniards and the Portuguese as the two controlling nations of the earth.

"How about Europe now ? " he exclaims.
Well, the practical man has to yield a point or two during cross-examination, but he has more to say for himself than philosophers have hitherto allowed.   For instance, Professor Münsterberg says that when a man of science speaks of progress and development he thinks of the transition from an acorn to a tree ; but that, to be consistent, he must acknowledge that there would be nothing worse and nothing better if the transition should be from the organism to the lifeless and from the cosmos to chaos.[1]   The practical man, unaccustomed to this kind of thinking, and believing that it is subversive of experience in the actuality of which the Professor himself reposes his daily life, imagines a reply ; and he has been known to construct an argument in a manner rude, rough, but strenuous.   He might, for instance, say that if the Professor received a royalty of twenty per cent. on his first book and only ten per cent. on his last, would that be

[1] *The Eternal Values*, p. 11.

" worse " or " better " ?   Indeed, why receive anything at all
if the lifeless is as good as the living ?   Even the Professor
might have to yield a point or two during cross-examination.
Whether we are monists, or dualists, or anything else, we
have to admit that life on the plane of the real is not the same
as that on the plane of the ideal ; a truth in thought may
not be a truth in action, and philosophies which refuse to
take this into account will be as diverting as they are untrue.
The Christian Scientist denies the reality of matter, but he
knows the right change out of a five-dollar note.

II

But let us return to the more direct question of the possibility of originality.   The answers given by scholars, philosophers, and historians are by no means unanimous, indeed
they form a highly interesting study in evasion, uncertainty,
and contradiction ; and although at the end of the debate we
may range ourselves with the optimists, it will not be because
the arguments on the other side have been few or lacking in
significance.   For instance, there is the well-known criticism
of C. H. Pearson in his *National Life and Character.*

" Certain kinds of poetry have become impossible ; certain
others are being rapidly exhausted.   Can anyone conceive
that an epic poem could be written in this age ? . . . The
pastoral is doomed. . . . The satire, as Horace and Juvenal,
Boileau and Pope fashioned it, has fallen into comparative
disuse. . . . Human nature, various as it is, is only capable
after all of a certain number of emotions and acts, and these
as the topics of an incessant literature are bound after a time
to be exhausted.   We may say with absolute certainty that
certain subjects are never to be taken again.   The Tale of
Troy, the Wanderings of Odysseus, the vision of Heaven and
Hell, as Dante saw it, the theme of Paradise Lost, and the
story of Faust are familiar instances . . ." (p. 298).

It would be possible to add a good many testimonies of
like character, but we will be content with two which deal

with the future of art. First, we have a declaration from Mr W. H. Mallock that "in art . . . after a certain point has been passed it can hardly be said there is any progress at all." [1] Next, we have a prophecy from Mr George Moore, dated 17th December 1912, to the effect that "art is going to cease. In fifty years' time there will be no art. Everybody will paint exactly the same as his fellow, unless you stop the railways and the motor cars, and I don't see any possibility of that. . . . People had better make the most of modern art while they can, for it is gradually petering out." [2]

III

Analysing these opinions closely we are led to ask the question why so pessimistic an outlook should be possible with men who are students of history or keen critics—or both. The answer is twofold : (a) because advancing years, in conjunction with historical study, predispose the mind to doubt the existence of continued progress ; and (b) because, within its limits, the opinion is true. It is at this point that originality and progress must be discussed together.

(a) The effect of advancing years, and of deep reflection, on the decisions respecting the problems of the future is, like most inquiries into mental operations, not easily measured. All we can do is to collect important facts and try to master their inward meaning. After fifty, sometimes before, there is a tendency to take rather pessimistic views of the world—we are speaking of leaders of thought as well as of men of average mind—not unhappy views, but views that are probably expressed with a sceptical smile. "You will never see anything better than this," they say—not gloomily, but somewhat sorrowfully. They have developed a fear that progressive forces have reached their limit of action ; they may even have assured themselves that all movement is in a circle, and that after some centuries of effort we find the world pretty much as it was in ancient days, except in the conveniences of civilisation. How far is such

[1] *Aristocracy and Evolution*, p. 253.
[2] Interview in *The Pall Mall Gazette*.

an attitude attributable to advancing age, and how far is it the outcome of careful investigation? for one must remember that a student of the history of thought and achievement is past middle life before he can be said to have mastered the details and arrived at an intelligent conclusion.

IV

Let us take a few illustrations. Herbert Spencer, in a letter to Tyndall in 1898, said: "I look at the state of the world in dismay; but I have for a long time past seen the inevitableness of the tremendous disasters that are coming." He was seventy-three when he expressed this view; and it will be observed it was not a recent view: he had probably held it since he was fifty-five or sixty. For our purposes we will suppose he was sixty when he first deliberately decided that civilisation was heading for disaster. We turn now to a very different man, with a very different kind of mental training: Gugielmo Ferrero. He is a brilliant Italian author whose piquant views, historical insight, and literary style have given his books a world-wide reputation—books which stand for long years of close study and deep reflection. In his *Ancient Rome and Modern America* he says: "The author . . . has not so much confidence in his own wisdom as to try to discover whether man is really progressing or not; whether he is moving down the valley of the centuries towards a fixed goal, or towards an illusion which retreats with each step he takes in its direction." Not a cheering outlook, truly. We cannot suppose that Ferrero disbelieves in the possibility of some great discovery by chance, or even in the future output of original work in the fine arts or invention; but his words convey the impression that in the main the world can hardly be described as changing for the better. Another earlier student of history, Professor F. A. Lange, takes a view that is rather more favourable. He says the progress of mankind is not continuous, and that every page of history supports this claim; but " it is still possible to doubt whether there exists upon the whole such a progress as we see unfold itself at some particular point and then disappear. Although to me it seems unmistakable in our present epoch that, besides the rising and falling of civilisation which we so clearly see in history, there is at the same time a continuous advance, the effects of which are only veiled by this fluctuation, yet this idea is not so certain as is that of progress at a particular point ; and we find able thinkers versed in nature and history, like Volger, who deny this progress." [1]

V

This is a step in advance. Progress may not always take place, but it does take place periodically. Lotze would not even go so far as that ; he says : " In history progress is hardly discernible " [2] ; and Leibnitz is not quite certain. " The human race," he remarks, " may possibly obtain in the course of time a higher degree of perfection than we can at present imagine." Max Nordau's chapter on " The Question of Progress " is a useful summary of opinions on this matter, and it also contains an intelligible theory that is worthy of consideration [3] ; but we have produced a sufficient number of judgments, by distinctive writers, for the purpose we have in view. The ages of these men at the time they issued their works from which the opinions have been taken were as follows :—

H. Spencer	. . .	60
C. H. Pearson	. . .	68
W. H. Mallock	. . .	49
George Moore	. . .	55
G. Ferrero	. . .	50
F. A. Lange	. . .	45
H. Lotze	. . .	47
Leibnitz	. . .	64

The average age, it will be seen, is fifty-four. Some readers, doubtless, are unable to believe that age has very much

[1] *History of Materialism*, vol. iii., p. 261.
[2] *Microcosmus*, vol. ii.
[3] *The Interpretation of History*. By Max Nordau.

influence on critical judgments, other than a good influence, but the instinctive hopefulness and expectancy of the young brain is absent from the older brain—which has become fixed, more or less, in its methods, with loss to the constructive imagination. Just as memory after fifty tends to dwell on the period of boyhood, so it shows a disposition to find its chief values in the past. Whatever be the ability shown during the first half-century of a man's life, and however much of that ability he may retain beyond that limit, it seems to be a fact that he will begin to regard the future apprehensively [1]; he may not sink into pessimism but he certainly is unable to retain the optimism of early manhood. But age is not the only factor. There is the long-continued study of history, and it does not appear to encourage a hopeful outlook. Does this scepticism arise from the manifest difficulty of interpreting past events? or is it because the truth is only too plain to the seeing eye—namely, that "progress," so far from being on an ascending arc, is on a level circle? Whatever be the reason, the fact is clear: few historians after fifty, who are fully acquainted with the social and political record of Europe and Asia, express themselves with strong conviction as to the definite advance in intellectual and moral things which the world may hope to see. For these sentiments we go to the Utopians and idealists of all schools, but not to the historian, critic, or philosopher. So far from seeing progress ahead of us, these writers are often doubtful as to its existence at any time; a profound knowledge of the past appears to create a disbelief in

[1] Dr Alfred Russel Wallace says: "In one of my latest conversations with Darwin he expressed himself very gloomily on the future of humanity on the ground that in our modern civilisation natural selection had no play and the fittest did not survive." See *Studies, Scientific and Social*.

Mr Benjamin Kidd, at thirty-nine, having studied history through the lens of a theory, sees life in rose colours. "Progress," he declares, "is a necessity from which there is simply no escape and from which there has never been any escape since the beginning of life. Looking back at the history of life anterior to man we find it to be a record of ceaseless progress on the one hand and ceaseless stress and competition on the other."—*Social Evolution*, p. 35.

advancement. Probably the deciding factor is neither age nor study entirely, but the personal equation. The historian who is a cynic by nature will find much to entertain him and to warp his judgment, just as the specialist with Christian or materialistic presuppositions will find everything he looks for. The biology of the brain cell determines our thinking.

But is there no possibility of escaping the influence of age, of shaking ourselves free from the dead weight of learning, and of adjusting differences due to the personal equation? Apparently not. Unless a man has formed a working theory of life and progress before the age of fifty, then, however much he probes the past, he is fairly certain to be either a mild or a pronounced pessimist as to the future. And the determining feature, after all, is not his age or his knowledge, but his temperament and the readiness with which he accepts an idealistic creed. Christian philosophy necessarily views the world as temporary and probationary; it sees no great hope for a universe which will be consumed in violent heat; and, naturally, its exhortation is: "Love not the world" [1]; but the eye of the Christian being set on the beauties of another life after death, the fate of earthly civilisations, their decay and death, do not create the hopelessness which must arise in the mind of a student whose views are bordered by the limits of the grave. The Christian view of progress is that of the fulfilment of a Divine programme, wherein some developments are regarded as inimical to the spirit of faith,[2] and must be eradicated. But the general tendency is to say, with Browning:

> "God's in his heaven—
> All's right with the world."

Consequently the Church members are optimists, even at seventy or eighty, not because they believe in progress so much as because they believe in Providence. With other

[1] Cardinal Newman said: "Our race's progress and perfectibility is a dream because revelation contradicts it."—*Idea of a University*, p. 73.
[2] *Protestantism and Progress*, by Prof. E. Troeltsch, p. 128 *ff*.

idealists we observe something of the same result but for different reasons.

VI

A sane view is that of Mr A. J. Balfour, who in his *Decadence* affirms that since decay is as natural as growth we cannot but expect to reach in many directions the boundaries of progress. "If there are whole groups of nations capable on their own initiative of a certain measure of civilisation, but capable apparently of no more, and if below them again, there are (as I suppose) other races who seem incapable of either creating a civilisation of their own, or of preserving unaided a civilisation impressed upon them from without, by what right do we assume that no impassable limits bar the path to Western progress?"[1] The matter is argued at some length, but the conclusion is that so far there are "no symptoms either of pause or of regression in the onward movement which for more than a thousand years has been characteristic of Western Civilisation." Mr Balfour was sixty-four at the time he issued his opinions on decadence, and it is noticeable with what definiteness he ascribes possible limits to developments. But he is equally positive in his final statement; the "onward movement" shows no sign of pause or retrogression. He recognises the existence of finalities here and there, but the whole world moves forwards. Mr Balfour believes in a rational universe; he has a teleology; the life of the planet has a traceable history, and a progressive destiny.

Other instances of the confident spirit of progress are found in the attitude of men like Sir William Crookes and the late Alfred Russel Wallace. Of the latter it was said that he was essentially a reformer, and that "nothing disturbed his cheerful confidence in the future, and nothing made him happier than some plan for reforming the house, the garden, the kitchen boiler, or the universe."[2] The former, at eighty-four, says : "I have no fears whatever about the future. The whole observation of my life has been that whatever happens is always progress." Both these men long

[1] *Decadence*, p. 38.
[2] *Letters and Reminiscences*, vol. ii., p. 108.

ago accepted the doctrine that personal life is continuous, and that after death it takes up the story again on another plane. They are not historians in the ordinary sense, but they may be said to know the history of the physical world at its best and worst; and, knowing it, they believe in its progress. Nevertheless, temperament exerted its influence, for both have been led by an idealism which is part of their nature.

VII

Mr Edward Carpenter, in his chapter on "How the World Looks at Seventy," [1] proves how a distant ideal affects one's estimate of mundane things: "The willing sacrifice of life, and the ecstasy of it, would be unintelligible if death did not indeed mean Transformation. In my little individual way I experience something of the same kind. I feel a curious sense of joy in observing—as at my age one is compelled to do—the natural and inevitable decadence of some portion of the bodily organism, the failures of sight and hearing, the weakening of muscles, the aberrations even of memory—a curious sense of liberation and of obstacles removed. I acknowledge that the experience—the satisfaction and the queer sense of elation—seem utterly unreasonable and not to be explained by any of the ordinary theories of life; but it is there, and it may, after all, have some meaning."

Once more, idealism changes the earthly scene.

We conclude, therefore, that although there are optimists of threescore years and ten, the general tendency after fifty is to expect little advance in the finer phases of civilised life, unless the personal outlook is profoundly affected by inward experiences of an ideal nature. It sometimes happens, however, that even these idealists have no deep interest or belief in the development of the world and worldly things; this life to them is "a vapour which appeareth for a while then vanisheth away." Were they to study history as others have done, they, too, might realise that continued immersion in bygone centuries is a disqualification for

[1] In *My Days and Dreams.*

estimating the future. At any rate it would seem to be better in every way to believe in the law of the unexpected rather than in the view that history repeats itself. For this reason one is inclined to agree with Havelock Ellis when he says : " Men have never known what the world is moving to. Who foresaw—to say nothing of older and vaster events —the Crucifixion ? What Greek or Roman in his most fantastic moments prefigured our thirteenth century ? What Christian foresaw the Renaissance ? We cannot be too bold, for we are ever at the incipient point of some new manifestation far more overwhelming than all our dreams." [1] Dreams ? If in 1918 some ardent follower of Lord Roberts had harangued a crowd to the effect that within two years 5,000,000 British soldiers would be enlisted to fight against Germany's assault on the freedom of nations, we should have laughed derisively, reflecting sorrowfully on the Utopian and fearful imagination of the scaremonger, or else scoffing at his ignorance of his fellow-men.

VIII

(*b*) We allowed that Mr C. H. Pearson's plea was, within its limits, true. The great poets and dramatists of the past are still unapproachable; at any rate they have never been excelled. Homer, Euripides, Dante, Goethe, Shakespeare— it cannot be said that names like these have been eclipsed, and will anyone claim that Phidias has been left behind as a sculptor, or that the works of modern painters have made the artists of former ages look like amateurs ? Let us admit, then, that in certain well-defined 'spheres it is highly improbable that we shall ever see any better work than that which has already appeared. But what does the admission mean ? It means that as the kind of life which gave birth to expressions of genius in the past is a life that has passed away, artistic embodiment of it is no longer possible. Take the epic. If our highly mentalised civilisation has made an epic impossible, there will, of course, be no epic to compare with those that arose during the days of instinct and passion.

[1] *Impressions and Comments*, p. 229.

ORIGINALITY

The epic, as such, has reached finality. To-day life is lived with most of its intensities directed inwards ; our love is for ideas rather than action, and the psychological novel, the character study, and the static theatre make a successful appeal to us. Art and life are inevitably bound up with each other ; and, maybe, some of the artists, sculptors, and poets of later generations may be judged to be as great in their interpretation of the life they knew as those of earlier times were in the embodiment of the life around them. Should this verdict be denied, then we must cheerfully confess that in certain of the fine arts the apex was reached long ago— unless the Great War shall produce *the* epic of all time.

This attitude need not disturb our confidence in the future. A profound student of the thought of Greece has said that " Platonism, if we understand the word in a broad and literal, and not in a narrow and pedantic sense, is not yet dead and cannot die, because its roots are struck deep in universal human nature." [1] We may boggle at such a statement, but we are compelled at last to accept it. Plato, as Emerson said, makes havoc among our originalities ; he plumbed the depths long before we knew there were any depths at all. He insists, and we cannot say him nay. Is it not so with the founder of Christianity ? So long as human nature exists, so long shall we be unable to unsay many of the things he said ; their vitality lies in their truth for all time. These admissions, however, do not constitute a denial of progress ; they affirm finality only in specific cases.

Literary forms, to take a very different sphere, are not a fixed quantity. The drama of action gives place to the drama of ideas, but it is still the drama. Let life be vigorous, internally or externally, and we shall find the forms of expression that we need. We may not find them at once, but eventually we shall, and in every art sphere, too. The first crude and blundering symptoms are seen in the work of the Futurists, the Cubists, the Vorticists, the Imagistes, and others. To regard these schools of effort, so positive and so partial, as final, is jejune in the extreme ; they are the forerunners of new developments whose outline is even now

[1] *The Vitality of Platonism.* By James Adam.

236

hardly discernible. Mr A. J. Eddy expresses the truth when he says that, "broadly speaking we are changing from the *perfections* of Impressionism to the imperfections of Post-Impressionism ; from the *achievements* of a school, a movement that has done the best it could, to the *attempts*, the *experiments*, the *gropings* of new men along new lines."

IX

The new man with the young mind—and mind is young up to forty-five—is instinctively progressive, hopeful, expectant; originality is always the great possibility. Optimism is more surely grounded in youth and maturity than in middle age and old age. The disposition to regard any achievement as final is almost repellent.

True, a number of young men and women, most of them abnormal in some way, have occasionally been disposed to indulge in pessimism, but this pessimism as to the new light and brilliant work of the years ahead has seldom interfered with their own progress. George Eliot is a case in point. At twenty-nine she was afraid originality was becoming increasingly difficult. She laments the fact that "great subjects are used up " and that "civilisation tends evermore to repress individual predominance, highly wrought agony, or ecstatic joy." [2] Eight years later she commenced *Amos Barton*, and eleven years later she surprised the world with her *Adam Bede*, and found there were still great subjects on which to write. Had she, at considerable length, expressed her views on the paucity of high themes, and embodied them in the form of an essay, supported by opinions from ancient and modern authorities, her later successes would have

---

[1] In *Cubists and Post-Impressionists*. See also an article on " The Impulse to Futurism," by H. W. Nevinson in *The Atlantic Monthly* (1910).

[2] See *Life of George Eliot*, by J. W. Cross. It is only fair to add the subjoined quotation from George Eliot's *Essays*: "It is foolish to be for ever complaining of the consequent uniformity, as if there were an endless power of originality in the human mind. Great and precious origination must always be comparatively rare " (p. 394).

disposed her to disavow the scepticism of her thirtieth year.

Some writers, basing their estimates of the future on too close a study of the analogy of Nature, are wont to regard the destiny of man as limited by the blind forces around us. That we depend on Nature for our very existence is obvious, but there is an element in our development in which the purely material factor has no part.

We cannot, indeed, accept Nature as any sort of guide to the intellectual future. Why should we ? So far as we can see, the planet has passed through its most changing periods and is now awaiting its last and final destiny. Every aspect of its past history compels us to realise how very old the earth is, and the story of evolution is the story of Nature's originalities ; how new species were evolved and how the older ones either died out or were included in the survival of the fittest. But new species are not evolved to-day, at least not by Nature alone. We go to Luther Burbank to see the new flowers and the new fruits. Nature herself has ceased to be original.[1] Perhaps it is better so. We should not care for a sudden departure from the law of gravity, and even if new flowers and fruits were always in a process of becoming, the advantage of an increase in flora might easily be discounted by an unpleasant increase in objectionable insects, and reptiles with a vicious cunning for ejecting poisons. The physical world has reached its limits so far as we can see ; only in the world of mind, and of matter as controlled by mind, can we look for that which we call progress. For the Universe as a whole there is bound to be change, but its scope is beyond imagination and therefore it is outside the narrower field of planetary development.

X

On the *real* plane of life : business, laws, social developments—in short, what we call civilisation—there has never

---

[1] It has been said that every sunset is original, and in the æsthetic sense we agree. But in science natural laws would appear to have no more variations in view.

been any doubt as to the possibility of originality. New ideas and new adaptations flow in a ceaseless stream. Not all of them are valued at their worth. The sewing machine idea of Howe was bandied to and fro across the Atlantic before it gripped the imagination and became a commercial reality. The Patent Office of every civilised country contains proof of steady industry in invention. As in other spheres, so in business, and the practical arts generally, finalities have apparently been reached in several directions. If the epic of the past is unapproachable, may we not say that it is unlikely we shall ever see superior applications of steam as a motive power? And yet new motive powers are not impossible. The explosive engine proves the contrary, and the new pump at Chingford Water Works is a triumph of imagination. The brain of man is not yet at the end of its tether; indeed whilst the literary critic discusses the question "Is Literature Dying?"[1] the engineer and the business man are trying to awaken their fellows to the great possibilities of development. Benedetto Croce affirms most truly that "there is progress whenever an activity declares itself, whenever (not to leave the circle of the practical) we pass from irresolution to resolution, from suspense to action."[2] And it is the practical person who in this respect is our salvation. He does not theorise overmuch. History fails to dominate him. He knows the present and works for a future. There is always the chance of some good thing ahead. His may be a rather narrow world, measured intellectually, but it is a real world all the same; and that any conjectures based on the past should govern present action pessimistically is not to be tolerated.

Looking back on the different aspects of the argument we have to confess that we believe in the possibility of progress in general and of originality in particular. New life means new thought; and as history ceases to dominate us so shall we cultivate a Greek directness and independence of inquiry, thankfully using the labours of those who have gone before us, but refusing to be bound by them. We can only believe that

[1] Article in *The Contemporary Review*, by Herbert Paul.
[2] *The Philosophy of the Practical*, p. 97.

the achievements of past eras are a prophecy of greater achievements to come. There may be sectional finalities in history, but history itself has no finality.

> " Guests of the ages, at to-morrow's door
>   Why shrink ye ? The long track behind us lies,
>   The lamps gleam, and the music throbs before
>   Bidding us enter, and I count him wise
>   Who loves so well man's noble memories,
>   He needs must love man's nobler hopes yet more."

CHAPTER II

ORIGINALITY IN THE FUTURE

I

To estimate the trend of originality in the future is a task of some magnitude, and we hesitate to deal with it; but our effort will not be misunderstood if the reader, however critical, will remember that we are seeking *tendencies*, not attempting to formulate prophecies.

Whatever be the cause, there can be no doubt about the fact that the thought movement of the present and of the future is, and will be, profoundly extensive and intensive—to use the language of the logician.[1] Long before the Great War this extension had begun to show itself in the use of words : we awoke to the fact that many words had com-·pletely lost their boundaries, and other words were being affected in the same way. Men nowadays believe in God, but they have no sort of belief in the Yahweh of the Jews, or the Father of Jesus Christ, or the First Person of the Trinity. Surveying the beauties of nature (and filled with Clifford's cosmic emotion), the soul of the observer compels an acceptance of a first cause who is called God—the god of

---

[1] Progress has been one-sided hitherto, at least in some respects. Prof. Marvin says: "At each of the previous great moments in the history of the West development has been secured by emphasis on one side of our nature at the expense of the rest. Visions of mankind in common progress have flashed on individual thinkers, a Roman Emperor, a Catholic Schoolman, a Revolutionary prophet. But the thing achieved has been one-sided, and the needed correction has been given by another movement more one-sided still. The greatest hope of the present day lies in the fact that in all branches of life, in government as well as in philosophy, in science as in social reform, in religion and in international politics, men are now striving with determination to bind the threads together."—"The Idea of Progress," in Marvin's *Progress and History*, p. 17.

pantheism. This indeed is no new thing, but the modern version of it is new. Immanence is more than the pantheism of the past. And there are men whose god is an Idea : the Idea of the Best they know ; others accept God as Right—He who will see justice meted out to the players when the game is over. Verily we have a Pantheon to-day in all civilised countries, and some good people have never recovered from the shock of hearing that Germany has a real German god—with a few old but inferior deities like Woden and Thor.

Take the word *life*. There used to be the life of the plant, of the animal, and of man : but now we have life where we never expected to find it. Life in the stone ; life in the inorganic ; life in forces that we call blind ; life everywhere—but what kind of life ? That question is the centre of acute discussion and the boundaries which we fondly hoped were fixed are breaking away.[1] Semblances of the organic coming directly from the inorganic are interesting, but confusing to our science. To some extent the same condition is found in mathematics. We believed we had in the phrase " mathematically exact " a truth as incontestable as any external truth could be ; but doubt is beginning to assert itself.[2] Exactitude can never be absolute ; it is always relative, but it is more relative, apparently, than it used to be.

II

Progress ? We had the notion that we *did* understand not only the word but the thing ; and yet we have begun a new quarrel about it. Some contend that there is no essential superiority in complexity over simplicity—or in the hetero-

[1] " I am willing to concede to Prof. Haeckel that all nature is alive."—Dr Paul Carus on " Panpsychism and Panbiolism," in *The Monist*, vol. iii., p. 235.

[2] Prof. Schubert, at the end of his chapter on " The Nature of Mathematical Knowledge," says : " The preceding reflections deprive mathematical knowledge of that degree of certainty and incontestability which is commonly attributed to it when we say a thing is ' mathematically certain.'"—*Mathematical Essays and Recreations*, p. 37.

geneous over the homogeneous; others affirm that evolution is merely the carrying through of a planetary programme and is therefore neither progress nor decline: others, again, contend that happiness is life's aim, consequently an advanced society which is less happy than one less progressive is not in a state of progress but of devolution. When we debate progress the word connotes different conceptions, because its boundaries have broken down. It is the same with many other words: law, morality, aristocracy, democracy, rights,[1] and a hundred more.

What is the true inwardness of this phenomenon? It means that some of our little systems have had their day and already have ceased to be. Not only has the theologian to prepare for an era of broadened ideas, but the man of science will have to bestir himself also. Frontiers are being pushed back because the boundary walls have been broken down. Wordsworth sang:

> "Death, life, and sleep, reality and thought,
> Assist me, God, their boundaries to know."

That was the nineteenth century. To-day there is a slump in dividing lines. We realise that life and the Universe are a whole, and we are hot on the track of unities. We are trying to find the formula for economic and political cohesion, and slowly we are perceiving that the issue is partly material and partly spiritual. But we approach the consummation steadily. When Mr Gosling was leading the big strike some years ago, the editors of the London papers thirsted for his scalp as a plotter against the State; to-day, one of those editors refers to Mr Gosling's latest address as a "wise and statesmanlike speech." That editor has learned something of the higher unity; so has Mr Gosling.

In science, in philosophy, in art, in business, the idea of extension is being pursued. Specialism has overreached itself and we have revolted against the worship of detail. Section-work will be continued, but as part of a whole-work.

---

[1] We could do with an up-to-date edition of Cornewall Lewis's *Use and Abuse of Political Terms*.

Distances, both long and short, cease to impress us. Instead of looking for the cause of epilepsy in the brain we go farther afield, so to speak, and discover the mischief in the intestines. Unity is all-embracing, and although Professor Jevons' notion that sun spots affect commerce may not be true, the tendency to look for operating causes at great distances from the effects is distinctly healthy. How long have we been trying to classify the sciences? Our difficulties respecting their boundaries ought to have taught us a good deal more than they have done: but in dull labour we plodded on— and with no imagination. There is no exact classification of the sciences or of anything else because there are no exact lines of demarcation. We used to dogmatise that sound is sound, and colour is colour, two absolutely distinct and different sensations and perceptions. And now? Well, we are giving serious attention to the colours of music. Soon we may be discussing the identity of perfumes and ideas— quaint notions which stir up the anger of the circumspect, who dislike the kind of research that breaks down the fences so carefully set up by the scientists of the past.

III

What was it that gave Froebel his hold upon the world of education? Just this, that "the desire for unity is the basis of all genuinely human development." He found that subjects were taught *as subjects*, and no one subject had anything to do with other subjects—*e.g.* Latin with Botany. So, he says, "I sought everywhere for recognition of the quickening inter-connection of parts, and for the exposition of the inner all-pervading rule of law." We could do with more of this spirit in present-day teaching. Boundaries are being set up in some directions; knocked down in others. For instance, *Educational Values and Methods* is a book the main object of which is to show that we cannot transfer the efficiency acquired by one mental power to another mental power. Then is each mental power—memory, for example— definitely marked off from every other power? If so, and if, further, its education can be advanced whilst that of neighbouring functions remains stationary, then we are back again in the world of "faculty" psychology; indeed we might as well call in Gall and Spurzheim at once, and develop our minds, bump by bump. Here is an alleged scientific result : "Specific memory training is specific in its effects ; there is no general memory function which can be developed, by feeding it upon any one material." [1] But an experiment conducted on school children and young students is not sufficient to justify so important an inference ; moreover, experiments conducted with adults point quite the other way. And why ? Because *interest* is deeper, and acting on a more acute intelligence it is found that concentration and method develop recollective power for faces, facts, figures, and words—things very different in themselves. There are no boundary lines between memory and the reproductive imagination, or memory and attention, or memory and an act of volition : the mind works as a unity, and it is its character as such which determines the tendency and the scope of its development. As Meumann says : "Our general capacity to retain and to reproduce depends . . . upon the development of other functions of consciousness, especially upon concentration and persistence of attention, the effort of will, the emotional condition and the like." [2]

IV

Another mark of the spirit of unity is the communising of *knowledge*, especially in the forms of natural science.[3] For a

[1] *Educational Values and Methods*, p. 72. By W. G. Sleight, M.A., D.Litt.

[2] *The Psychology of Learning*, pp. 6, 356. Münsterberg is of the same opinion. "Our general retentive and reproductive capacity is strengthened and improved by every act of memory."—*General Psychology*, p. 168.

[3] "The effect of these international labours has been to destroy the clearly marked differences of national thought. At least in the domain of science the peculiarities of the French, German and English schools are rapidly disappearing. The characteristics of national thought still exist ; but in order to find them in the present age we

long time music has been internationalised, or nearly so : now science is following suit, and, ere long, we may see a true cosmopolitanism which allows the national spirit to express itself without grating on the feelings of the rest of the world. And this tendency to abolish frontiers is nowhere more marked than in the relationship between East and West. Strictly speaking, there is no frontier at all, and there never has been ; nevertheless the dividing line between the mind of the Orient and the Occident has always been recognisable. But there appears to be a spirit of give and take in both directions ; the Western intellect goes East and sympathetically enters into its mysticism, its civilisation, and its other-worldliness ; and the Eastern intellect comes West with as few prejudices as may be, beholding our haste and hurry, and trying to fathom our materialism. What then ? Well, we get a new kind of *littérateur* ; Kipling, Lafcadio Hearn, Rabindranath Tagore. Perhaps the original literature of the future will come from a fusion of East and West.[1] Life is not all of it contemplation, neither is it action : it is a union of the two. And when we come to reflect on this thought, looking backwards meanwhile, we see how much we owe to the East ; the formal and informal philosophers have drunk deeply at the wells of Oriental thought—Spinoza, Berkeley, Hegel, Schopenhauer, Emerson, Nietzsche. Their success lay in their search for the universal ; it was to them

should have to study the deeper philosophical reasonings, the general literature, and the artistic efforts of these nations."—J. T. Merz, *History of European Thought*, p. 305.

[1] Prof. Dowden has thus illuminated this principle : " No folly can be greater than that of fancying that we shall strengthen our literary position by living exclusively in our own ideas, and showing ourselves inhospitable to the best ideas of other lands. Nor is that hospitality the finest which constrains the guest to assume the garb and adopt the manners of his entertainers. The shock of strangeness is inspiriting. Every great literary movement of modern Europe has been born from the wedlock of two peoples. So the great Elizabethan literature sprang from the love-making of England and Italy ; the poetry of the early part of the nineteenth century from the ardour aroused in England by the opening promise of the French Revolution."—"Hopes and Fears for Literature," in *The Fortnightly Review* (1889).

a finer thing to discover the oversoul than to discover the soul. East and West, as terms, lost their hard exactitude. Professor E. A. Ross offers us an interesting list of boundaries in the world of interpretation, and it shows that they are as delusive, finally, as those which are more material. "St Augustine makes the history of humanity turn on the anti-thesis of the pre-Christian and post-Christian epochs; Bossuet, on the contrast of the chosen people with the heathen peoples; Cousin, on the opposition of the Finite and the Infinite. Among the crude attempts at the differenti-ating of social phenomena are Hegel's balancing of Orient against Occident; Renan's opposition of Semite and Aryan; St Simon's alternation of 'organic' with 'critical'; Buckle's broad contrast of the Asian with the European en-vironment; Benloew's division of history into periods ruled respectively by the ideals of the Beautiful, the Good, and the True."[1] That such provisional boundaries may render a temporary service we do not deny, and approximate classi-fications are a real need; but we have often used them as if they were final, and new knowledge has been rejected in consequence.

V

It has been declared that man's originality is due to his perception of new unities. From this it follows that the pulling down of barriers of all kinds is likely to assist in the development of creative thought; for sharp lines of demarca-tion—armed frontiers where passports are demanded—tend to restrict intercourse, to prevent the growth of knowledge, and consequently to cause an absence of intellectual stimulus. Along with the more elementary facts we have just noticed there are the favourable influences of the war. We shall know our Allies better than ever before. Along with great industrial activity will come a Renaissance of a more spiritual kind: Russia, Italy, Belgium, Great Britain, and France will have a free trade in thought the effects of which, confused at first, must end in much more than mere enlightenment. The least good achieved would lie in the abolition of racial

[1] *Foundations of Sociology*, pp. 76-77.

prejudice; and yet that is a very important change. Prejudice kept us apart, but the defence of liberty brought us together. Out of that struggle will issue a true understanding. The boundaries once so definite have become indefinite, and from the ease of interchange thus established we may hope to see a broader mental horizon effecting great things in organised knowledge and still greater in the creative sphere.

But along with this extensive influence there works the *intensive*. Enlargement without is accompanied by enlargement within. In the nineteenth century the word soul was for long most unfashionable. None of us had a soul. But nowadays even Europe itself has one—according to Mr M'Cabe.[1] Nations have souls; and Mr Gibbs[2] thinks the war has one. What does it all mean? It means that the inner life of man is coming into its own, and that the outward things which represent man's aspirations are complimented by being given an analogous soul. About forty years ago psychology became a serious study in this country, not only on the part of university students and teachers, but, slowly, on the part of the general reader of books. The effect on theological thought was, at first, not salutary; some religious phenomena of alleged divine origin were seen to be quite explainable on naturalistic grounds, and this, as might be expected, was not a welcome retreat for the dogmatists. But the later developments of psychology have all been in favour of religion, and even the dogmatists have felt more comfortable than they did. Truth to tell, the theologian owes a debt to the psychologist which he has not been too ready to pay. Both, however, bear witness to the new intensity with which the inner life is lived, perhaps not with the many but certainly with the few—the few that will soon expand into the many. Let us be plain. The life of the mind, and of mind as it concerns what we call soul, is a life that has received an amount of attention infinitely greater than it did when the inner life was confined mostly to meditation on sin,

---

[1] *The Soul of Europe.* By Joseph M'Cabe.
[2] *The Soul of the War.* By Philip Gibbs. In all about twenty-five books were published in 1916 dealing with the Soul of Nations and Things.

forgiveness, and life after death.[1] We are not superfine idealists, and yet we are men and women who stand in the presence of intellect and soul—thought and emotion—with a new reverence. Man may be a trembling reed, as Pascal said, but he is a reed that can think, and though the sun should destroy him he would be greater in his death than the sun would be in its victory—for he would be conscious of his experience : the sun would not. In this old-world thought we are discovering new meanings. Consciousness has ranges, even on the plane of intellection, which we have not yet reached ; and maybe the mystics, when we can bring them down to hard pan and brass tacks, will show us the truth of realities which we have hitherto denied.

VI

Is it the message of the East once again ? It may be. All the deep thought movements that have profoundly affected mankind have arisen in the East and moved West-wards. Apparently the movements from West to East have not been so successful : the curve begins at the wrong end, so to speak. Japan was never more Japan than it is to-day : the superfices are changed—the depths remain, and those depths (in India also) give the chief value to the inward life of being. Man must always transcend reality, if he can, and the thought world is his opportunity. We cannot stay to analyse and illustrate this phenomenon ; our object is specific—we ask in what way it will affect originality in think-ing and in action. Taken in conjunction with the extensive movement already referred to, this intensive accompaniment must issue in multiplying conditions favourable to the creative mood. To put it concretely, science and poetry will live and grow together. We shall not be realists or idealists, men of science or poets, materialists or transcendentalists ; barriers will have been burned away and the impulse towards

[1] One aspect of the tendency to detail is seen in the new schools of art and poetry where mental impressions, considered sectionally, appear to be the chief consideration. The Imagistes, for instance, take a part and make it into a whole.

comprehensiveness will be as natural to us as it used to be to the Greeks. There will be less disposition to worship one section of life at the expense of others, or to deride all material things in favour of the spiritual. When Pindar said: " Strive not to become Zeus : a human lot becomes a man," he built better than he knew. Every effort to cram existence into a formula, whether religious, scientific, or economic, is an effort to become Zeus—to deify a section of life, and thus degrade the others. Life is a whole, and in spite of the obvious difference that a system of values is bound to make in our appreciations of mind and matter, it cannot be denied that all our wars and persecutions have been due to sectional idolatry—*i.e.* we declare a scheme of salvation and punish those who will not accept it ; we announce a theory of government and imprison the people who refuse it ; or we set up an economic god and start a revolution. These actions spring from ideal tendencies ; they endeavour to remedy evils and promote happiness, and to that extent they are right. But they are often too drastic, like the deeds of the Russian *Skeptsi*, who get rid of temptation by mutilating themselves. In the future there will be no slackening of ideal effort, but it will be more rational and sympathetic than hitherto because the inner life itself will be more reconciled to the human lot —reconciled not by a weak yielding to unpleasant facts but by seeing through and beyond them.

VII

One outcome of the combined extensive and intensive movement will be the creation of an atmosphere favourable to the activity of talent and genius. It must not be supposed that every man of parts has his opportunity ; indeed it may well be true that genius is not always self-assertive, rather the reverse ; and until the conditions are congenial, some men of great ability will remain mute and inglorious.[1]

[1] This is argued by Prof. C. H. Cooley in his *Genius, Fame, and Comparison of Races*. He says: "Every able race probably turns out a number of greatly endowed men many times larger than the number that attains to fame " (p. 3).

Those conditions are an amalgam of (*a*) sympathy on the part of the public, (*b*) opportunity for the individual, (*c*) sentiment on behalf of progress, and (*d*) practical facilities for developing the best talent. The last phrase suggests eugenics, but for many years to come eugenics can do little more than prevent inefficient and imperfect lives from reproducing their kind ; a century would be necessary to prove in a satisfactory manner the idea that High Masculine talent + High Feminine talent = genius, or anything like it. We do not know how chance works in these matters, and analogous cases among carefully bred animals do not foster any confidence whatever.[1] Mr Whetham, agreeing that good qualities tend to be inherited, admits they are complex in character. "It needs," he says, "the conjunction of many different factors to produce a man of ability, a woman of beauty and charm. Hence we cannot, at present at all events, trace the descent of ability, moral character or beauty in the same precise way we can follow from generation to generation certain bodily diseases or mental defects." [2] We are therefore all the more dependent on those conditions which experience has taught us are favourable : sound health ; personal hygiene ; intelligent vocational oversight ; love guidance and control ; public esteem. Even then we must expect a sense of failure, for the great men of past eras, as well as the men of mark, have sprung up suddenly and without apparent reference to conditions, prepared or otherwise. And yet reason tells us that if the ground is cultivated, the yield will be greater,[3] and there is nothing so successful

[1] A writer well acquainted with the pedigree of race-horses says, after giving many illustrations of uncertainty : " It is the aim of the figure theorists to prove there is no such thing as lottery in breeding. The cases here cited will not help them to force their pragmatic lessons home." Some of the cases concern Sceptic, Pretty Polly, Hammerkop, La Fleche.

[2] " The Extinction of the Upper Classes," in *The Nineteenth Century* (July, 1909). A more positive view is found in Schuster's *Eugenics*, p. 135.

[3] Prof. W. James, in his chapter on " Great Men and their Environment," says : " Sporadic great men come everywhere. But for a community to get vibrating through and through with intensely

as success. Let the national life be lived as it *could* be lived
—with a fine balance between the claims of the Real and the
Ideal—and the tendency thus set up would reach its goal in
a phalanx of original leaders as distinctive as any group of
which history can boast.

VIII

But to many observers the future is not so easy, so rosy,
or so probable. Some of them are obsessed with the effect
of governments on intellectual growth and advancement.
They echo Heine's saying : " If democracy really triumphs
it is all up with poetry." Or, adopting a more philosophic
view, they say that democracy and original thought are in
complete opposition ; that knowledge is not obtained *by*
the people *for* the people, but *by* the aristocracy of intellect
for the common good ; and that, therefore, democracy when
all-prevailing has a blighting effect on every kind of superiority. Even a writer like Mr J. M. Robertson admits :
" It is true that if a democratic society to-day does not
make express economic provision for a scholarly cultured
class it is likely to lack such because the leisured or idle class
in all countries grows less capable of and less inclined to such
intellectual production as it contributed to the serious literature of England during the nineteenth century. But such
economic provision has been still more necessary in monarchic
communities." [1] The debate, then, is as to the respective

active life, many geniuses coming together, and in rapid succession,
are required. This is why great epochs are rare—why the sudden
bloom of a Greece, an early Rome, a Renaissance, is such a mystery.
Blow must follow blow so fast that no cooling can occur in the
intervals. Then the mass of the nation grows incandescent and
may continue to glow by pure inertia long after the originators of
its internal movement have passed away. We often hear surprise
expressed that in these high tides of human affairs not only the
people should be filled with stronger life but that individual geniuses
should seem so exceptionally abundant. This mystery is just about
as deep as the time-honoured conundrum why great rivers flow by
great towns."—*The Will to Believe*, p. 243.

[1] *The Evolution of States*, p. 139.

merits and demerits of aristocracy and democracy in fostering original minds. If we take history as a guide—always uncertain—we shall find the balance very slightly in favour of aristocracy, but the margin of superiority is hardly worth talking about. Indeed, you might find a monarchical country so immersed in politics as to prevent the blossoming of its best intellects, just as to-day, in at least two of our foremost republics (England might also be included), the waste of energy consumed in governing is colossal.

Now democracy and aristocracy make very little difference to the progress and expression of mind ; but the time consumed in governing is another matter. Ireland is a sad illustration. If that country could have forgotten politics for five years—any five years in the last century—it would—well, no one knows how beneficial the effect would have been. England has not gone scatheless,[1] and America is still in the bonds of an elementary system of electing a President, judged by the standards of efficiency of which that country was the prime originator. Stewart, Gilbreth, Harrington Emerson, and others could invent a method less costly, less involved, briefer, and more satisfactory in every way. Talent thus consumed in the roundabout ways of modern politics would bear much fruit in literature, science, and industry. But there is very little in the *form* of government itself that is repressive of originality.

IX

This outcry against democracy has no sound basis. Lord Bryce, who has made a specialised study of America, says : "All things considered, I doubt whether democracy tends to

[1] " So much of the national energy spent itself in politics, religion, and science, during the Reform era that less remained available for imaginative literature and history. Brief lyrics, brilliant review articles, and novels of episodical rather than concentrated interest were most in request among readers of little leisure and most readily supplied by writers on whose time there were many demands."— *Modern England*, vol. i., p. 201. Prof. L. P. Jacks' article on "A Bad School for Statesmen" (see *Land and Water*, 15th June 1916) is an excellent criticism of modern parliamentarianism.

discourage originality, subtlety, refinement in thought and in expression, whether literary or artistic."[1] Professor Brander Matthews is more positive: "Nor is democracy hostile to genius or slow to recognise it."[2] Professor Dowden in arguing this question gave prominence to opposing views such as those of De Tocqueville and Scherer. The former said: "In America the majority draws a formidable circle around thought. Within the determined limits a man is free; but woe to him if he should pass beyond them." Scherer said: "The general level rises with democracy . . . ; and by a parallel movement, all that is superior is lowered and the average of which I speak is the result of the lowering of the minority as well as the elevation of the masses"[3] Dismal notions, but quite wrong: it is not the number of votes in a country that causes the mischief, but the canvassing of them, printing for them, speechifying to them, reporting for them, counting them, and kow-towing to them. The one writer who has, in our opinion, arrived at the truth is Dr J. Beattie Crozier. He had his doubts and fears (he says), "but on going on to inquire how the balance stood between Aristocracy and Democracy in their power to push on civilisation to higher and higher stages, I was hampered by a vast array and complication of considerations which detained me long and gave me much trouble to resolve; but in the long run I ended by perceiving, as I have so often done in other lines of speculation, that what actually has occurred in the world on a large scale in any given epoch or period, was the best thing, the right thing, the thing wanted there: and that although Democracy would, in a world destined to stand still and become stereotyped, give greater energy, range, and expansion to the spirit than aristocracy, which confines its finer sense of personal dignity, its more refined culture and standard of manners, to the few; in a world intended to advance, and with Progress as its end and not stagnation,

[1] *The American Commonwealth*, p. 828.
[2] "Literature in the New Century"— article in *The North American Review* (1904).
[3] "Hopes and Fears for Literature "—article in *The Fortnightly Review* (1889).

this need not be so, but on the contrary all forms of government must be brought into requisition in turn according to the necessities of the place and hour and the obstructions that have to be cleared away—now a military despotism, now a limited monarchy, here an aristocratic, there a democratic regime." [1] Precisely. A king may foster education or he may not ; a premier may be reactionary or merely neglectful of his opportunities ; and a referendum may have a good result or a very bad one. England may be a Republic in disguise, to use Bagehot's phrase, and it is probably the one thing that is suited to us ; centuries hence it may be the one thing that is dangerous to our unity.

We believe that the intense culture of class-consciousness of any kind is the really serious evil so far as political feelings are concerned. We remember listening to the diatribes of a working man in Hyde Park, a year or two back, and although he spoke well he spoiled the whole thing by advocating the development of class-consciousness. This compound word seemed to hypnotise him : he rolled it out lovingly and unceasingly, failing to observe that `he was urging his hearers to form a ruling conception the existence of which in the aristocracy he had so severely criticised.[2] There can be no doubt that in the past the aristocrats have lost half their possibilities of influence, simply because they were out of touch with the middle and working classes ; but if those classes intend to repeat the conduct of the aristocrats we are not likely to make much progress, indeed the possibilities of social mischief would be considerably increased. How ridiculous it sounds to-day when we read that Tycho Brahe, of noble birth, apologised to his audience for the

---

[1] *My Inner Life*, pp. 482-483. Dr Crozier will have modified his views on " a military despotism."

[2] Mr P. G. Hamerton rightly says : " Is it not that the love and pursuit of culture lead each of us out of his class, and that class views of any kind, whether of the aristocracy, or of the middle class, or of the people, inevitably narrow the mind and hinder it from receiving pure truth ?` Have you ever known any person who habitually lived in the notions of a caste, high or low, without incapacitating himself in a greater or less degree for breadth and delicacy of perception ? "—*The Intellectual Life*, p. 277.

affront he offered them by taking an interest in astronomy ! Authorship, too, it seems, involved him in a threat of social degradation. But, as Mr Hamerton points out, Robert Burns was in danger of going to the other extreme, by referring to " honest rusticity " and by telling gentlefolk that he " was bred to the plough and independent."

X

A more serious hindrance to the welfare of the mental life, and all that it means, is the predominance of sports and recreations. This predominance has its good side, and its drawbacks have not been as mischievous as some of our pessimists prophesied : but in the new era, where war will be transferred from the battle-field to the counting-house, the factory, and the workshop, we shall need a better perspective. Men who are engaged in occupations where the foreigner has a grip will have to put more brains into *affaires* than they have done, and less time into sport and recreation. We do not advocate no sport or recreation—the kill-joy has no place in our scheme of life ; but we do advocate a better time-table for work and play. How else is this country to keep pace with the probable and actual originalities of other peoples ? These other peoples are much less addicted to vicarious athletics than we are ; they will not stand for hours in the rain watching a football match and call it physical culture.[1] Such criticism is not very welcome, we know, but, after all, that is not a grievous matter. Indeed, we shall venture to aggravate the remark by adding a further criticism : this crowd interest in sport—this worship of physical fitness and skill in other men—is a sign that there is no ability to endure solitude or to profit by it.[2] Here are two extremes :

[1] *Vide* article in *The Quarterly Review* (July, 1910), on " Sport and Decadence."

[2] Nietzsche's notion that there should be " Retreats " for all of us, not merely for the pious, is excellent. He argues for " detachment from the tyranny of stimuli " and for " severe seclusion from all letters," and in favour of " a kind of profound introspection and self-recovery."—*The Will to Power*, ii., p. 337.

the 40,000 crowd shouting itself hoarse, and the solitary individual meditating a theme of high importance as he treads a lonely country lane. We are not setting up the contrast to bring discredit on the group and to exalt the individual; we simply ask the question as to whether the man in the crowd or the man in the country is getting the better form of recreation and rest; and whether, in addition, the man in the country is likely to produce something of greater intellectual worth. There can be but one answer. England in the past, prior to 1914, has had too many in the crowd; we want a few more of the thinking solitaries, and we shall have to grow them. Once in the crowd, always in the crowd. Ask such men to sit in a room with their own thoughts for company and you punish them with the utmost severity. They are afraid of themselves. It takes a Bunyan or a Raleigh to endure confinement, and even they had books and visitors to solace them. Besides, we are naturally gregarious (it is claimed), and without society we could not live. All very true, as the quaint Zimmermann [1] told us a hundred years ago, but as we have oscillated too far in the crowd direction, it is high time we began to curve the other way. The merit is not in solitude itself but in the leisure and silence it gives for mental enlargement, and for the more practical benefits of maturing plans for professional and commercial advancement. We have watched many types of business men in action, and have learned to respect the sort of man who knows how to rest and to profit by a few silent hours away from his fellows. They always beat the "bangers" eventually.

XI

But let us look at this matter nationally. The crowd is too much with us: getting, spending, we lay waste our powers. We can go to a meeting of a most deserving kind every night in the week: we have thousands of leagues, societies, guilds, clubs, centres and what not, the result being

---

[1] Zimmermann wrote a book on *Solitude considered with Respect to its Dangerous Influence upon Mind and Heart.* 1798.

that we are losing the inestimable benefits of our own firesides, or the more rigorous and apparently selfish solitude of our own four-walled study. We are obsessed with the social spirit. We must talk or we die. Now, over against this, we urge another plea : it is that if we talked less we should think more and to better purpose. These meetings and lectures are only half efficient in carrying out their allotted tasks ; not enough time is spent in digesting material and formulating right conclusions. Take, for instance, the various socio-logical societies. They do not appear to do much more than discuss themes in an academic manner ; and the men who are, so to speak, *making* sociology—Cabinet Ministers, for example—are seldom asked to contribute from their experience to the science of society. Stipendiary magistrates are learned in human nature because they are studying it every day, and yet what sociological society has ever had the audacity or the originality to canvass stipendiary magis-trates with a view to testing sociological theory by practical experience ?

Here is a question : " Are people more honest in the morning than they are in the later hours of the day ? " It is a question at once interesting and rather surprising, and we much doubt whether anyone but a stipendiary magistrate could answer it. But Mr Cecil Chapman of the Tower Bridge Court was able to do so. He tried a case where a man was alleged to have stolen some rings, and who, when in danger of capture, had thrown the rings into a crowd coming out of a music hall. Mr Chapman said in Court : " The crowd was so honest that out of nineteen or twenty rings scattered in the street only two were returned "; but to a Press repre-sentative he dived more deeply into the subject :

" It is not at all a question of drink ; with late hours a species of subtle change seems to come over people's char-acter. If I were to drop ten sovereigns in a frequented spot of London I should quite expect to receive back a number decreasing with the hour—eight, perhaps, in the forenoon, six later in the day, and so on till I wonder whether I would get two back at midnight."

ORIGINALITY IN THE FUTURE

That is sociological material which is too good to be lost, but unless a magistrate is persuaded to write his reminiscences, and to state his theories based on Court experience, such material dies with the man who created it. Hence our plea that the wastage of superfluous meetings should be stopped and that more solid results be obtained by individual and group investigations.

XII

We have had a surfeit of archæology and of the study of modern conditions : we want more prophecy. Here is a question in the immeasurable : How much more imagination has been spent in reconstructing the life of Rome and Athens than in forecasting the future of London ? No one can say. Athens and Rome have an undying interest for us, but London is imperative. It is here and now. We have to take part in it, pay its taxes, endure its fogs, preserve its art treasures, and ensure a healthy life for its inhabitants. And yet we are sure that the past of Athens and Rome has had, and still has, more imagination spent upon it than has been given to the future of London. It is another instance of the dominance of the sense of history. There are books galore that tell us of the Greeks and of the Romans ; only once in a while does some rather shy man venture forth from his study to paint a picture of the Metropolis a hundred years hence. Sir Aston Webb, in his address on "London of the Future" (20th January 1914), told his hearers that in A.D. 2014 there would be a salmon weir at London Bridge, that there were two great railway stations, one for the North and one for the South ; that the great roads out of London were 120 feet wide, with two divisions, one for slow-moving and the other for fast-moving traffic ; that a huge belt of green fields surrounded the London of to-day ; that there was a Ministry of Art, and that a score of other developments, real and ideal, had been compassed. We need not pause to discuss these, one by one ; the point is that originality in town-planning and in remodelling communal life can only come from the exercise of the constructive imagination.

ORIGINALITY

Of course there is nothing new in that contention : it is as old as the hills, but like most commonplaces it is overlooked because it *is* a commonplace. The town council is elected on a political basis—at any rate it is too often so elected. Will the time ever come when civic imagination will be a requisite in the mental outfit of a councillor or an alderman ? A group of such men would never allow the continued existence of that frightful anachronism called Covent Garden. It is a disgrace to the first city of the world. The original buildings became too small for the immense business that had to be transacted, so the market was allowed to slop over into the adjoining streets, which now until eleven A.M. are a picture of uncleanliness and disorder. It is no argument to say that we manage to rub along somehow ; there is no doubt we do ; but how much are we losing in other ways ? How do we *know* that the transit and sale of produce is as good as it can be and that the present arrangements could not be bettered ? It is the old English cry of "It will do"—the cry that comes from the native love of the rule of thumb. For greater efficiency, for the sake of dignity, for the saving of our national reputation in civic things, this eyesore should be blotted out and a new and satisfactory building set up worthy of the most densely populated of world cities.

XIII

If all progress is governed by the same laws then we may at any time expect to see a new outburst of intellectual activity. Periodic advances are easily traceable in the records of history, and they have generally originated in the transcendent ability of one individual or of a group ; indeed all Advance would appear to be on the basis of the plateau. On page 261 is a figure roughly representing the idea.

At A there is an upward and progressive movement ; X stands for the uniform level of a period in which there is no change of note ; B represents another outburst of originality, and Y for a further level of comparative mediocrity. Educational psychologists have observed this gradual ascent in the individual development of manual skill and mental ability [1] ; and mathematicians and physicists like Poincaré have noticed seeming discontinuities in the evolution of natural forces—progress has a kind of " leap " in it. " A physical system," we read, " is susceptible only of a finite number of distinct states ; it leaps from one of these states to the next without passing through a series of intermediate states." [2] We may not know the cause of this sudden leap, but it is not without analogies in human evolution. Variations announce themselves and we do not know how, except that the factors reside in the species itself. Very well : in

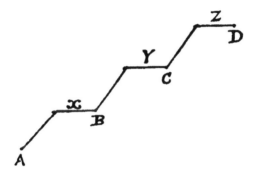

Nature there are sudden appearances which in some mysterious way have for a long time been in preparation and which quite suddenly burst upon us as *faits accomplis*. May there not be similar periods of hidden preparation in the mental life of peoples, times when inertia is more apparent than real ? If there be no such thing as slow and leisurely progress but first an ascent, then a plateau, then another ascent, are we not justified in cultivating a spirit of hopeful expectancy with regard to the immediate future ? The present age may be, probably is, the beginning of one of the periods, *A, B, C,* or *D.*

The answer to the question is affected by the personal equations of age, of education, and of experience, but every opinion must surely be affected by the thought : In what way shall we come out of the crucible of war ? We cannot expect

[1] Swift, *Mind in the Making*, p. 169.
[2] *Revue Scientifique* (24th February 1912).

to be the same people, governed by the same standards, controlled by the old values, however unchangeable human nature may be. Our character will have undergone a change, and a change in that respect means something of a mental revolution.[1] There will be first of all a new and long-continued impulse towards achievement. The spirit of the people will be conquest in the battles of peace—a fair fight, but still a real fight and no favour. For a decade we shall be more awake than we have been for centuries, and after the first hard period of readjustment to civil life has been completed, the new era, despite characteristic weaknesses, will begin to be. The originalities, or the changes which pass for originalities, will come first in economics, then in science and in education. Perhaps it will not be wise to expect very much until the new education shall have had its chance, but we need not be surprised if the older men who did not fight (as well as the younger men who did) join the youngest of all in a rebirth of the national spirit. Such forces cannot be measured, but their primary function is to liberate intellect. Many a man will aspire to-day who never hoped for much before. Scattered intelligence will get a focus. Drift will give place to destiny. Half-a-century of this endeavour should yield a harvest of new and wonderful results, not for their own sake but for the sake of our common life.

But even if this progress is not of a kind with a "leap" in it, there are discoveries which, though improbable in themselves, to many of us at any rate, are nevertheless not impossible, and not absurd as propositions for serious discussion. One is the scientific proof of a life after death ; another is the obtaining of satisfactory evidence that other planets are inhabited. Further, if communion with the dead should become incontrovertible, and if, moreover, the knowledge of the philosophy of another planet could be passed on to us, is it not clear that such an access of wealth to our spiritual

[1] " It is character and not intelligence that goes to the founding of societies, religions, and empires. Character it is that enables people to feel and act. They have never derived much advantage from too great a desire to reason and think."—Le Bon, *Psychology of Peoples*, p. 34.

nature would not only revolutionise our thinking but exercise a profound effect on our conduct ? In one short year we should make an advance equal to centuries under the regime of steady progression. The sages and mystics say we are not yet ready for these things. Perhaps not. We are hardly ready for universal telepathy; for if every man in business could read "the other fellow's" mind, be he buyer or seller, how could commerce continue ? And if in every drawing-room the women knew each other's thoughts to the very last "notion"—well, social life would collapse.

XIV

Leaders of thought, especially our professors, are in need of a better forward look. We have few university exponents of sociology compared with America, France, Germany, and other European countries, and those we have are as yet in the regions of analysis : their work is too recent to have reached a really constructive period. But chairs of philosophy and science have been established for centuries, and yet their holders are not notable, with few exceptions, for the manner in which they use their learning to build up the life of the future. The men of science are, indeed, much better than the philosophers, but both would be no worse for a little more enthusiasm. We do not mean that they should imitate the German professors, but that they should be more closely identified with the life of the people and with advance movements in general ; for no safe action can be carried out without sound knowledge, and we expect the university professor to supply this—not the impetus : *that* will always come from below. It is perhaps invidious to use names, and if we do so it must be understood as being without prejudice to other names unmentioned whose character and work we highly esteem. Professor Patrick Geddes has always appealed to us as possessing the right temperament and the right method for effecting a happy union of three things not often found together—namely, the scientific mind, the constructive imagination, and a genius for communication. We look upon his views on Cyprus as almost a model of thought at its best. In *The Contemporary Review* for June, 1897, he expressed his ideas on " Cyprus, Actual and Possible," and in connection with this article he said to an interviewer :

" ' I have been specially interested in the history of the Mediterranean lands and peoples—*e.g.* in the association of the decline of ancient Rome and of modern Spain and Turkey with the gradual deterioration of their soil.'

" ' In what way ? '

" ' Chiefly by the cutting down of trees, which has altered not only the soil, but even the climate, of the countries bordering on the Mediterranean. It is everybody's obvious interest to cut down trees, so for the sake of immediate gain the interest of the future is sacrificed. Under the great maritime civilisations, from the Phœnician to the Venetian, the country was recklessly stripped of its forests. The peasant, too, did it to make a clearing, the shepherd to find grass. Then came the torrential rains of every autumn and spring, the soil was washed away, and the slopes were completely denuded, so that now we find barren rock where once was fertile soil.'

" At this point the Professor showed me a number of very curious photographs of Cyprus, showing how by the destruction of forests the rocks have gradually been laid bare. The work of afforestation in Cyprus or the East generally will be, of course, a slow affair, but, so he says, a holy war, a war lasting over centuries, but one which, as it goes on, will bring back wealth, health, and happiness to the impoverished and degenerate Eastern races." [1]

And Professor Geddes thus began his work in the island. The philosophy of natural history formed the basis of a new principle of regeneration. How often do professorial thinkings end in such reasonable and useful originalities ?

XV

If we are to do our best for the Empire we must have some kind of organisation whereby the best men are put to the

[1] *British Weekly* (8th July 1897).

right kind of work, consistent, of course, with our native love
of liberty and of freedom of action. The future of original
thought in science, for instance, must no longer be left to
chance. We must organise. Organisation is of two kinds :
mechanical and directive. Good results are possible by the
former, but the latter yields a supply infinitely higher and
better. It does not make men into mere machines : it
avoids the evils of a rigid system, and it allows free play for
individuality. The State should discover its most promising
science students and set them to work on the problems that
urgently need solution for commercial and other reasons.
The rule of thumb is intolerable in a sphere where the
scientific method is like a divine commandment.

The State should also have a staff of psychologists who
can discern mental ability of an unusual kind and take advantage of it before schooldays are over. A schoolmaster
cannot always do this, nor can a psychologist, unless he has
trained himself to diagnose mental and moral character.
The need of such a staff is pathetic in its urgency. The
London County Council has appointed a psychologist to serve
its schools in an advisory capacity, but—strange comment
on our sense of values—he gives far more attention to the
feeble-minded than those who are highly talented. Are the
latter unworthy of any guidance, and why is it better for
the country to have a psychologist for the dullards and none
for the gifted ?

XVI

The modern business man, strange as it may seem, uses
his imagination more fully, and perhaps more successfully,
than would be conceded by the average critic. In America,
and in all new countries, this is particularly true : the constructive impulse is deep and ranges far. The outcome may
in part be novelty rather than originality, but when that de-
duction has been made there is a good margin of originality
left. A business man would admit the result but not the
method. He has a rather cheap way of depreciating any
kind of ability that is not business ability : he speaks of
"the newspaper chaps that write," and of "the B.Sc. analysts

who are never worth more than two quid a week." But changes are coming fast. He is already enamoured of the psychology of buying and selling, and does not object to the formal analysis of a proposition as his father did. His father was " guided by experience—and be damned to your philosophy." The son is different, and is growing still more different. He knows that in opening a new branch he must take a shop on the right side of the street. Which is the right side ? His instinct, confirmed by observation, will tell him that, but he is curious to go deeper down. He once read in a newspaper—he treasures these cuttings—that " it is a peculiar unexplainable psychological fact that there is a right and wrong side of the main thoroughfare in every big city and the Café Sorgon happened to hit the wrong side. The café had to be closed down in consequence." The old father would have said: "Bosh"; the son says: " I wonder ? " He thinks of Piccadilly and the Strand ; of Kingsway and Oxford Street. On which side do shops change hands the more frequently ? On which side of the Strand are to be found the most prosperous cafés, and why ? What is it that gives the northern side of Oxford Street a "pull" over the other side ? Does the success of one man cause traffic to move on his side, thus creating other successes near by ? or is there a helpful factor in the planning of other streets ? Why should a house agent believe in "lucky" streets ? These are interesting questions—not superficial or fanciful.

But the business man is not likely to lose himself in studying the deeper aspects of his affairs. The new spirit is practical as well as philosophical. The Designs and Industries Association, whether it lives long or dies early, is a good sign ; it shows what is going on mentally when an association of traders, manufacturers, designers, and consumers can be found to improve the quality of merchandise and of everything that is sold at a price with a view to profit. Not averse to machinery or the factory-made article, it is keen on better design and just as solicitous for better rewards for the workers. The intention is to create a wave of idealism that shall raise the status of all productions in regard to originality and beauty, and that shall bring a new zest and happiness into work. Ambitious? Yes; properly so. The scheme may never affect the huge factory with orders for 50,000 of this or that, to be shipped in a month's time; but it will begin with the smaller manufacturer, and gradually extend its influence until the larger demand will inevitably produce the larger supply.

The critic will say: "Are you going to do all this betterment work by means of factory regeneration?" No; by means of the individual. You do not obtain originality from a factory. If you ever by chance find a departure it will be easily traced to an individual. We met a friend one day to whom we put the question: "Have you read Wilson's *On Workmanship*?" He said: "No; there are so many Wilsons and there is nothing exciting in workmanship." We disagreed, and handed him a copy for perusal. He brought it back a week later, declaring it was a pamphlet that ought to be in the hands of every worker engaged in production, no matter what kind of material he handled. Mr Wilson is an idealist who believes that all the earlier and greater works of man were beautiful and that we have lost the tradition. "The first workers were the first thinkers," he says, "and because poet and worker, singer and shaper, seer and workman were often one and the same, their poetry was like etherealised sculpture or gem-work, their painting and sculpture like poetry materialised." He devotes many pages to the exemplification of these claims. He argues that beauty of expression or supreme workmanship is part of the cosmic process bound by the same laws as those which round the dewdrop and shape the crystal. "They are laws whose operations we cannot escape," declares the author. "We must create or perish; develop or disintegrate; shape, or be shapen from. Who lives, labours; who labours not, is dead, is as true of the simple organism as of the complex being." Do British workers feel they are influenced by such beliefs? We fear not. Nor are they blameable. The system must bear that responsibility. Until better life is made easier of attainment work will be a necessary nuisance, and only a comparatively small number of people may be expected to rise to the dignity of "creation." But the number will increase, slowly yet surely. And the Eastern spirit will in part be responsible for the change : we shall battle with the modern spirit of haste in the endeavour to secure sufficient repose of mind to conceive and produce art works in the sphere of industry.

XVII

We do not think that in these random guesses at the future we have been too hopeful, and it has been our endeavour to offer reasonable ground for such optimism as we have expressed. If the nations become possessed of new ideals, held vitally, then since thoughts are real forces, ruling the world, we can expect new manifestations of the individual mind ; for the conditions will favour original persons, of both sexes, despite the probable growth of the democratic spirit. Mr Kipling, in a most interesting adventure in constructive thought, has told us that in a little over two hundred years— to be exact, in A.D. 2150 [1]—we shall have so far advanced in scientific discoveries that civic life, the politics of the nations, and the government of continents, will have been codified on a universal basis. The Aerial Board of Control is the world's army and navy centralised, and it subjugates recalcitrant populations by using physical forces, especially unendurable light and noise. War, as such, has disappeared. It is an age of science, a little unromantic, the sort of scientific world where a prayerless man might drop on his knees and ask for a dose of the unexpected ; but still a world without stark evils, and one where suffering is reduced to a minimum. For ourselves we have imagined no such line of development, but we confidently believe in development, and that it will find its first and last impetus in the brain of the original thinker.

[1] *The London Magazine* (April, 1912).

SECTION VI

PRAXIS

SOME REFLECTIONS ON MENTAL ATTITUDES AND METHODS

I

To suppose that originality of thought can be made the subject of a curriculum is to suppose an impossibility. It is as if one attempted to teach personality itself—*i.e.* how the individualism of a remarkable intellect can be reproduced in another mind by a course of lessons under the guidance of a tutor. A man's literary style is as much a part of himself as the colour of his eyes or the manner of his walk; and in the same way his originality is his own—no one can take it from him. We can *imitate* it, but imitation is the very thing we wish to avoid. To be original is to be oneself, and although our originality may not be of much value, it is nevertheless *ours*. Such phrases as "The poet is born not made" have always seemed to us beside the mark. That some men are born with great gifts is undoubted, but, by this time, it is clear that those gifts are trained by experience, and that, in consequence, even the poet is *made* just as he himself is a *maker*.

This effort to establish genius as something outside mental laws, and as a quality that descends from God fully wrought and ready for use, is a psychological superstition. So far from being lawless, genius is the law of mind in the very perfection of its fulfilment. Therefore the question we have now to answer is not: How may originality be taught? but: What are the conditions of life, mental and physical, which will enable a man to produce the originality that is in him, be it distinctive, or otherwise?

It is not a puerile question: it is, on the contrary, one of the utmost importance both to the individual and to the nation. Much intellectual wealth has been lost to the world because we have made no effort to develop it—no effort, that is, of a truly scientific character. Professor Giddings has produced some remarkable figures showing the small number of distinguished men and women during the last twenty-two centuries. To him the word *distinguished* applies to those "who are of such intellectual ability and of such developed social nature that they succeed in making great contributions to human well-being." He estimates that 45,000,000,000 people lived and died between the age of Pericles and A.D. 1870. How many of these were distinguished? He answers: "1 in every 450,000"; adding that, "in these startling figures there is a practical lesson of the greatest importance. In nothing whatever can a nation so ill afford to be wasteful as in her men and women who combine genius with highly developed social nature. What, then, shall we say of those governments that in times past have deliberately destroyed such elements in the population by death, imprisonment and other forms of persecution on account of differences in religion and political belief?"[1]

II

For ourselves we do not apprehend losses in the future on the same grounds as in the past; nor do we think true genius is ever likely to be wholly obscured. We fear the loss not only of a higher average because we are content with a lower average, but of the highly talented, and of the whole genius whom our neglect condemns to be a half genius. We have a pitiful faith in the notion that ability will in every case announce itself and make a place for itself; we believe that we have no need to seek for it, to nurture it, and to see that it gets a just reward. The real truth is that twenty-five per cent. of our national inventiveness in every sphere—literary, artistic, and commercial—escapes us completely; hence a systematic plan to discover it and put it to national service is a duty that ought to be as pleasant as it should be

[1] *Elements of Sociology*, pp. 114-116.

successful. We cannot hope in these pages to do more than state the need for such a programme, although we shall try to outline some of those more subtle conditions of original thinking with which education has no time to concern itself. We may have to suffer a few gibes in the attempt, but, after all, *training* is a word that has higher connotations than it had in the last and some preceding centuries. We are going back to the earlier notion of which Professor Butcher speaks, when he remarks that "the Greek poets themselves seem to have thought of their own aptitude more as the result of trained skill than of abnormal inspiration. It is remarkable how the word σοφία, ' wisdom,' ' skill,' is selected by them to denote the poetic gift where we should be disposed to speak of genius." [1] True, and who can doubt that there is a σοφία of mind to which every man can attain, and by which he will achieve—it may not be superlative ends, but—ends that otherwise he would never have accomplished, due to ignorance, lack of confidence, or of hope ?

III

There are two factors, physical and mental, and they constitute a partnership. As to which is the senior partner there may be some doubt. Destroy the body and the mind is also destroyed. There is no mental life without physical life, from which we might suppose that the body is the chief partner in the combination. And yet the mind exerts the real control, and it can wield unusual power even in lives where the physical element is weak. That is a commonplace of our experience. But perhaps the truth about the senior partnership is not important ; at any rate, a more pertinent question is this : Can one partner increase his powers at the expense of the other ? For instance, does the severe training of an athlete prejudice the development of his mental ability ? We are compelled to reply in the affirmative. Observations carried out for a number of years seem to prove conclusively that the Spartan regime of physical discipline uses up the reserve energy that would otherwise be available

[1] *Harvard Lectures on Greek Subjects*, p. 129.

for mental culture. A reserve cannot be used twice, but a period of rest, and of abstinence from great exertion, will create a new reserve that may be used for intellectual advancement. Nevertheless the general law still holds: that super-excellence in athletics prevents the athlete from developing his mind to the full *at the same time.*[1] Violent exercise for students is thus a serious mistake in hygiene; recreative pursuits should be thorough but not exhausting. The oxygenating of the blood is of deeper import than the strengthening of muscle; the tense action of very vigorous and long-continued exertions uses up the reserve force needed for physical endurance during mental labours. Consonant with the general position we have taken up is the finding of Sir William R. Nicoll, a close observer of student life. He remarks that "it has been said very truly that vitality is hardly compatible with the student life. The literary man soon discovers that if he is to do anything with his profession he must observe a very strict routine. I have noticed that men who are very vital in their writings are generally very quiet in company, slow to speak, and uninteresting when they do speak. Their wit seems to lie like fire in a flint and to need a strong evocation." Speaking of Hazlitt, who was a vital writer but whose physical vitality was dry and scant, Sir William says that his "was perhaps a case where there was plenty of vitality, but it went in one channel, and it needed times of silence, times of repose, in order to renew itself."[2]

[1] We were interested to find a similar view in Mr W. R. Greg's *Enigmas of Life*. "No one of the three elements of our composite being can reach . . . fullest development except at the expense of the others. . . . Let the practised student or the trained literary man examine himself as to the times and conditions in which he finds himself capable of the highest flight, or the most severe and sustained toil. Is it when the *animal* part of him is in the healthiest and most natural condition . . . when limbs are wearied with salutary exercise ? . . . On the contrary . . . he feels less capable than usual of concentrated thought, less disposed for patient and prolonged research, more ready to enjoy, less ready to contemplate and to soar."[1] James Hinton lost his abnormal memory, as a youth, after an ultra-strenuous game of cricket.

[2] *The British Weekly* (12th July 1906).

MENTAL ATTITUDES AND METHODS

The attention given to physical culture in recent years is so good a policy that it seems impertinent if not dangerous to criticise it ; and yet we are bound to say that it has too often overstepped the mark, ending in muscle development, in speed efforts, and weight lifting. But along with excess—that is, excess in cases where special aims were not entertained—there has been a more rational movement in favour of *health* culture ; and although scores of people have been injudicious in the severity they have inflicted on themselves, an equal number have received nothing but good. The ideal is to secure enough exercise to keep every organ in a healthy working condition, and to prevent superfluous weight. Thus equipped on the physical side a man may justly expect his brain to give the best of which it is capable.

IV

But suppose that instead of becoming an athlete a man devotes all his leisure to the building of his brain, will such a course adversely affect his physique ? Does it not follow that if physical culture, pursued with the utmost ardour, results in lowering mental power, mental culture, pursued with the same ardour, will end in lowering physical power ? In one sense it does, and over-study has been known not only to destroy health but to destroy the mind itself. And yet it is also true that we may develop mental ability, to the limits of which we are capable, without injury to health, provided we take rational exercise, and conform to physical laws. Indeed, the all-round vitality of the brain worker has become a common experience ; and if men and women were to continue their education systematically, as opportunity served, up to sixty, or even over that age, they would find that mental industry increased the chances of prolonged good health, as well as developed mind-power more fully.[1] The notion that use enfeebles or destroys the power used has

[1] The mental side is interestingly set out in an article by Mr Archibald Marshall (*Daily Mail*, 4th September 1913), called "Learning by Heart at Forty." How many men ever attempt such a feat ?

been proved to be a delusion. Use develops and enlarges. It is *disuse* that brings decay and death, and there is evidence to show that the reflex influence of intellectual activity on the body is not only promotive of the best interests of the partnership, but tends to lengthen the term of their joint action. [1]

But every man should have his physique valued in relation to any work he has to do. In this respect we are sadly unscientific, except in the military sphere and in matters of insurance. John Stuart Mill's scheme for a science of ethology does not appear to have been carried out, although a society for its discussion is, or was, in existence ; as for a psychography—there is no such thing. And yet we are in absolute need of both : for in business and the professions there are literally thousands of misfits, all of which could have been prevented had we possessed a means of gauging physical and mental powers in relation to occupations. America makes a better showing.[2] Thayer, in his *Life of Garfield*, says that the President-to-be, when a youth, went to a doctor and requested that probably surprised medico to give him an estimate of his physical and mental possibilities. The doctor complied, and Garfield left the consulting-room to work out his destiny with confidence. " Very American," the reader chuckles. Yes ; but very sensible, provided a medical man can be found who has the requisite knowledge and sympathy. How many youths of eighteen to twenty-five can render a fair statement of what they can do mentally, and endure physically ? How many *know* themselves as to their limits and possibilities ? Only

[1] " Use is the great preservative, not destroyer, of strength ; and the use of the brain protects and develops the nerve power of which it is the reservoir, and on which, in part, longevity depends. The man who has used his brain all his life, say for six hours a day, has in fact trained his nerve power, and placed it beyond the reach of early decay, or that kind of feebleness which makes so many apparently healthy men succumb so readily to attacks of disease."
—*Spectator* (15th April 1893)—article on " The Effect of Culture on Vitality."

[2] We refer to the work of the Boston Vocation Bureau, and Prof. Hollingworth's *Vocational Psychology*.

a small number. The great majority drift ; they take chance as it comes. At thirty or thirty-five reflection shows that some of the best years of life have been lived on a rule of thumb method in regard to both mind and body. " If I had only known what I know now "—*that* is the common phrase of disillusionment. As early as possible, therefore, men and women should know themselves—that is, they ought to understand their powers and use them in those directions where the best work can be accomplished.[1] In the absence of expert guides we have to follow methods of our own devising, poor and inadequate though they may be. By-and-by the vocation professor will arrive, and, equipped with a full knowledge of mind and body, he will save the world from much wasted and misspent effort. His popularity will be instantaneous—the vogue of the phrenologist is but a strong testimony to the felt need for professional advice on the direction of ability. Meanwhile we have to use the *Questionnaire* which, as the name implies, is a series of questions so formulated and stated that even to the reader himself they are almost self-revealing.[2] It is not necessary to discuss theories—like those of Dr Thooris—that physiologic-ally we are by temperament cerebral, muscular, respiratory, or digestive, although there is a good deal to be said in favour of the new classification. All that we need do is to become acquainted with physiology and the laws of health, then learn from experience what are our mental limitations and advan-tages—that is, learn these things properly and not leave them to chance.

V

For instance, can you think better, in every sense, when

---

[1] Individual differences in mental constitution are now receiving some attention, but as yet there are few results of service to the public. Prof. E. B. Titchener says that " the creation of a scientific psychology of these differences is, in my opinion, one of the principal achievements of the experimental method."—*Experimental Psy-chology of the Thought Processes*, p. 7. But it is one thing to trace the differences ; another thing to apply them.

[2] A copy of this *Questionnaire* will be sent on application to the publishers of this book.

recumbent, when sitting in an easy-chair, or when walking ? We have asked many a student that question, and only four were ready with an instant reply. A wise man makes experiments and acts accordingly. Dr Russel Wallace was not a sound sleeper, but he did not allow himself to be dominated by occasional insomnia until it became frequent ; some people become sleepless by auto-suggestion. He thought out and planned some new work; indeed he found the lying down position helpful to reflection.[1] His son says that " he often told us with keen delight of some new idea or fresh argument which had occurred to him during those waking hours."[2] Le Vasseur, on a visit to Descartes, found the philosopher in bed at eleven in the morning, raising himself at intervals to write and then lying back to meditate.[3] Business men, more accustomed to action, perhaps, find a lonely country lane full of the right stimulus, or a sharp walk, instead of the usual drive to the city.

Again, does not Leffingwell's *Influence of the Seasons on Conduct* suggest that those same seasons must also influence brain—else how could they influence conduct ? " I work more easily when the barometer is high than when it is low," said Goethe to Eckermann. Perhaps genius is more sensitive to atmospheric influences than the average intellect, but brain workers who have to work whether the season is helpful or not are better prepared to combat the heaviness of a muggy day if they have by experience discovered sound means of circumventing physical depression. Then there is the subject of fatigue, so fully investigated by Mosso[4] : Do we

---

[1] Thackeray's amanuensis says : " He was sometimes in doubt and difficulty as to whether he should commence operations sitting, or standing, or walking about or lying down."—E. T. Mason, *Personal Traits of British Authors*, p. 292.

[2] *Letters and Reminiscences*, vol. ii., p. 121.

[3] *Descartes*. By J. P. Mahaffy.

[4] An investigation conducted by Prof. E. G. Martin, of Cambridge (Mass.) had results to which men who persist in working on Sundays should take heed. Experiments conducted on nine students showed that " from Monday to Saturday there was a tendency for the nervous tone of the subjects to diminish progressively. There were, of course, occasional departures from this tendency, but, on the whole, the

know what fatigues us more than anything else, and why ? Have we traced the effect of music on thought, and how far sounds in general unconsciously, as well as consciously, affect our concentration ? These and other matters are being scientifically investigated in the interests of manual labour, but we do not appear to investigate them for ourselves. We use artificial light, and yet we have no exact knowledge of the influence of light on the thinking process, or why it is that darkness often brings with it a spirit of creativeness. Is there *no* explanation of twilight as the mood for poetising, for fancies, for those apprehensive glimpses of worlds far off ? It may be said that the knowledge of the conditions favourable to the best results comes to us from experience without our seeking it. Acquaintance with a few conditions no doubt comes in this way, but some of the most serviceable escape us : we have not formed the habit of observing, classifying, and summarising our mental efforts and their outcome.

VI

The immense importance of the physical element in the life of thought is expressed by Professor Fraser Harris, who traces most mental excellencies to the quality of the nervous system, and that quality, of course, is partly an inheritance and partly a training. "We shall increasingly recognise," he says, "that breeding, fineness of temper and amenability to the influences of culture, are as much the outcome of neural molecular dispositions as they are the responses to appropriate surroundings. Style in all its individuality and inimitableness, whether that of the painter, the poet, the

downward trend was unmistakable. Between Saturday and Monday on the other hand (rest period) the nervous state showed marked improvement. . . . A single night's rest did not suffice to prevent the nervous tone from showing a decline, the longer interval of Sunday not only arrested the decline but restored the nervous system to its normal condition."—"The Day of Rest in Nature and Human Nature," in the *Bibliotheca Sacra* (April, 1916). We can now understand why so many business men, by instinct, or experience, or both, arrange their important interviews on Mondays.

preacher, the musician, the actor, or the orator, is inherent in their nervous systems, and is before and beyond the teacher's art." [1] We may demur a little to the small place allowed for the effect of training, and still more to the large place given to inheritance—a sort of nerve fatalism—but the view is otherwise sound : and every man should regard his physical education and its relation to his mental efficiency as part of his religion. Professor J. L. Myres has outlined a scheme for a "Bureau of Biometry," [2] excellent in itself, still more excellent in its spirit of adapting means to ends. One of these days man-measurement, physical and mental, will come into being.

VII

The inner problem of knowledge may be insoluble, but there is no difficulty in understanding how knowledge itself comes to us : it arrives by way of the senses, chiefly through sight and hearing, and any discussion of ways and means of enlightenment must therefore concern *sensibility*. The word itself need not present a difficulty. It means practically the same thing as sensitiveness ; a neuralgic area, we say, is sensitive to the touch—*i.e.* it has great sensibility, responsiveness to external pressure, however light. In the mental sphere this sensibility means a peculiar susceptibility to impressions : a glorious sunset is not merely something we have seen—it becomes a potent memory ; and the dawn seen from a mountain-top is changed into an inspiration. Suffering is not merely a picture of want or the spectacle of a pain-ravaged body—it is a message from the gods. To be deeply affected by phenomena of all kinds means that consciousness is sensitive—like a photographic plate. To be lacking in sensibility is to miss the true inwardness of such things as we experience ; we are mentally dull with the dullness that can see the moon reflected in the lake without any other emotion than that of curiosity—it "dodders" : the dullness that can witness the pathos of struggle with no more

[1] *Nerves.*
[2] *Oxford and Cambridge Review* (June, 1907).

philosophy than "that is how the world wags"; or is only responsive to the kind of music that pleasantly jangles the nerves.

We are brought back to the previous standpoint—namely, that the deciding factor is the range of consciousness; and this is nowhere more marked than in the range of sensibility. All our inquiries up to the present have proved the fundamental importance of feeling; genius, in all that is creative as distinct from that which is discovery, has always had an emotional, an affective basis. The reason is not far to seek. As Professor Jastrow says, quaintly and truthfully: "Feeling is older than knowing."[1] When we examine life our first impulse is not to *reason* about it; we value it according to its effect on us. Attraction and repulsion are earlier facts than logic, and all attempts to found a system of living, or a religion, on Reason (with a capital R) have been failures, and always will be. Feeling is fundamental, not sinfully, as many rationalists would have us think, but rightfully; it is a law of human nature. Syllogisms are mental rules to guide our steps through dark and uncertain places, but beyond this they tell us nothing about those places; they are the instruments of the survey, not the promised land itself.[2] Education has often failed because it taught the use of instruments but said little about the more important things. Perhaps we expected too much of the pedagogue, forgetting that he had little time for the many tasks which a system imposed upon him; but however that may be, the

[1] *The Subconscious*, p. 26. This primary nature of Feeling, several times referred to in our pages, has an interesting illustration in Bergson's *The Meaning of the War* (p. 17). "*Comprendre et ne pas s'indigner*: this has been said to be the last word of philosophy. I believe none of it; and, had I to choose, I should much prefer, when in presence of crime, to give my indignation rein and not to understand."

[2] "It comes, therefore, to this, that if we are to think fluently and harmoniously upon any subject into which change enters (and there is no conceivable subject into which it does not) we must begin by flying in the face of every rule that professors of the art of thinking have drawn up for our instruction."—Samuel Butler, *Luck or Cunning*, p. 30.

training of the emotions has been left to the Churches, to poets, and to reformers. In good hands ? Yes, so far ; but chance has ruled here as elsewhere, or if not, the life of feeling—we use the words feeling and emotion synonymously for the moment—has been warped by connecting it with dogmas that can no longer be defended.

VIII

We will suppose that the importance of sensibility has now been understood and that a desire has been aroused to become alert to the possibilities of finer impressions than have heretofore been realised. What is the first danger ? That sensibility will be confused with observation. It is possible to see much and to remember it, and yet have no insight, no vision, no enlargement of soul. The aim is not to amass information so as to write a guide-book to existence : that would be useful, no doubt, as organised knowledge always is, but it would not be individual ; it would be stored material, not eyesight.[1] What we need may be expressed in three words : wonder, admiration, and rapture. These are the things we cannot teach, but they are primary mental conditions of all original thought, because such thought has its commencement in feeling. Leonardo da Vinci, one of the six great intellects the world has produced, often broke out into apostrophe, but if we think this came *after* his achievements and not before them, we have drawn a wrong conclusion. When he exclaimed : " O wonderful, O stupendous Necessity, thou by thy law constrainest all effects to issue from their causes in the briefest possible way," [2] the wonder

---

[1] We are so far from decrying the need of keen observation that we deplore the lack of it. Prof. James Ward has well said that " As a first stage towards a well-ordered mind it is desirable to secure as vivid and as varied an experience as possible of the facts on which our minds are to be exercised." He refers also to " the faintness and unimpressiveness of ideas that have not been derived direct from things."—" Mental Culture," in *Essays, Mock Essays and Character Sketches* (p. 91).

[2] *Thoughts of Leonardo.* By E. M'Curdy. Speaking of the tendency of the subconscious to act according to æsthetic principles—

did not begin with the revelation; it was the primary cause of it. If that claim should need further support let us go back to Aristotle, who declared that "Wonder is the first cause of philosophy,"[1]—in fact, the spirit of wonder gave Greek thought its initial impetus. Goethe realised the truth when he affirmed that "he who does not begin with wonder and admiration will never find his way into the Holy of Holies." Is this the spirit in which the intellectuals of to-day approach the mysteries of existence? In a few cases it is, but with the majority the spirit of wonder has gone out of fashion. It is too simple, too childlike, too yielding. So they go to the other extreme, and we get the spirit of *antagonism*. But wherever we see it at work it never satisfies us. The men who mouth its paradoxes or scribe its spitefulnesses are palpably missing the mark. Their attitude suggests artificiality—a lack of the human touch—they are *poseurs*.

IX

To measure the possible range of consciousness, calculate the degree of its spirit of wonder. If the degree is low the range will be circumscribed; if it be high, then self will not be prominent for it will be merged in wonder. Need we be surprised that genius is often so impractical and so other-worldly? Concentration in the form of absent-mindedness only means that self-consciousness has been lost in the consciousness of phenomena. This is what Türck calls disinterestedness. "The genius," he says, "is distinguished from the ordinary average man only by being permanently and intensively in this state of disinterested absorption, whereas the average man is able only transiently and usually for some special reason, so far to forget himself and his earthly needs as to be carried away by contemplation, by hearing,

and the tendency does exist—Poincaré says: " It is this special æsthetic sensibility that plays the part of the delicate sieve of which I spoke above, and this makes it sufficiently clear why the man who has it not will never be a real discoverer."—*Science and Method*, p. 61.

[1] *Metaphysics*, I.

or by imaginative impressions." [1]   It is not an absorption
due to fear, or anxiety, but to admiration.   That is another
important word in regard to sensibility.   Maeterlinck has
it that "if we take care not to make our admiration subordinate to so many circumstances of place or of origin we
shall not so often miss the chance of unclosing our eyes to the
wonder of things, and nothing is more beneficial than so to
unclose them."   Besides, it is a mental law that we tend to
become like that which we admire ; at any rate the admired
object exercises a shaping influence upon us : the beholding
of the transfigured is itself transfiguring.   Hence the feeling
of rapture which is the finale of all great sensibility.   Have
not our moralists missed a fine opportunity here—missed it
because they have discussed solely the theory of right and
wrong, thus giving little attention to the impulse towards
ecstasy ?   The devout Christian, the hard drinker, the
sensualist, the miser, and a score of others are all seeking the
moment of rapture ; so are the inventors, the men of science,
and the reformers.   It is a different kind of rapture in each
case, but in another sense it is the same ; the aim is an
elevation of feeling accompanied by warmth and illumination.   The elevation may come when a few drops of alcohol
pass the lips and tingle the nerves ; or when the sordid
spirit is cheered by the addition of another fifty pounds to
an already exaggerated income ; or it may come when after
years of effort the glory of a discovery reveals itself to a
hard-working scientist, or when the mystic, leaving the earth
behind him, realises his first experience of the Eternal.
Sensibility !   Yes, it is fundamental.   Jastrow, who has dug
deeply into the subject, affirms confidently that "first, last
and throughout . . . sensibility makes the man." [2]

[1] *The Man of Genius*, p. 12.   Türck bases much of his contention
on the following deliverance of Schopenhauer : "*Genius* is simply
the completest *objectivity*, *i.e.* the objective tendency of the mind,
as opposed to the subjective, which is directed to one's own self—
in other words to the selfish will."
[2] *Qualities of Men*, p. 142.

MENTAL ATTITUDES AND METHODS

X

Herein lies one of the secrets of Walter Pater. Nothing which has ever interested living men and women—he said—can wholly lose its vitality. He was a man of books and a recluse, but also a man of rare and fine sensitiveness; indeed the stimulus of his art criticism lay in his power to express and elaborate "all those vivid, human intimations, vague half reminiscences, or visionary historic administrations which with most of us form the ground of our deepest pleasures, but which in most cases can never become articulate." [1] But if we recall Pater's own words from the famous "Conclusion" about which he once had doubts as to its possible dangers,[2] we shall see his mind in its purpose and operation alike; not challenge, not antagonism, but appreciation, valuation, the evocation of the greatness that lies in simple things, especially the overlooked and forgotten things. To some he was a Hellene, to others he was half Hellene and half Hebrew,[3] but to-day Arnold's terms have lost much of their meaning. And, after all, why should we attach labels to our minds? Classifications of mental outlook are more hopeless than any other classifications. Once we were either Platonists or Aristotelians; nowadays we are neither, despite Coleridge's assertion that we must be either one or

[1] *Walter Pater*. By Ferris Greenslet, p. 52.

[2] " Every moment," he says, " some form grows perfect in hand or face ; some tone on the hills or the sea is choicer than the rest ; some mood of passion or insight or intellectual excitement is irresistibly real and attractive to us—for the moment only. Not the fruit of experience, but experience itself is the end. A counted number of pulses only is given to us of a variegated dramatic life. How may we see in them all that is to be seen in them by the finest senses ? How shall we pass most swiftly from point to point, and be present always at the focus where the greatest number of vital forces unite in their finest energy ? To burn always with this hard, gem-like flame, to maintain this ecstasy, is success in life."—*The Renaissance*, p. 239.

[3] Prof. T. G. Tucker gives an illuminating yet popular account of the two standpoints in his chapter on " Hebraism and Hellenism." See *Platform Monologues*, p. 68. Melbourne.

the other.[1] Once we were Kantians or Hegelians ; then we were Neo-This and Neo-That. We became Pragmatists and Anti-Pragmatists, and as to the future it doth not yet appear what we shall be. But we do need a larger number of men and women who decline to be labelled, not because a label is wrong—it is not—but because to attach oneself to a school of thought has a narrowing and restrictive influence.

We are reminded of the queer intellectual straits in which theologians of all countries found themselves during the Great War, and of the strained defence which Professor Muirhead had to offer when, as a Hegelian and a Briton, he tried to show that Prussia and Hegel were very different things.[2] We want less of the dogmatic spirit and more of the attitude of Sir Thomas Browne when he said : "I am of a constitution so general that it consorts and sympathiseth with all things." Our sensibilities have then a chance of complete activity, and we are not called upon to defend a position (which secretly we feel to be weak) because we have identified ourselves with a people or a society, and must perforce fight for the system that is involved.

XI

Moods, as mental phenomena, have not received the attention which their importance demands. A mood is that which gives temperature and direction to consciousness. Usually it has a physical origin—witness the irritability that comes with certain forms of nervous disorder ; but essentially a mood is a thing of the mind—it may be pleasurable or otherwise ; it may be creative or stagnant. To know the secret

---

[1] The passage in his *Table Talk* (p. 102) says: "Every man is born an Aristotelian or a Platonist. I do not think it possible that anyone born an Aristotelian can become a Platonist and I am sure no born Platonist can ever change into an Aristotelian. They are the two classes of men, beside which it is next to impossible to conceive a third. The one considers reason a quality or attribute ; the other considers it a power."

[2] *German Philosophy in Relation to the War.*

of one's best moods is to know the best of which we are capable; to have no moods at all—of an elevating kind—means a serious intellectual loss; it shows that consciousness is being restricted in its range of activity.

The great enemy is the haste of modern life. Haste is quite natural in itself. It is our effort to keep pace with the rapid development of thought and of material progress. But what a price we pay for that effort. We seldom discover ourselves in quiet meditation because we so seldom give the factors a chance to form a mood.[1] We are " in action " all the time — money-making, pleasure-seeking, recreating, working. And yet it is often when we are temporarily out of action—walking by the stream or on the mountain, or talking in the half light, that the newest and best thoughts " come."

Art, music, rhythm—these will surely find a place in our feeling-consciousness ? We say *surely* because we are afraid some people see the dangers of æstheticism and have no eye for its great opportunities. They say that decadence always overtakes the artistic spirit more quickly than it does in any other sphere of emotional life—which is not a true statement; besides, what of ancient and modern *Agapemones* —and why do society and the Churches tolerate the community at Spaxton ? As we shall show, every idealist impulse needs balance, the σωφροσύνη of the Greeks as applied to more mundane things, but we cannot afford to dispense with impulses on that account. Plato, in that well-known passage in the *Republic*, says : " Is not this the reason, Glaucon, why musical training is so powerful, because rhythm and harmony find their way into the secret places of the soul ? " He is referring, of course, to the education of the young as affected

---

[1] Prof. G. T. W. Patrick, of the University of Iowa, who has given much attention to the subject of relaxation, says that all civilisations need a more restful policy—*e.g.* more outdoor life, more walking, and less riding, the individualising of sport and play, more holidays and festivals, less reading, more tranquil music, more art, and more religion. The noteworthy feature of this pronouncement is that he is not thinking of promoting the higher mental activities, but of conserving the health of the community. See *The Psychology of Relaxation*, p. 258.

by beautiful surroundings, especially education considered as movement or action.

Remembering what the Greeks meant by music,[1] one can hardly realise the objections which have been urged against Plato's doctrine by Adam Smith and many others. It may be that æsthetic cannot nowadays be a prominent feature in the school curriculum, but it ought to be a prominent feature in the life of the adult. Before the days of huge factories, with their ear-splitting noise of machinery, it was possible to use rhythm and song as an accompaniment of labour—perhaps in a rather utilitarian sense—but modern work has become too monotonous and too mechanical for song. The man at the office desk has no illusions about his duties; even when he is well paid those duties are a drudgery unless he is working to achieve an ambition, in which case the music arises from a knowledge of the fact that some day his friends will hail him with *See the Conquering Hero Comes.*

XII

But how can the æsthetic spirit be brought into the life of men and women of sound health and mental ability, even though their circumstances are not propitious? It is confessedly a difficult question to answer, although Goethe attempted it. "Every day," he said, "we should hear at least one little song, read one good poem, see one exquisite picture, and, if possible, speak a few sensible words."[2] There is nothing essentially impracticable in such a programme, despite the pessimism of the critics who claim that twenty-three hours of drudgery and sleep are more than a match for

[1] " But what the ancients called *music* in the wider sense must be held to include a knowledge and recitation of good poetry as proper training in that figured dancing which was the most usual service of the gods. Indeed, a good musical education in Greece, much in contrast to ours, included every graceful æsthetical and intellectual accomplishment." — *Old Greek Education*, p. 41. By J. P. Mahaffy, M.A.

[2] Darwin said : " If I had to live my life over again I would have made a rule to read some poetry and listen to some music at least once every week."—*Life and Letters*, p. 100.

one hour of idealism. It needs but a small outlay to possess the best poems the world knows, and to have good copies of the greatest pictures ; as for song and sensible remarks, the one is hardly ever quite out of our reach, and the other . . . we do not think it is unattainable when we have swallowed Goethe's cynicism. At any rate some such scheme—the practical piety of æstheticism shall we call it ?—is both possible and necessary if the finer forces of the mind are to reach their highest standard [1]—that is, the highest of which the individual is capable.

We have studied closely what may be called the mentality of uneducated men who have nevertheless obtained positions of importance in the world. Looked down upon by the scholar as ignorant, their success, whatever it is, has been explained by luck or sheer physical energy. This is the usual and superficial view. But is it not true that the men who have not filled their minds with facts and thoughts gathered from books have given their intellects a chance to live, provided, of course, they have any intellect at all ? To our surprise the uneducated man who, in his talk, made many slips in grammar and could never spell the word psychology, knew some of the deeper truths of the mind that do not make much show in our text-books.

But because they have used their knowledge commercially we have denied them the possession of it, alleging that their success was due to the whim of chance. It is not. They have gauged the taste of the public partly by the dry facts of buying and selling prices but more by a sense that comes close to intuition. " I had a feeling the public would come back to this sort of goods," they would say, if you pinned them down by close questions. They have no system by

[1] " Few things are more striking in adult life than the number of persons who have no means of artistic expression or appreciation at all ; who are driven for relaxation to futile pursuits such as card-playing, and who, as their higher feelings atrophy, become, in success, fonder of their food and drink and possessed of a morbid craving for rapid motion ; or, in failure, gloomy, listless and irritable."— *Studies in Education*. By M. W. Keatinge, M.A., chapter on " Education and Æsthetic," p. 103.

means of which they decide when to follow such feelings and when not—wherein they are wise.

XIII

It will have been noticed that up to the present we have dealt with various aspects of the emotional life—*i.e.* sensibility, wonder, admiration, rapture, and moods. A hint was thrown out that the emotional life needs a stabiliser ; we find it in *balance*. This is partly a gift, partly an acquisition. In his interesting chapter on "Education," Professor Campagnac tells us the difference between good and bad rhythms. "In both we are to recognise the action and reaction of freedom and of control ; but in the good, control and freedom are kindred from the first, and time and experience discover more and more fully the intimacy of their relation ; whereas in the bad, control is mere necessity and freedom mere licentiousness." [1] Balance, then, must be good rhythm—a kind of gyrometer that silently and inevitably restores a movement that has been lost from the centre. The notion is primarily ethical, and the power, as just intimated, is partly inborn and partly the outcome of experience ; there is a tendency to seek compensations. Much of the eccentricity of genius is due to defective rhythms. Rousseau literally wallowed in feelings of all kind, but had a penchant for tears—or he said he had ; De Musset lived for rapture, and many a man has followed in his steps, to reap the same reward. Probably all of us would like to build charming chalets on the Mount of Transfiguration and live in ecstasy ; but if we did our final destiny would be the asylum. We need drudgery as a balance, not merely in a moral sense but as a mental adjustment. To come down from the Mount and pull a long face as we scan the demands of the Surveyor of Taxes is excellent hygiene. To leave our books and sit on the magistrates' bench is to have a shock that brings strength. Of Machiavelli, Lord Morley says : "Like Bacon and some others who have written the shrewdest things on human conduct and the arts of success, he

[1] *Converging Paths*, p. 84.

made a sorry mess of his own chances and gifts."[1] Bacon lived the life of thought too ardently; Machiavelli had educated himself too freely away from principles—both had lost that fine balance which is so difficult to hold when men occupy positions of leadership. All moral errors, indeed, are primarily a loss of balance; and all intellectual limitations that are not congenital spring from the same cause. We have known men who have resolved to develop what they called their will-power, or their " minds "—perhaps their æsthetic sense. In one instance Will became a Deity; force was worshipped for its own sake, and as a consequence the man's common-sense sank to a minimum. He was a Boanerges in doing anything he undertook to do, but then he never knew the difference between what was a good thing and a bad thing. He was unbalanced—like every other man who has been devoted exclusively to one cult. The little crowd who indulge the artistic temperament never arrive ; they are too narrow in life, too disdainful of average things, seeking beauty and originality in the artificially new and in that alone.

XIV

Will-worship crops up in unexpected quarters. Mr Clutton Brock, in a fine essay on Progress in Art,[2] suggests that as all progress is due to the exercise of the human will in a right direction, therefore progress in art will come about by that agency. But the Will, apart from elevated feeling and disciplined thought, is merely blind energy. Why should we split up the forces of intelligence as if one alone could effect great changes ? Even granting that the power of action is final, and that without it nothing would be accomplished, there is not sufficient justification for the isolating of Will as a Thing-in-itself. Mr Brock himself admits that " no man can make a scientific discovery by the pure exercise of his will. It jumps into one mind and not into another just like an artistic inspiration." Surely, then, there is less chance of progress in art by Will ? The fact is our

[1] *Machiavelli*, p. 15.
[2] In Marvin's *Progress and History*.

new developments of all kinds depend less on Will than on *Illumination*; and this in turn depends far more on sensibility than on the motive tendencies.

XV

The more subtle conditions which favour illumination have already been hinted at, and we may now suggest one or two considerations of a more obvious but still important character. Will it be forgiven us if we use a worn phrase and insist on the right environment as a *sine qua non* of mental development in all its forms ? However individual we are, we can do little until we come in contact with the surroundings that are needed for the creation of new ideas. We are not referring to the advantages of a change from society to solitude or from solitude to society, but to the more permanent associations. They often make or mar us, because they give us the atmosphere we are compelled to breathe. Some people seem to depress us—they silently but unconsciously steal our physical vitality and smile amiably whilst they do it ; in a literal sense they make us tired, and we are never at ease in their presence. Some places, some streets, some houses are impossible : when there—we can do nothing. Other situations are quite the reverse. We feel at our best, for we are *en rapport.* This sense of dependence is not a bit of ignorance or a wilful upholding of a fancy as if it were a truth ; it is reality itself. Musicians understand it perhaps better than anybody else. The pianist who on one occasion says : "I simply could not help playing well—the audience made me do it," will say, on another occasion : "They were like stones—they would not let me play."

All excellence is made up of *self plus surroundings.* Do we not read that Jesus Christ went to a place where He could not perform any of His mighty works because of the people's unbelief ? Even the greatest genius finds a limit ; superlative power cannot be exercised if the environment is wrong or unready.

Professor Yrjö Hirn, in his *Origins of Art,* has provided us with an interesting illustration of this fact. Art, he says, is, in its innermost nature, a social activity. There is a natural tendency in every feeling-state to manifest itself externally, and this externalising effect creates a similar feeling-state in the consciousness of the audience; "the sympathetic feeling acts upon the author of the original manifestation, heightening in him the feeling - state which gave rise to it " (p. 302). Very true; the audience is, in part, creator of the work; minus its sympathy and response, even genius is half impotent; it cannot blossom in a frosty atmosphere.[1]

There are no self-made men. There have been men with tremendous initiative, and that is to their credit; but in amassing wealth or acquiring fame and position they owe much to their fellows—to the staff who stood by them in those dark days when the creditors held the keys of life and death—or to the kindly friend who paid the promising scholar's university fees, asking for no return. The unfortunate man, the man who, though clever enough, never seems to make headway despite his diligence, the men whose life is a series of misfits—these are often the victims of the wrong environment. One of them might have been a star of magnitude if . . .; the other might have been a Cabinet Minister if . . .; a third changed his occupation so often that he almost lost his identity, and yet if . . . ? We claim to have a science of life, but where is it when all the obvious futilities of this kind are before us ? If genius is dependent on its audience, so is talent, and so is average ability. We have heard sermons preached in obscure country churches and chapels that vastly eclipsed the deliverances usually

---

[1] " Originality in art . . . is an affair of individual endowment and thought, and of social recognition and confirmation. It is not that the art impulse is exhausted in self-exhibition . . . the social judgment which a work of art has to sustain finds its correlative impulse in the self-exhibition of the producer. Only thus can his own judgment be instructed. The reaction of this social recognition upon the producer is not alone the fountain of his stimulus and the test of his success ; it is also the very source of his test of values."
—J. M. Baldwin, *Social and Ethical Interpretations in Mental Development*, p. 150.

heard in St Paul's or the Metropolitan Tabernacle; these preachers (we gathered) were misunderstood by their congregations—actually they had not found their true audience. We have seen an organ in a country cottage, cunningly devised and constructed by a shy youth who absented himself when the instrument was played, and who, by way of daily toil, hoed turnips and milked the cows. His shyness was in part due to the criticism of friends who in the earlier stages of his organ-building complained of his waste of time. Truly, he needed an audience, and with its sympathetic support what might he not have done?

Some day our intellectual economy may find a way of avoiding waste in ability by providing suitable surroundings for its nurture and growth. Meanwhile every man will have to discover his own right environment. No one can tell him exactly how; he must follow his own instincts and the guidance of intelligent friends. His great enemy will be the Society for Repressing Ambition—branches everywhere. If he can overcome its machinations he may hope, after numerous mistakes, to find himself in true correspondence with those people and those conditions that favour self-expression.

XVI

Of the purely mental habits which favour illumination one that is worthy of notice is the alternate use of *focus* and *distributive observation*. It is like leaving the study of an atom for the study of the heavens—renouncing the microscope for the telescope, the infinitely little for the infinitely great. A minute analysis of parts followed by a comprehensive survey of the whole is the secret of many a discovery. It is also the method of all fine interpretations of life. The law of the minute thing may provide the key to the vaster thing; and the complex may be a mystery until the simple has been thoroughly understood. Too easily we pass by the simple, the usual, the fact that is all too familiar; and yet to focus on it may bring the revelation we seek. As Professor Dewey says: "Our progress in genuine knowledge always consists in part in the discovery of something not understood in what had previously been taken for granted as plain, obvious, matter-of-course." [1]   But the wide survey is equally necessary.   The universe is made up of the Many in the One ; the plan has details but the scheme itself is infinite.   It is well to watch the falling apple ; let us also consider the orbit of the planets.

Again : to seek the highest standard, then to look for something better beyond it—that, surely, is one of the unconscious methods of genius.   Talent, seeing a standard, emulates it, and tries to equal it ; to surpass it is hardly ever considered seriously.   That is why so few of the talented ever cross the border-line and become men of genius.   They lack the impetus which causes others to be dissatisfied with attainment and which results in efforts to advance beyond it.   Then are we justified in encouraging the average man to go forward where the man of talent fails ?   We are justified in urging *every* man to make the best use of his powers ; and the best use is the enlightened use.   Not every man will succeed, but effort itself is educative, and without effort we, as a country, are bound to lose a certain percentage of mental ability because of ignorance and inactivity, and the individual is minus a percentage of possible wealth and culture.

XVII

A final word.   Looking back over the ground we have covered it may truthfully be said that we have no message for the man of genius.   He follows his own light, discovers truths for himself, and sets up his own laws of conscious action. But we have endeavoured to show that in his most inspired moments, those moments when he is most strikingly original in the fullest sense, he is not above law, but is the fulfilment of it.   He is a superman and yet a man.   His mind works like other minds but in a manner that is superlative.   His is not a mind plus a mental halo called genius.

We found it possible to base certain conclusions on these findings, supported as they are by known facts in physiology,

[1] *How We Think*, p. 120.

psychology, sociology, and the data of geography. We have ventured to offer counsel to men and women in the belief that if they would leave a wider margin for individuality, conventionalities need not be the less secure, and originalities of value might be multiplied. As to whether we have justified ourselves in this enterprise must be left to the judgment of others. But that the social, commercial, and political conditions of the future call for a new emphasis on the creative function of the mind will not be disputed. Is Britain, and the Empire, to be behind the rest of the world in enterprise of every kind? It is not probable, but it is not impossible. Measured by the likelihood of original products in other countries, Britain's chances are as good as ever, *if she will rise to them.* When the call went forth to serve King and Country the response was startling in its readiness and impressive in its magnitude. The call now is for the service of the highly trained mind, not merely the possession of applied science, but the ability to create. "What can you *do*?" is a truly serious question for every executive individual; but a question just as serious is: "How far can you *see*?" We need more men with vision, not for the commercial sphere but for every other sphere, and we believe we shall get them.

Eighty-three years is the lifetime of a very old man, and yet it is a period that does not stagger us by its length when we read the daily obituary notices in the Press. But in eighty-three years' time we shall be in A.D. 2000. What may happen between then and now? Who will have discovered the war weapons that will make war impossible? To what nation shall we owe the abolition of frightful diseases, and who will have done most to solve the problems of capital and labour? Can we hope for a new philosophy and for the advent of brilliant departures in literature, drama, and the arts? If so, from whence will come the great inspiration? These are questions no man can answer confidently, but such is the cathartic power of a war-cataclysm that, despite its sordid residue, there is the glimpse of a world redeemed. Every nation, small and great, may contribute its share, and all nations will be unfeignedly glad; for a new humanity with true cosmopolitan feelings will have been born, and the glory of one country will be the glory of the others. The national spirit will not die, rather will it be enlarged ; but it will be enlightened also, and instead of conflict we shall expect harmony. Every originality will then be welcomed in the service of man.

INDEX

A

ABILITY, 35, 36, 37
Abstraction, mental, 129, 130, 131
Ackermann, Carl, 27, 110
Activity, physical and mental, 138
Adam, Prof. J., on Platonism, 183, 236
Adams, 4
Addison, 107
Æsthetic sensibilities, 46
Æstheticism, alleged dangers of, 285
Age, affects ideas of progress, 228; its effect upon brain power, 133; and originality, 134; and pessimism, 231
Alfieri, 128
Alverstone, Lord, *Recollections*, 215
Amiel, 136
Analogy, 108, 115
Angelo, Michael, 12
Antagonism *v.* sympathy, 281
Anti-war suffragettes, 146
Aquinas, Thomas, 89, 150
Aristotle, 10, 37, 72, 128, 150, 165
Arkwright, 16, 72
Army and navy officers and originality, 218–222
Army training, mental effects of, 219, 220
Arnold, Prof. Felix, 85
Arnold, Matt., 96, 97
Art, a social activity, 291; originality in, 291
Artistic temperament, vagaries of, 95, 96, 289
Asceticism, its effects on original thought, 139, 140, 142
Association of ideas, 85
Athletics and mental efficiency, 271
Atmosphere favourable to talent and genius, 250, 251
Austin, Lady (Cowper), 142
Avebury, Lord, 72

B

BACON, 8, 105, 148, 289
" Bad Form," 167–168

Bagehot, Walter, 113, 192–193
Bain, Prof. A., 108, 113
Baldwin, Prof. J. M., 38–39, 291
Balfour, A. J., 73, 233
Balzac, 32, 131
Barker, H. A., case of, 208
Barker, J. Ellis, 166
Barrie, Sir James, 113
Beauty, elusiveness of, 41
Bellarmine, doctrine of mental reservation, 15
Benson, A. C., 168
Benson, Robert Hugh, 31
Bergson, philosophy of, 27, 50–51, 84, 177, 279
Berkeley on mathematics, 40
Berlioz, 87
Billia on psychological failures, 23
Binet, Prof. A., 49
Bismarck, 148, 175
Blake, William, 91–92, 131
Bloomer, Mrs, 16
Böhme, 29
Books and the average man, 176
Boole, Prof. G., 111
Bonheur, Rosa, 145
Bosanquet, C., 19–20
Bossuet, 107
Boutroux, 22, 42, 51
Brandes, Georg, 131, 150
Branford, Benchara, *Janus and Vesta*, 161, 170
Brett, G. S., 26
Brill, Dr, 57, 114
Brinton, D. G., 17
British Weekly, 264, 272
Brock, A. Clutton, will and art, 289
Brontë, Charlotte, 46, 47, 90
Brougham, Lord, on duty to clients, 214
Browne, Sir Thomas, on sympathy, 284
Browning, Oscar, on education, 168
Browning, Robert, 129
Bryce, Lord, on democracy and originality, 253
Büchner, 24
Buddha, 174
Buffon, 107
Buller, General, and Boer tactics, 218

INDEX

Burbank, Luther, on new flowers, 238
Burns, 141
Business low standards, effect of, 198–201
Butcher, Prof. S. H., 6
Butler, S., on the art of thinking, 113, 279
Byron, 105

C

Cæsar, 175
Campagnac, Prof., on education, 165, 288
Campbell, R. J., 31
Carlyle, 4, 96
Carpenter, Dr W. B., 84
Carpenter, Edward, on old - age optimism, 234
Carr, Dr H. Wildon, 49, 51
Carson on mathematical education, 85
Carus, Dr Paul, 39
Case, Professor, of Oxford, 23
Cerebration, 77
Cervantes, 134
Chapman, C., on public honesty, 258
Charron, 139
Chateaubriand, 93
Chesterton, G. K., 191, 194
Christian scientist and matter, 227
Christianity as compared with Judaism, 6
Christianity and optimism, 232
Civil service and originality, 216–218
Class consciousness, evils of, 255
Coleridge, Lord, 122
Coleridge, S. T., 38, 101, 283
Competition, 199
Complex, 57, 58
Concentration, 95, 129, 130, 131, 281
Conditions favourable to growth of talent, 251
Confession of an opium eater, 47
Conscious action, suspension of, 88
Consciousness, essential inscrutability of, 23; finer reach of, 33; governed by temperament, 31; growth and reduction of, 21; range of, 32, 35; stream of, 53, 55; unity and trinity of, 25
Cook, T. A., on " Curves of Life," 112, 205
Cooley, Prof. C. H., on racial genius, 250
Coomaraswarmy, 127

Cooper, Prof. Lane, 175
Covent Garden (an anachronism), 260
Cowper, 141
Creative mind, the need of the Empire, 294
Croce, B., 31, 177, 239
Crookes, Sir Wm., 30, 233
Crothers, S. M., on the courage of being ignorant, 181–182
Crowd, dominance of, 257
Crozier, Dr Beattie, 148, 254
Cunningham, Prof., 27
Curie, Madame, 100, 144

D

Daguerre, 116
Daily Mail, 273
Daily News, 191
Dante and Beatrice, 142
Darwin, 12, 13, 80, 82, 92, 105, 134, 286
Daudet, Alphonse, 118
Deane's *Pseudepigrapha*, 174
Dearborn, Prof., 143
Defective home training, 153
Defoe, 134
De Goncourt, 135, 136
De Morgan, William, 134
De Musset, 128
De Quincey, 47, 114, 126
Descartes, 24, 95, 107, 111, 276
Dewey, Prof., 26, 121, 178, 292
Dickens, 131
Diderot, 104
Diodorus Siculus, 105, 106
Discoveries, accidental, 115, 116, 117, 118
Disraeli, 38, 148
Dividing lines, disappearance of, 243
Doctors and prejudice, 208
Dogma, mistake of, 156, 158
D'Orbigny, 117
Dorland, W. A., 133
Dostoievsky, 93
Douglas, Jas., 192
Dowden, Prof., on literary movements, 246, 254
Drummond, 113
Durkins, A. M., Miss, 144
Dwelshauvers, Prof. Georges, 46
Dyer, Thiselton, 165

E

East, message of the, 249
Eccentricity, 12
Eddy, A. J., on Impressionism, 237

298

INDEX

INDEX

INDEX

INDEX

INDEX

17 – 30 – 36 – 47⁶ – 60' – 74⁸ – 83 – 92 –
99 – 104 – 107 – 110 – 114 – 125 – 152 –